Public Spending in the 20th Century

This book discusses the changing role of govern.. ... ...ance in the 20th century. It documents the enormous increase in government spending in that century across all industrialized countries. However, the authors find that the growth of government spending over the past 35 years has not brought about much additional social and economic welfare. This suggests that public spending in industrialized countries could be much smaller than it is without sacrificing important policy objectives. For this to happen, governments need to refocus their role on setting the rules of the game. The study provides options for institutional and expenditure policy reform. After a detailed account of reform experiences in several countries and the public debate regarding government reform, the study closes with an outlook on the future role of the state, a period when globalization may require and people may want "leaner" but not "meaner" states.

Vito Tanzi has been Director of the Fiscal Affairs Department of the International Monetary Fund since 1981. He previously taught economics at various universities before joining the IMF staff in 1974. Dr. Tanzi is the author of numerous books, including *Inflation and the Personal Income Tax* (1980) and *Taxation in an Integrating World* (1995) and hundreds of articles in professional journals and edited collections. He served as president of the International Institute of Public Finance in 1990–4 and is now honorary president of that association. Dr. Tanzi's ongoing research focuses on public finance. He holds a PhD in Economics from Harvard.

Ludger Schuknecht is Principal Economist in the Fiscal Policies Division of the European Central Bank in Frankfurt, Germany. Dr. Schuknecht previously served on the staff of the World Trade Organization's Research Department and of the IMF, where he worked in the African and Fiscal Affairs departments. He was a Fulbright Scholar at George Mason University. He is the author of *Trade Protection in the European Community* (1992) and has published widely in professional journals including the *American Economic Review*. Dr. Schuknecht's research interests include public expenditure policy and international trade, particularly in financial services and electronic commerce.

Advance Praise for *Public Spending in the 20th Century*

"Vito Tanzi and Ludger Schuknecht have made a valuable contribution by documenting and analyzing the enormous growth of government in the Western world during the past century. Many of their proposals for public sector reform will be seen as controversial, but the policy makers of the twenty-first century will surely have to confront the pressing issues raised in this well-articulated book."

Peter Birch Sorensen, *University of Copenhagen*

Public Spending in the 20th Century

A Global Perspective

VITO TANZI
International Monetary Fund

LUDGER SCHUKNECHT
European Central Bank

CAMBRIDGE
UNIVERSITY PRESS

PUBLISHED BY THE PRESS SYNDICATE OF THE UNIVERSITY OF CAMBRIDGE
The Pitt Building, Trumpington Street, Cambridge, United Kingdom

CAMBRIDGE UNIVERSITY PRESS
The Edinburgh Building, Cambridge CB2 2RU, UK   http://www.cup.cam.ac.uk
40 West 20th Street, New York, NY 10011-4211, USA http://www.cup.org
10 Stamford Road, Oakleigh, Melbourne 3166, Australia
Ruiz de Alarcón 13, 28014 Madrid, Spain

© Vito Tanzi, Ludger Schuknecht 2000

First published 2000

Printed in the United States of America

Typeface 10.5/13 Times Roman   *System* QuarkXPress [BTS]

A catalog record for this book is available from the British Library.

Library of Congress Cataloging in Publication Data

Tanzi, Vito.
Public spending in the 20th century: a global perspective/Vito Tanzi,
Ludger Schuknecht.
p.   cm.
Includes bibliographical references and index.
ISBN 0-521-66291-5 (hb) – ISBN 0-521-66410-1 (pb)
1. Expenditures, Public.   2. Government spending policy.
I. Schuknecht, Ludger, 1962–   . II. Title.
HJ7461.T36 2000
336.3′9 – dc21   99-40258
                                                            CIP

ISBN 0 521 66291 5 hardback
ISBN 0 521 66410 1 paperback

To Maria, Jyoti, and our children

Contents

List of Tables

xi

Preface

The idea for this book came about four years ago when one of the authors was invited to a conference and asked to write a paper on the future of the welfare state. The writing of that paper required a kind of mental exercise that addressed the question of what would be given up if the welfare state were scaled down. This exercise inevitably led to the related question of what kind of societies and, more specifically, what level of public spending the industrial countries had had before some of them became welfare states? It was surprising to find that the level of public spending in the early part of this century had been very low even compared to the levels common in the present day's developing countries. Yet, at that time several of the industrial countries had vibrant and modern economies and societies.

Various programs that account for the lion's share of the current budgets of industrial countries, such as those for education, health, pensions, unemployment, and some others, were of marginal importance early this century. This realization led us to speculate on the relationship between public spending and social welfare. When public spending increases, it generates two effects. First it leads to a higher level of taxation and thus to a fall in the disposable income of individuals. Second, it reduces the need for the individuals who benefit from the public spending to take actions, in their capacity as private individuals, to protect themselves against various risks. Thus to some extent the public action replaces the private action. If this is true, and it must be true for many, though not all, individuals, more public spending will not automatically increase public welfare and it may even reduce it. The book speculates on some of these issues.

Writing this book required a great effort at data collection. We believe that some of the information available in this book is not available in any other single source. Solita Wakefield was very helpful with the statistical part of the book. We were also greatly advantaged by the library resources available at the International Monetary Fund. We would like to thank especially Yvonne Liem and Deirdre Shanley of the Fund's Fiscal Library for their great help in tracing books and articles not easily available. Ms. Shanley was also particularly helpful in putting the finishing touches to the bibliography.

Much of the burden of typing various drafts of the manuscript was borne by Champa Nguyen, to whom we owe a great debt of gratitude. We also wish to thank Beulah David who helped with the final draft and Deirdre Shanley, who helped with the bibliography.

Part of the work on this book was done while one of the authors (V. Tanzi) was spending a sabbatical period at Collegium Budapest, Institute for Advanced Study (in Budapest). The Institute provided a congenial environment for thinking and for writing, and the authors wish to thank the Institute for the hospitality granted. Finally, four referees provided very valuable comments on an earlier draft. These comments helped improve the final product.

This acknowledgment would not be complete if we did not mention our families, who paid a heavy price, as much of the work was done in the evening and on weekends. We wish to thank our children and especially our patient wives, Maria and Jyoti.

It is obvious that the views expressed in this book are strictly those of the authors and do not reflect the official views of the institutions with which the authors were associated during the writing of this book.

Vito Tanzi, Washington, D.C.
Ludger Schuknecht, Frankfurt

PART ONE

The Growth of Government: A Historical Perspective

The first part of this book, comprising Chapters I–III, is focused on the growth of public spending in industrial countries over a period of about 125 years, from 1870 to the mid 1990s. The first chapter breaks the period in several parts: 1870 up to World War I, the interwar period, the period up to 1980, and the more recent years.

Chapter II provides a breakdown of the various government programs that contributed to the growth of spending. It shows that areas that had not been the responsibility of the government in the past came to play an increasingly important role in public spending with the passage of time. Some of these programs became the most important reason why spending grew significantly.

The growth of public spending had to be financed mostly by tax revenue. Chapter III describes the changes in tax revenue and in tax structure that made possible the financing of the growing expenditure. It also shows that when tax increases were not sufficient to finance higher public expenditures, governments resorted to debt financing. This led to the increase in public debt and, because of the need to service the debt, to another demand on public revenue.

The main conclusion of Part One is that the growth of public spending was not caused by inevitable forces that made it imperative. It was thus not inevitable as assumed by some theories about the growth of spending such as Wagner's Law or Baumol's disease. On the contrary, it is argued that growth was nothing but a response to changing perceptions about what the government should do. In a way the growth of government reflected a lack of confidence in the private

1

sector's ability to deal with some problems and a belief that public spending was the best way to deal with several risks faced by individuals. The action of government was always assumed to be additive to or complementary of the action of individuals. It was almost never assumed to be substitutive.

I   The Growth of Government since 1870

Economists' and society's views of the role of the state in the economy have changed remarkably over the past two centuries. Because of this, public institutions and the government's involvement in the economy have changed as well. Since 1870, government spending has increased considerably in all of today's industrialized countries. Although this increase has not been equal in all countries, it is nevertheless remarkable that the growth in public spending has been a general phenomenon despite the considerable institutional differences and geographic and language barriers that have existed among industrialized economies. Government spending increased most rapidly until about 1980. Since the early 1980s, it has been growing more slowly and in some instances has even declined. We shall argue in this book that, in spite of pressures for more public spending due to the less fiscally friendly environment that will prevail in future years because of demographic developments, public spending is likely to fall in the future.

1. THE PERIOD UP TO WORLD WAR I

The Dominance of Laissez-Faire

In the nineteenth century classical economists and political philosophers generally advocated a state with minimal economic functions. This attitude was in part a reaction to the major distortions

3

that governmental intervention had caused in the eighteenth century.[1] As Keynes put it: "Almost everything which the State did in the eighteenth century in excess of its minimum functions was, or seemed, injurious or unsuccessful" (Keynes, 1926, p. 12). Classical economists thought that the government's role should be limited to national defense, police, and administration because government "cannot have any other rational function but the legitimate defense of individual rights" (Bastiat, 1944–5). In 1776, Adam Smith had described his views on the role of the state in providing public goods or, in his words, "erecting and maintaining those public institutions and those public works, which, though they may be in the highest degree advantageous to a great society, are, however, of such a nature, that the profit could never repay the expense to any individual or small number of individuals. . . . [These public works are mainly] those for facilitating the commerce of the society, and those for promoting the instructions of the people."[2] Thus, in some ways Smith introduces an early version of the concept of a public good.

Furthermore, classical economists "were [. . .] among the most forceful advocates and pioneers of state education" (West, 1970). Referring to the lower "classes," Smith already recognizes the importance of education for modern states: "The state [. . .] derives no inconsiderable advantage from their instruction. The more they are instructed, the less liable they are to the delusions of enthusiasm and supposition, which among ignorant nations, frequently occasion the most dreadful disorders." Many people of the time also stress the importance of education for keeping young people from doing-mischief.[3]

For classical economists, the government role should be small and essentially limited to the allocation of resources (see Robbins, 1962). The countries' institutional frameworks, such as the U.S. Constitution,

1. On this see a little known book by Keynes (1926).
2. Adam Smith, *The Wealth of Nations* (1937, p. 681). By the beginning of the nineteenth century, private charity was already considered inadequate, and public relief and punishment programs for the poor were introduced, mainly to maintain law and order (Rimlinger, 1971). Distributional policy interventions during crisis periods also occurred. See Rothbard (1962) on debt relief in the panic of 1819 or Hammond (1957) on banking and politics before the Civil War.
3. See West (1970, pp. 112–13). However, West also writes that the degree of state intervention as developed over the past hundred years would have not been approved by classical economists.

did not specify any other economic role for the state. Consequently, in the last century, public spending was minimal in a number of industrialized countries for which data for 1870 could be found (Table I.1).[4] Around 1870, unweighted average public expenditure amounted to only about 10 percent of gross domestic product. In the United States, government expenditure was about 7 percent of GDP, and, in most newly industrialized European countries of the period, such as Germany, the United Kingdom, or the Netherlands, expenditure did not exceed 10 percent of GDP. By the standards of classical economists, Australia's, Italy's, Switzerland's, and France's public expenditure share, in the range of 12–18 percent of GDP, was considered as heavy state involvement in the economy. A leading French economist of the time, Paul Leroy-Beaulieu (1888), addressing the question of the proper share of taxes in the economy, suggested that a share of 5–6 percent was moderate while a share beyond 12 percent had to be considered "exorbitant" and would damage the growth prospects of an economy.

In the latter part of the nineteenth century, however, classical economists started to be challenged by Marxian thinking, which strongly influenced the socialist movement in Europe. By the end of the century, the German economists Schmoller and Wagner had added redistribution of wealth to the legitimate and normal government functions. They justified government policies aimed at redistributing wealth from the rich to the less fortunate. Up to that time, policies with redistributive effects had been mostly ad hoc and aimed at protecting some groups in particular situations such as famines, banking crises, and so on. By that time, the government role in providing *primary* education was already predominant (Connell, 1980) even though a large share of the population still did not have access to and thus did not attend the schools. The first social security system, albeit with minimal eligibility and benefits, was introduced in Germany in the 1880s (Altenstetter, 1986). It has been argued that "by the end of the nineteenth century, the setting was prepared for the modern concepts of social protection" (Rimlinger, 1971).

---

4. In a recent paper, one of the authors has warned that the role of government is not limited to spending but can be pursued through quasi-fiscal activities and regulations (see Tanzi, 1998c). In this book, we focus on spending and taxing and thus largely ignore that warning.

Table I.1. *Growth of General Government Expenditure, 1870–1996 (Percent of GDP)*

	Late 19th Century about 1870[a]	Pre World War I 1913	Post World War I 1920	Pre World War II 1937	Post World War II			
					1960	1980	1990	1996
General government for all years								
Australia	18.3	16.5	19.3	14.8	21.2	34.1	34.9	35.9
Austria	10.5	17.0	14.7[b]	20.6	35.7	48.1	38.6	51.6
Canada	...	...	16.7	25.0	28.6	38.8	46.0	44.7
France[c]	12.6	17.0	27.6	29.0	34.6	46.1	49.8	55.0
Germany	10.0	14.8	25.0	34.1	32.4	47.9	45.1	49.1
Italy	13.7	17.1	30.1	31.1	30.1	42.1	53.4	52.7
Ireland[d]	...	...	18.8	25.5	28.0	48.9	41.2	42.0
Japan	8.8	8.3	14.8	25.4	17.5	32.0	31.3	35.9
New Zealand[b]	...	...	24.6	25.3	26.9	38.1	41.3	34.7
Norway[d]	5.9	9.3	16.0	11.8	29.9	43.8	54.9	49.2
Sweden[c]	5.7[b]	10.4	10.9	16.5	31.0	60.1	59.1	64.2
Switzerland	16.5	14.0	17.0	24.1	17.2	32.8	33.5	39.4
United Kingdom	9.4	12.7	26.2	30.0	32.2	43.0	39.9	43.0
United States	7.3	7.5	12.1	19.7	27.0	31.4	32.8	32.4
Average	**10.8**	**13.1**	**19.6**	**23.8**	**28.0**	**41.9**	**43.0**	**45.0**

*Central government for 1870–1937,
general government thereafter*

Belgium	...	13.8	22.1	21.8	30.3	57.8	54.3	52.9
Netherlands	9.1	9.0	13.5	19.0	33.7	55.8	54.1	49.3
Spain	...	11.0	8.3	13.2	18.8	32.2	42.0	43.7
Average	**9.1**	**11.3**	**14.6**	**18.0**	**27.6**	**48.6**	**50.1**	**48.6**
Total average	**10.7**	**12.7**	**18.7**	**22.8**	**27.9**	**43.1**	**44.8**	**45.6**

Sources: Compiled by Tanzi and Schuknecht based on Fernández Acha (1976); Andic and Veverka (1964); Australia, Bureau of Census and Statistics (1938); Institut National de la Statistique [Belgium] (1952); Brosio and Marchese (1986); United States Bureau of Census (1975); Butlin (1984); Norway, Statistisk Sentralbyrå (1969, 1978); Delorme and André (1983); Flora, Kraus, and Pfenning (1983); IMF, *Statistical Appendix*, New Zealand; IMF, *Switzerland: Recent Economic Developments* (1996); *Historical Statistics of Japan* (1987); Mitchell, *International Historical Statistics* (various years); Neck and Schneider (1988); The Netherlands, Centraal Bureau voor de Statistiek (1956); New Zealand Official (1938); OECD, Economic Outlook (1996, 1997); Italy, Istituto Nazionale de Statistica (1951); *Österreichisches Statistiches Zentralamt* (1935).

[a] Or closest year available for all columns. Pre-World War II data sometimes on the basis of GNP or NNP instead of GDP.

[b] Central government data for this year, New Zealand: 1960 = 1970, and 1994–95 = 1996.

[c] 1996 data; calculations are based on the Maastricht definition, and are smaller than that published by the INSEE, the national statistical agency.

[d] 1995 instead of 1996, because of break in data calculation.

Nevertheless, laissez-faire attitudes continued to predominate and the role of the government remained limited. The average share of public expenditure in GDP increased slowly between 1870 and World War I growing from 10.7 percent in 1870 to 11.9 percent in 1913. This share included central, state, and local government spending for most countries (see details in Table I.1). The arming of Austria, Germany, France, and the United Kingdom in anticipation of World War I is reflected in higher public expenditure levels in these countries, while expenditure in Japan, Norway, the Netherlands, and the United States was still below 10 percent of GDP. In a few countries, the share of government expenditure in GDP even declined over this period. The remarkable feature is that these low shares of government spending were achieved in a period when much of Europe was becoming modern and when many large public works (railroads, metros) were completed.[5]

The Effects of World War I

The first World War brought about a considerable increase in average levels of government expenditure. This increase was largely a result of military and other war-related spending. As governments had expanded their revenue base to finance at least part of their war efforts, they could maintain higher expenditure levels after the war (Peacock and Wiseman, 1961). They also had to pay back their war-related debt or reparations. By 1920 or shortly thereafter, public expenditure had increased to an average of 18.7 percent with only Sweden, Spain, and the United States staying near 10 percent of GDP. In France, Germany, Italy, and the United Kingdom, the countries most affected by the war, expenditure exceeded 25 percent of GDP. Australia, Austria, Canada, Ireland, Japan, the Netherlands, Norway, and Switzerland belonged to the group of "medium-sized" governments with expenditure levels below 20 percent of GDP.

---

5. A note of warning on the data is perhaps necessary. Obviously, there are problems of comparability of data. However, these problems are not likely to change the basic trends reported.

2. THE INTERWAR PERIOD

The End of Laissez-Faire

After World War I, general attitudes toward the role of the government started changing as reflected by the title of Keynes's 1926 book, *The End of Laissez-Faire*. In that book, Keynes wrote that: "The important thing for government is not to do things that individuals are doing already, and to do them a little better or a little worse; but to do those things which at present are not done at all" (pp. 46–7). He implied that there were many things that were not being done at that time.

By the late 1920s many European countries had introduced rudimentary social security systems, and the Depression resulted in a wave of expansionary government expenditure policies including social programs (Ashford and Kelley, 1986). The Depression was seen by many as a monumental failure of the market economy and of laissez-faire, a failure that justified governmental intervention and made many intellectuals look with varying degrees of admiration at the economic experiments going on in Russia and in Germany and Italy. The United States introduced major public expenditure programs with the New Deal (such as Aid for Families with Dependent Children), and other governments authorized higher spending on the unemployed and on public works partly to create employment in the context of the Great Depression. Starting from the mid-1930s, growing military spending in response to the threat of Hitler's Germany also contributed to the rise in public expenditure in European countries.

By 1937, public expenditure had increased to an average of 22.8 percent or about double the 1913 level. Expenditure had increased in all countries and the increase was most pronounced in Canada, Germany, Japan, the Netherlands, Spain, Sweden, Switzerland, and the United States. However, part of this increase was due to the fall in GDP caused by the Depression rather than to a real increase in public spending.[6] With the exception of Australia, Norway, and Spain, public expenditure exceeded 15 percent of GDP in all countries. By

---

6. The increase looks even less dramatic when account is taken of the fact that in 1937 some countries were already preparing for war.

1937, the minimal state committed to laissez-faire policies was on the way out. The ground had become fertile for the future growth of the welfare state, and in this growth income redistribution would play a large role.

3. THE PERIOD UNTIL 1980

The Growing Influence of Keynesianism

The post–World War II period, and particularly the period between 1960 and 1980, saw an unprecedented enthusiasm for activist expenditure policies coupled with rapid growth in the involvement of the government in the economy. In his influential book, Richard Musgrave (1959) described the allocative, stabilizing, and redistributive functions that a modern government should undertake. The development of the theory of public goods and of the concept of externality suggested a growing allocative role for the state. The popularity of socialism among Western intellectuals and some political leaders made the redistributive role a progressively more appealing and more important one.

In *The Ethics of Redistribution*, Bertrand de Jouvenel (1952, p. 73), a French political philosopher, would write:

Public finance generally is a dull subject, but public finance in the first half of the twentieth century is entrancing: it has been revolutionized and in turn has been the means of a revolution in society. Out of many new aspects of public finance, the two most notable are, first, that it has been used to alter the distribution of the national income between social classes, and, second, that the fraction of national income passing through public hands has increased enormously.

It should be noted that he was writing in the 1950s, well before the real expansion in public spending had taken place.

Keynes's *General Theory,* popularized through influential works by Alvin Hansen, Abba Lerner, Lawrence Klein, and others, provided the tools for stabilization and, yet, another powerful reason for governmental intervention. The great fear of unemployment after the Great Depression came to be tempered by the belief that the application of Keynesian demand policy could eliminate or at least reduce business cycles and unemployment. The enormous impact of Keynes's writings on policymaking in the 1960s and 1970s (if only as a pretext for expansionary special interest policies) made this period the Keynesian era. To some extent, the influence of Keynes may have confirmed his own prediction that "the ideas of economists and political philosophers, both when they are right and when they are wrong, are more powerful than is commonly understood. Indeed the world is ruled by little else."[7]

Galbraith's politically influential book, *The Affluent Society* (1958), written during the fiscally conservative Eisenhower administration, expressed in a pointed and well-articulated fashion the attitude of the economic avant-garde at that time. Influenced by the experience of the Great Depression and the seeming success of expansionary fiscal policies before the war, Galbraith backed the view that "in the event of insufficient demand, taxes should be cut and public outlays [should] be increased, as is now widely accepted." In his view, the previous "conventional wisdom of balanced budgets at all times" had become obsolete (p. 18). Galbraith was particularly unhappy about the insufficient government activity in the production of public goods and services. Thus, in a way he was building on the views of Keynes expressed in 1926 in the *End of Laissez-Faire*. As Galbraith put it, "the myopic preoccupation with (private) production and material investment has diverted our attention from the more urgent questions of how we are employing our resources and, in particular, from the greater need and opportunity for investing in persons" (p. 332). To Galbraith, "public poverty" prevailed not only in education but also in basic research, education, pollution control, and foreign assistance for relieving starvation. In other words, public poverty could be alleviated by more public spending. He concluded that "government expenditure is likely at any given time to be near the minimum which the community regards as tolerable" (p. 241). This conclusion seems far from more recent views about the level of public expenditure.

To Galbraith, opposition to social insurance and legislation was another liberal fallacy that reflected Ricardian and Malthusian gloom and social Darwinism (1958, chapter V). By the late 1950s, only a few decades after the introduction of social legislation and social

---

7. Keynes continues, "Practical men, who believe themselves to be quite exempt from any intellectual influences, are usually the slaves of some defunct economist. Madmen in authority, who hear voices in the air, are distilling their frenzy from some academic scribbler of a few years back." In 1966, Walter Heller wrote about "Lord Keynes's spectacular rescue of economics from the wilderness of classical equilibrium" (p. 4).

insurance in most countries, he observed approvingly that "the basic uncertainties of life had been eliminated" (1958, chapter VIII). In this statement he anticipated one of the important justifications for government spending, namely the reduction of risk for most citizens.

This strong faith in the role of government was shared by Francis Bator, another influential economist at that time. In *A Question of Government Spending*, he stated his view of a good society as follows: "My conception of the good society . . . lead me to believe that we are dangerously shortchanging ourselves on defense, foreign aid, education, urban renewal, and medical services; that we badly need to increase allocations to these and a variety of other tasks" (Bator, 1960, p. xiv). In other words, there was a strong need for more public spending. Similar views were expressed in 1958 by James Tobin, who wrote that "Orthodox fiscal doctrines have again dominated our policies during the five years since 1953, and again have brought the nation to the brink of catastrophe . . ." (in Tobin, 1966, p. 57). Writing in 1960, he added that: "Increased taxation is the price of growth" (ibid. p. 87).

The forceful stance for bigger government involvement in the provision of goods and services by the aforementioned economists and others was accompanied by new developments and techniques in the evaluation of government programs and in budgeting. See Merewitz and Sosnick (1971). Earlier decades mainly dealt with institutions and accountability in the budgeting process, sometimes using rules of thumb to assess the benefits of government programs. In the 1950s and early 1960s, some came to believe that planning, programming, and budgeting systems and other techniques would increase the efficiency of public expenditure (Premchand, 1983).

Cost/benefit analysis of public projects, for example, was considered a major breakthrough in economic planning techniques. New techniques were assumed to remove political discretion from budgetary decisions so that public money could be properly and efficiently allocated by the government. It is difficult now to convey the excitement of that period in this area. "An air of mystery began surrounding it through expressions like input-output, linear programming, discounted cash flow, critical path analysis," leading some economists to predict that these will be "as revolutionary in [their] policy implications as was the Keynesian revolution in economics" (Peters, 1973, p. 10). Smithies (1964) emphasized the role of program budgeting in determining national program goals and suggested that budgets can be a "precise instrument for planning, appropriation, administration, and control" which could help "to clarify and refine government objectives and the allocation of resources." An engineering approach to public policies and social welfare emerged as the evaluation and implementation of policies were assumed to become more and more efficient.[8]

It was also believed at the time that progressive taxation, presumably with a stable tax base and no serious disincentive effects, could provide the financing for these more ambitious expenditure policies. Furthermore, these expenditure policies could identify and target potential beneficiaries at low administrative and efficiency costs. It is remarkable that, at the time, most studies did not find any negative impact on the economy deriving from high marginal tax rates. The so-called second generation analyses of the impact of high marginal tax rates were still some years in the future.

The Decline of Fiscal Institutions

This intellectual belief in a positive role of the state and its power to carry out such a role came to be embedded in the legal-institutional framework for countries' policymaking. Some erosion of constraints on government expenditure policies had already begun in the late nineteenth century (Moser, 1994). Before World War II, the Great Depression was the main cause for an erosion in constraints on fiscal deficits, when, for example, in the United States, the Supreme Court ruled that "the power of congress to authorize appropriations of public money for public purposes is not limited by the direct grants of legislative power found in the Constitution." Thereby it provided the judicial opening for extensive public works and the developing of welfare programs (Niskanen, 1992).

The erosion in the legal-institutional constraints on fiscal deficits accelerated after World War II when many European countries came to accept welfare rights as constitutional rights. Several countries

---

8. On Schumpeter's view of the beneficial effect of economic uncertainty and recessions, Galbraith comments that "government inactivity was equal to not calling the fire department when a house is on fire because the fire had work to do" (Galbraith, 1958, p. 46). This image of the economy in recession as a burning house with government demand policies as the fire rescue squad is a typical example of a social and economic "engineering" approach to government.

made strong legal provisions for interventionist policies in their constitutions (e.g., Germany and Switzerland) or through their legislature (e.g., Germany and the United States), and supreme courts supported such policies when interpreting the consistency of activist legislation with the existing legal framework (Moser, 1994).

In Germany, the new postwar constitution stressed the role of the state in shaping the "social market economy." In the late 1960s, the stabilization law extended the role of government to the promotion of macroeconomic stability. After the first oil crisis, the German supreme court exempted the government budget from the constitutional deficit limit. Article 81 of Italy's constitution also provided some formal constraints on fiscal policies, including the requirement to match new or higher expenditure in the budget with means to finance them. The vagueness of this rule on what constitutes appropriate "means" probably facilitated its relaxation in the 1960s (Eusepi and Cerioni, 1989). In Switzerland, the most far-reaching revision of federal powers was introduced in 1947 that included the subsidization of industry and agriculture. In 1971, the Swiss court permitted state intervention for social policy motives.

The U.S. Constitution has no strong provisions against economic and social legislation and is very difficult to change. The Supreme Court of the United States de facto helped in changing constitutional rules by permitting, first, the New Deal legislation and later, postwar activist legislation such as the 1946 Employment Act (Moser, 1994). The Employment Act of 1946 declared that the federal government was responsible to promote "maximum employment, production, and purchasing power" (Okun, 1970, p. 37). This was indeed a major departure from laissez-faire.[9] In the words of James Tobin: "with this Act as a solemn expression of national policy, no Administration, Democratic or Republican, can avoid a modest amount of economic planning" (1966, p. 10).

The growth of government was also facilitated by the dynamics of the political process in democratic societies. Expenditure growth was furthered by interest groups lobbying for spending programs and by bureaucrats demanding larger budgets. Monetary financing of government deficits weakened expenditure control. Additional institu-

---

9. These few examples show that there is surprisingly little discussion on how the legal-institutional framework underlying fiscal policymaking in industrialized countries changed to accommodate expansionary fiscal policies and deficits.

tional factors led to asymmetries in the political costs of taxing and spending. In democracies, legislators typically have an incentive to enhance their political support by voting for spending projects in their districts, because wealth is transferred to their voters while the costs are borne by all voters in the country. By the same token, they are reluctant to increase taxes that affect their constituencies. In some countries, certain changes in the federalist decision-making processes have increased expansionary pressures on the budget.[10]

A number of other reasons for the growth in public spending have been advanced (for a survey see Holsey and Borcherding, 1997). Rapid urbanization in industrial countries is likely to have facilitated increasing taxation and to have created more demands for public spending. More recently, the aging of the populations in industrialized countries has started to contribute to the growth of spending although the full pressure from aging will only be felt in the coming decades. Wagner's Law (named after a publication by Adolf Wagner in 1876) has been probably the most prominent but not very convincing explanation for government growth. Wagner argued that a rise in public spending was a kind of natural development that would accompany the growth of per capita income. Wagner's Law fails to explain why public spending did not grow between 1870 and 1913. In this book, we argue that the growth in public spending resulted from changing views on the role of government in the economy.

It is important to maintain a historical and institutional perspective when assessing the expansion of public expenditure since World War II. Between 1937 and 1960 public expenditure, as a share of GDP, increased at a relatively slow pace and much of the increase was probably related to the growth of defense spending especially during and after World War II. Average, unweighted public spending grew from about 22 percent of GDP on average in 1937 to 28 percent of GDP by 1960. In Japan, Switzerland, and Spain, public expenditure was still below 20 percent of GDP in 1960. Public spending even declined in Germany, Japan, and Switzerland. The growing role of government,

---

10. For a number of theoretical and empirical articles on this subject see Forte and Peacock (1985); Mueller (1986); Buchanan, Rowley, and Tollison (1987); Frey (1988); Winer and Hettich (1991b); and the essays in Breton, Galeotti, Salmon, and Wintrobe (1991). Wildavsky (1985) provides a "cultural" explanation for the growth of public spending. Lindert (1994) shows that political economy factors were already relevant for explaining the growth in social spending between 1880 and 1930 in various countries. For a survey of the literature on deficits see Mueller (1997) and Alesina and Perotti (1995a).

however, manifests itself at the same time in considerable spending growth in Australia, Austria, the Netherlands, Norway, Sweden, and the United States.

The rapid expansion of public expenditure between 1960 and 1980 is remarkable because it occurred when most countries were not engaged in war effort; there was no depression, and the demographic developments were generally fiscally friendly. That expansion reflects mainly the previously mentioned change in attitude toward the role of the state. The 1960s and 1970s was the heyday of Keynesianism and the time when governments were perceived by many to be efficient in allocating and redistributing resources and in stabilizing the economy. This was also the period when basic social security systems acquired some of the characteristics of the welfare state.[11] Consequently, public expenditure as a share of GDP increased from around 28 percent in 1960 to around 43 percent in 1980. The share almost doubled in Belgium, Ireland, Japan, Spain, Sweden, and Switzerland, and increased rapidly in most of the other industrialized countries. By 1980, public expenditure exceeded 50 percent of GDP in Belgium, the Netherlands, and Sweden. No industrial country kept public expenditure below 30 percent of GDP and only Japan, Spain, Switzerland, and the United States stayed close to this level.

The 1960–80 period could be described as the golden age of public sector intervention. It was a period much influenced by perhaps naive perceptions of how governments operate (Tanzi, 1997). Normative views of how the government should act prevailed over positive views of how governments actually act in the real world. The public choice literature had still not had much influence. More recent experience has shown that the romantic or idealized view of how policy is made and is carried out is, at times, far removed from reality. In some ways extreme versions of this romantic view were implicit in the work of Tinbergen (1952) and Johansen (1965). What were these naive perceptions of how government operate? Implicitly or explicitly it was assumed that:

(a) The actions of the policymakers were generally driven by the

---

11. In many countries the social security systems expanded their activities outside the field of insurance for old age. Also, the link between contributions and pensions became more tenuous for individual contributors. Thus, social security contributions came to be seen as taxes by many of those who paid them.

objective of promoting social welfare. Thus, rent seeking on the part of those who formulated the policies was assumed to be insignificant or nonexistent. The literature on rent seeking would appear only in the 1970s and would not become influential until later.[12]

(b) The public sector was monolithic and with an obvious nerve center where all the important economic decisions for the whole sector were made in a rational and transparent way. Therefore, policies could not be inconsistent among them. For example, the policies pursued by the public enterprises or by other decentralized entities (such as local governments, stabilization boards, and social security institutions) could not be at odds with those pursued by the central government; and, of course, within the central government, there was consistency in the policies promoted by the various ministries.[13] It is puzzling how little interest there was until the 1990s in issues of fiscal federalism and policy coordination *within* countries.[14]

Policies were assumed to be consistent not only in space but also in time. The political horizon of governments would be long enough so that current policies would not conflict with future policies. Such conflicts can result either from mistakes or from political considerations (such as winning the next elections) that may lead policymakers to choose, in the short run, policies that are clearly inconsistent with long-run objectives. Once again, the literature on the time inconsistency of economic policy is a product of more recent years.[15]

(c) Policy decisions were reversible. Thus, government employees could be dismissed when no longer needed; public wages could be cut as well as increased; incentives could be removed when their objec-

12. See Tullock (1967) and Krueger (1974).
13. For examples of inconsistent or uncoordinated policies within the U.S. government, see Krueger (1993). An extreme example for the United States was provided by the subsidies given to the producers of tobacco at the same time as the government was trying to discourage smoking.
14. For examples of inconsistent policies between the central government and the local governments, see Tanzi (1996c) For recent surveys on practices in fiscal federalism, see Ter-Minassian, editor (1997). For a historical study on fiscal federalism, see the collection of essays in Musgrave (1965), and, in particular, Rafuse's study on the destabilizing expenditure and revenue dynamics at the state and local level in the postwar United States.
15. See Calvo (1978). There is now a large literature that confirms the existence of political cycles in public expenditure behavior.

tives had been achieved or their implementation time had expired; entitlements could be ended; and so on. During the 1980s, governments had to face the unpleasant reality that it is far easier to increase benefits (such as pensions and wages) than reduce them; or to hire civil servants than to fire them.

(d) The policymakers had full control over the policy instruments. They could rely on honest and efficient public sector employees who would implement efficiently and objectively the policies decided at the top. The literature on corruption, principal-agents problems, and rent-seeking is relevant here and is, once again, a product of recent years;

(e) Finally, it was assumed that the policymakers had a good and correct understanding of how economies operated. The certainty of Keynesian economics, with the addition of the Phillips curve, had not yet been challenged in a convincing way, either empirically or theoretically, as it started to be in the 1970s.

4. THE 1980s AND THE 1990s

Growing Skepticism of Government Intervention

Skepticism about the proper role of the state, in many of its activities, started emerging in the late 1960s and the 1970s. It was then that shortcomings in the underlying theoretical models which favored activist government policies in allocation of resources, in stabilization, and in income distribution became evident, at first, to a small group of critics (Buchanan, Friedman, and a few others) and then to a growing number of observers. Some critics also started to question the practical implementation of these policies.

The failure of government policies to allocate resources efficiently, to redistribute them in a well-targeted manner, and to stabilize the economy in the stagflation of the 1970s was coupled with results of new studies that highlighted the disincentive effects of high taxes and the growing underground economies.[16] The usefulness of the new programming and budgeting techniques was also called into question. Policy formulation had not sufficiently recognized the institutional

---

16. Once again, it is strange that the phenomenon of the underground economy was not discovered until the late 1970s.

and systemic constraints. Moreover, difficulties arose in defining government objectives or assigning monetary values to many costs and
benefits (Premchand, 1983). As deficits and public debt were rising,
many economists argued that government had grown much beyond
its justified role, undermining economic incentives, property rights,
and economic freedom, and "mortgaging" the income of future generations (Buchanan, 1975).

The new skepticism about "benevolent" government making the
"right" policy choices, and about its technical ability to conduct efficient policies, reawakened the academic interest in the role of
political institutions and in the incentives for policymakers. Especially the public choice and new institutional economics literature has
discussed the importance of constraints on fiscal policymaking. This
debate initially focused largely on the United States. In recent years,
however, renewed interest in institutional constraints on fiscal
deficits, public debt, and public spending has emerged in other
industrialized countries.[17]

At the political level, in the 1980s the tide turned in favor of a
smaller government role. With Margaret Thatcher as prime minister
of the United Kingdom and Ronald Reagan as president of the
United States, two forceful and articulate opponents of big government came into power in two very influential countries. From their
powerful positions, they carried out a determined political attack on
large government.[18] Over the course of the 1980s and early 1990s,
more and more social and political groups began attacking what they
considered excessive government spending and expensive welfare
states, and many reforms promised and initiated by the government.[19]
Also many OECD countries started a strong attack against
regulations.

17. Suggestions for the United States have included more inclusive majority rules for
spending and tax increases, a line-item veto for the president, limiting the Senate's
power to cutting (but not raising) expenditure, and, most prominently, a balanced-
budget amendment to the constitution (Wagner and Tollison, 1987; Buchanan, 1985).
The new literature on the role of institutions is discussed in more detail in Part Three
of this study. In Europe, some attention has also been paid to constitutional limits on
tax rates. Switzerland, for example, has imposed such limits on the rates of the recently
introduced value-added tax. See also Forte (1989, 1998).
18. Reagan popularized the view that, far from being a solution to problems, the
government could be a cause of them. For a critical account of Reagan's contempt for government see, for example, *New York Times Magazine*, August 11,
1996.
19. See Assar Lindbeck (1997) and Chapter X of this book.

New Trends in Public Spending

With some noteworthy exceptions, relatively few countries, have so far accompanied their antigovernment rhetoric with successful shifts in their policy regimes toward less state involvement and cuts in public expenditure.[20] In part because of the tyranny of past commitments, and because of the power and resistance of groups with strong entitlements on public spending, on average, public expenditure levels have continued to increase, but the pace has definitely slowed down (see Table I.1). In 1990, unweighted average public expenditure reached 44.8 percent of GDP. In 1996, it reached 45.6 percent of GDP. Over the 1980–96 period, the share of public expenditure in GDP declined in Belgium, Ireland, New Zealand, the Netherlands, and the United Kingdom. It increased by another 5 percent of GDP or more in Canada, France, Italy, Norway, Spain, Sweden, and Switzerland. Italy and Norway have increased spending by another 10 percent of GDP or more in the 1980s, but in the past six years, spending has come down in both countries as well as in Canada. The long recession in Switzerland and the German unification also caused public expenditure to increase significantly as a share of GDP in these two countries in the first half of the 1990s. Despite the considerable rhetoric and public perception, the United Kingdom and especially the United States have not been very successful in reducing public spending since 1980.

When the overall developments between the late nineteenth century and the late twentieth century are compared, it is noticed that half of the growth in government expenditure – from 10 percent of GDP around 1870 to 28 percent in 1960 – occurred during the two world wars. Expenditure growth to 46 percent of GDP in the thirty-six years after 1960 equaled the expenditure growth in the previous ninety years even though the post-1960 period was free of major wars or depressions.

5. THE SYMMETRY OF EXPENDITURE GROWTH

Governments grew rapidly in all industrial countries over the past 126 years. However, growth in public spending was not fully sym-

---

20. However, some progress has been made in reducing regulations on economic activities.

metrical across countries. In 1870, Switzerland, France, and Australia had the highest levels of public spending. Today, Australia and Switzerland have among the smallest governments in this group. The United Kingdom had one of the largest governments in the interwar and post–World War II period but by the mid-1990s, it showed a relatively low level of public spending. The most striking change in the size of government took place in Sweden and Norway, which had among the smallest governments until World War II and which, by the 1990s, had among the largest governments. New Zealand, Norway, and Ireland are the first industrialized countries that, since the late 1980s, have reduced public expenditure considerably.

When looking at the reasons for these asymmetric developments, it comes as no surprise that public spending in countries with stronger institutional constraints on taxation and spending grew more slowly than in those without such binds. In Switzerland, for example, the power to tax is restricted by the constitution and these constraints were not relaxed much over recent decades. Laws setting income and indirect tax rates, for example, are only valid for ten years. After that period they need to be extended (or changed) via a popular referendum. The limited power to tax has probably contributed to government expenditure growing much more slowly than elsewhere in Western Europe.

Japan is also an interesting example of how institutional constraints can slow the growth of government. Recall, that in Japan, government expenditure grew only from less than 20 to about 36 percent of GDP between 1960 and 1996. The political system in Japan after World War II resulted in the dominance of one party with extensive checks and balances. This party seemed to encompass all the important social groups that balanced the interests of various factions (Olson, 1982). The system also included a relatively autonomous and a generally considered effective and powerful bureaucracy.[21] The number of institutional changes, especially those facilitating the expansion of government, was limited. Thereby, policymakers seemed to reflect a desire to promote the countries' overall welfare (rather than the welfare of selected special interests) and to keep government lean and efficient. However, this view may need revision in light of recent

---

21. More recently, the ability of this bureaucracy has been put into question by a series of scandals and by the problems that the Japanese economy has been experiencing. Also, the Japanese have been pressured to increase public spending to stimulate the economy.

developments that have indicated that the bureaucracy may have been less efficient than previously thought.

There is very little discussion in the literature on institutional changes in countries which saw the most rapid increases in public spending, especially the Scandinavian countries.[22] In Italy, the constitutional constraints probably prevented major increases in public spending (and in deficits) until 1960. Afterwards, and especially in the Keynesian heyday of the 1970s, public expenditure started to increase rapidly, perhaps because these constraints were relaxed or were no longer effective (Eusepi and Cerioni, 1989).

6. CONCLUDING REMARKS

In this first chapter we have documented the increase in public expenditure across industrialized countries in the past 126 years. While initially, the two world wars permitted some significant increases in revenue and expenditure levels, it was the period between 1960 and 1980 that saw the most rapid expansion. Changes in public expenditure levels largely followed changes in attitudes toward the role of the state and changes in the institutions which constrain government intervention in the economies. These changes in attitude characterized both policymakers and economists. The 1980s and early 1990s have witnessed once again another change in attitudes toward the role of the state. This period has witnessed, perhaps, the first attempts at reversing the trend of expenditure growth. In the rest of this book, we shall argue that this change in attitudes is likely to lead to a reduction, over future years, in the share of public spending in GDP in most of the industrial countries. This would happen in spite of a relatively less fiscally friendly environment due to demographic changes and other factors.

22. But see Lindbeck (1997).

II The Composition of Public Expenditure

The growth of government over the past century has been accompanied by considerable changes in the composition of public spending reflecting the changing perceptions of what the state should do. A century ago, spending was mostly limited to the maintenance of law and order, external security, and to some very limited amount of government services and investment. Over the subsequent decades, the provision of government goods and services was extended considerably. In recent decades, however, *real or exhaustive* government spending did not grow much in most countries.[1] Instead, especially cash spending often associated with social programs grew rapidly. Most of this increase resulted from explicit policy decisions and, thus, was not the result of some technical factors such as the "Baumol's disease" or even of Wagner's Law. In other words, there was nothing automatic or inevitable about it that could not have been prevented by determined governments. In more recent years, unemployment and demographic changes have also contributed to the growth of public spending. If current policies persist, the growth of social spending, including pensions and health expenditure, will continue and, together with the growing real interest burden on public debt in several countries, could push public spending to unsustainable levels.

---

1. This is spending that *directly* absorbs real resources that could be used by the private sector. It is distinguished from spending that is in the form of cash, such as pension payments or interest on the public debt.

23

1. GOVERNMENT REAL EXPENDITURE

Government real expenditure[2] has grown considerably over the past 125 years, with the bulk of this growth having taken place by 1980 in most countries. At the end of the nineteenth century, government real expenditure ranged between 2.5 and 6.7 percent of GDP for the seven countries for which data are available (Table II.1). Comparing these numbers to total expenditure in Table I.1 from the previous chapter, it is evident that, at that time, between one-half and two-thirds of total expenditure fell into this category. The very low level of expenditure suggests that governments provided just a minimum of services beyond "the administration of justice," defense, and some expenditure for infrastructure. Defense expenditure accounted on average for over half of real expenditure and about one-third of total expenditure in the pre–World War I period. Public education and spending for infrastructure were probably the other main expenditure categories in the late nineteenth century. This was the period when major public projects such as railroads, underground systems, and waterworks, were built, when power plants were created, and when the provision of universal schooling up to a certain age became an important objective of governments.

The level of public employment (including military personnel) is another indicator of the limited role of government a century ago. In 1870, on average, only 2.4 percent of the total employed population worked for the government compared with 18.4 percent in 1994 (Table II.2). In Japan and Germany, this share was only about 1 percent. The United Kingdom had the largest public work force, about 5 percent of total employment. This was probably due to the needs connected with its large and widespread colonial empire.

Government real expenditure increased from an average of 4.6 percent in 1870 to 11.4 percent of GDP in 1937. In 1937, government real expenditure as a share of overall public expenditure continued to average about 50 percent. Public expenditure programs following the Great Depression – such as the New Deal in the United States –

---

2. Defined as the sum of government wages and salaries and materials and supplies purchased by the government. This is the part of government spending that absorbs or uses economic resources *directly*. It is an economic definition that does not identify the function of the expenditure. It may thus include social spending provided in kind (i.e., public housing or public education) rather than in cash.

Table II.1. *Government Real Expenditure, 1870–95*
(Percent of GDP)

	About 1870[a]	1937	1960	1980	1990	1995
Australia	4.8	5.5	11.2	17.6	17.1	17.5
Canada	. . .	10.1	13.4	19.2	19.8	19.6
France	5.4	15.0	14.2	18.1	18.0	19.3
Germany	. . .	21.0	13.4	20.2	18.4	19.5
Japan	. . .	12.4	8.0	9.8	9.1	9.7
Netherlands[b]	6.7	12.3	12.6	17.9	14.5	14.3
Norway[b]	2.6	3.2	12.9	18.8	21.0	20.7
Spain[b]	4.9	10.7	8.3	12.5	15.5	16.6
Sweden[b]	5.5	10.4	16.0	29.3	27.4	25.8
United Kingdom	. . .	11.7	16.4	21.6	20.6	21.4
United States	2.5	12.9	19.4	18.7	18.9	16.2
Average	**4.6**	**11.4**	**13.3**	**18.5**	**18.2**	**18.2**
Austria	. . .	. . .	13.0	18.0	17.8	18.8
Belgium	. . .	. . .	12.4	17.8	14.5	14.8
Ireland	. . .	. . .	12.5	19.2	15.1	14.7
Italy	. . .	. . .	12.0	14.7	17.4	16.3
New Zealand	. . .	. . .	10.5	17.9	16.7	14.3
Switzerland	. . .	. . .	8.8	12.7	13.3	14.0
Average	**. . .**	**. . .**	**11.5**	**16.7**	**15.8**	**15.5**
Total Average	**4.6**	**11.4**	**12.6**	**17.9**	**17.4**	**17.3**

Source: Complied by Tanzi and Schuknecht, based on Andic and Veverka (1964); Butlin (1984); Delorme and André (1983); Foster and Stewart (1991); Mitchell, *International Historical Statistics* (various years); OECD, *National Accounts* (various issues); Okawa Shinohara, Unlmura (1965–79).
[a] Or closest year available for all columns.
[b] Central government data for 1870 and 1937 column.

the extension of government services, for example in education, and war preparations in a number of European countries explain a large share of the expenditure growth in this category.[3]

Public employment over the 1870–1937 period doubled to 5 percent of total employment. Austria, the United Kingdom, and the United States had the highest share of public workers. The fact that government employment increased more slowly than expenditure on public consumption could be due to depression-related public expen-

3. In Germany and Italy, defense spending absorbed almost 10 percent of GDP in 1937, and France and the United Kingdom also stepped up military spending considerably.

Table II.2. *Government Employment, 1870–1994[a]*
(Percent of Total Employment)

	About 1870[b]	1913	1937	1960	1980	1994
Australia	1.4	1.7	. . .	23.0	26.0	20.9
Austria	1.9	4.7	7.6	10.6	17.3	22.4
Belgium	2.2	4.8	. . .	12.2	18.9	19.4
Canada	. . .	. . .	. . .	18.4	18.8	20.4
France	2.5	3.0	4.4	. . .	20.0	24.8
Germany	1.2	2.4	4.3	9.2	14.6	15.1
Ireland	2.5	2.6	1.8	. . .	14.5	14.0
Italy	2.6	4.4	5.1	7.7	14.5	16.2
Japan	1.0	3.1	5.0	. . .	6.7	6.9
Netherlands	3.5	4.6	5.8	11.7	14.9	12.7
New Zealand	. . .	. . .	. . .	17.9	19.2	18.1
Norway	2.2	3.4	4.7	. . .	23.2	30.6
Spain	. . .	. . .	. . .	. . .	11.9	15.1
Sweden	2.2	3.5	4.7	12.8	30.3	32.0
Switzerland	2.4	5.7	5.8	7.3	10.7	14.1
United Kingdom	4.9	4.1	6.5	14.8	21.1	15.0
United States	2.9	3.7	6.8	14.7	15.4	14.5
Average	**2.4**	**3.7**	**5.2**	**12.3**	**17.5**	**18.4**

Sources: Compiled by Tanzi and Schuknecht based on Bird, Bucovetsky, and Foot (1979); Flora et al. (1983); Japan Statistical Association (1987); Liesner (1985); OECD *Historical Statistics* (1992, 1996).
[a] General government based on U.N. national accounts definition, includes military personnel.
[b] Or closest year available for all columns; New Zealand 1994 = 1985, and selected countries 1994 = 1993.

diture programs that provided temporary public works but did not affect much regular government employment.

By 1960, government real expenditure had increased modestly to 12.6 percent of GDP and had fallen slightly below 50 percent of total expenditure. The average increase would have been higher if it had not been moderated by the elimination of some public expenditure programs because of the end of the great depression and World War II. In some countries (mainly Germany, Japan, and Spain), a decline in defense spending explains much of the reported decline in real expenditure for the 1937–60 period.

If we look at the change in public employment over the 1937–60 period, we find indications of some substitution among spending programs. Government employment doubled between 1937 and 1960 without leading to an equivalent increase in real expenditure. This may reflect the fact that the extension of government services in the postwar period created new public employment while the postwar disarmament and the demise of depression-related expenditure programs reduced spending but did not affect the size of the civil service.

Still, a few countries, such as Australia, Norway, Sweden, the United Kingdom, and the United States expanded real government expenditure considerably during this period. In the United States (and to a lesser extent Australia), this increase was largely due to an increase in defense spending which, in 1960, was much higher than in 1937 (Table II.3). In fact, in 1960 the highest share of real government expenditure in GDP was reported by the United States (19.4 percent of GDP). In this country, in 1960 defense spending was relatively high. The second largest share in government real expenditure was shown by the United Kingdom with 16.4 percent of GDP. Japan, Switzerland, and Spain spent only between 8 and 9 percent of GDP on this category, less than half of what the United States spent. Again, the difference in spending levels between these countries can largely be explained by differences in defense spending.

The next two decades saw further increases in government real expenditure, with the average increasing from 12.6 percent in 1960 to 17.9 percent of GDP in 1980. By 1980, only Japan maintained a spending level around 10 percent. In Sweden, Germany, and the United Kingdom, government real expenditure had exceeded 20 percent of GDP. The change was especially remarkable in Sweden, from 16 percent of GDP in 1960 to 29.3 percent of GDP in 1980. In the United States and to a lesser extent in other countries, nondefense spending had replaced a considerable share of military spending in this category. In fact, in the United States, the fall in defense spending has substantially hidden the increase in nondefense public spending. Also, in France and in Canada the increase in government expenditure would have been even larger had it not been for a marked decline in military expenditure.

Public employment increased in line with real expenditure. By the mid-1970s, on average, one-sixth of the labor force of the industrial countries was employed by the government. The

Table II.3. *Public Expenditure on Defense, 1900–95*
(Percent of GNP)

	About 1900[a]	1920	1937	1960	1980	1995
Australia	0.2	1.0	0.6	2.4	2.3	2.4
Austria	...	0.7	1.3	1.2	1.2	0.9
Belgium	...	2.4	...	3.4	3.1	1.7
Canada	...	...	...	4.3	1.6	1.6
France	6.5	1.9	5.5	6.3	3.3	3.1
Germany	1.7	0.9	9.6	4.0	2.9	1.7
Ireland	...	5.1	1.2	1.4	1.9	1.4
Italy	7.4	2.7	9.9	2.7	1.7	1.9
Japan	6.0	4.1	5.3	1.0	0.9	1.0
Netherlands	...	...	...	3.9	3.2	2.1
New Zealand	...	...	3.9	1.4	1.6	1.3
Norway	...	0.9	0.8	3.2	2.6	2.6
Spain	...	5.8	3.8	2.9	1.6	1.5
Sweden	...	2.0	1.6	2.8	3.2	2.5
Switzerland	...	...	1.8	2.4	2.1	1.6
United Kingdom	5.4	2.6	5.3	6.4	4.9	3.1
United States	0.8	0.6	1.1	8.8	5.2	4.0
Average	**4.0**	**2.4**	**3.7**	**3.4**	**2.5**	**2.0**

Sources: Compiled by Tanzi and Schuknecht based on Fernández-Acha (1976); Andic and Veverka (1964); Australian Bureau of Census and Statistics (1938); Norway Statistisk Sentralbyrå (1969, 1978), IMF, *World Economic Outlook* (1995); League of Nations *Statistical Yearbook* (various years); Stockholm International Peace Research Institute, *Armaments, Disarmaments and International Security: SIPRI yearbook, 1996*; United States, Arms Control and Disarmament Agency, *World Military Experience Transfers* (1996).
[a] Or closest year available for all columns.

governments of Australia, France, Norway, Sweden, and the United Kingdom had 20 percent or more of the labor force on their payrolls.

Some authors have argued that the increase in real expenditure may overstate the increase in real spending because productivity growth in the public sector is generally assumed to be slower than in the private sector. Thus, a larger share of GDP must be spent to purchase the same real share of inputs. Levitt and Joyce (1987), for example, have argued that although government real expenditure in the United Kingdom increased from 16.5 percent of GDP in 1964 to 21.8 percent of GDP in 1984, the price-adjusted increase was negligible: at 1980 prices, government real expenditure increased only from 20.7 percent to 20.8 percent.[4] Similar arguments have been made for other countries. This would suggest that in a real sense government consumption may not have increased much since the 1960s in many industrialized countries. However, the higher spending still requires more taxes to finance it, and higher taxes impose real costs on the economy and reduce the income that the taxpayers have to sustain their standards of living.

The increase in real expenditure explains only part of the growth of total government spending in this period. The share of real expenditure fell from almost 50 percent of total public expenditure in 1960 to 42 percent in 1980. Since 1980, average real expenditure has remained broadly constant within the 17–18 percent of GDP range and has even declined moderately in Belgium, Ireland, New Zealand, the Netherlands, Sweden, and the United States. This decline reflects changes in the perceived role of the state as mentioned in the previous chapter or, in the United States, the United Kingdom, and a few other countries, a further fall in defense spending. Privatization or subcontracting of services to the private sector in recent years has reduced the government's direct involvement in the economy in a number of countries. In addition, several countries have reduced their role in running enterprises. The share of state enterprises in the economy, for example, declined in Germany, Italy, and most prominently, the United Kingdom during the 1980s.[5] This decline has reduced the subsidies that these enterprises receive from the government.

While real expenditure has been relatively stable as a share of GDP, it has continued to shrink as a share of total public expenditure over the 1980s and early 1990s. In 1995, real expenditure constituted only 37.8 percent of total public expenditure. In the next section it will be shown that this reduction reflects the growing importance of cash subsidies and transfers in the budget. In fact, one could speculate that the relative stagnation or reduction of real expenditure reflects policy substitution toward (politically more important) transfer payments.

---

4. This divergence in productivity growth between the public and the private sector is sometimes referred to as Baumol's disease (see Baumol, 1967).
5. For more details on the issue of public enterprises, see World Bank, *Bureaucrats in Business* (1995), or World Bank, *World Development Report* (1997).

2. SUBSIDIES AND TRANSFERS

The most remarkable change in the composition of government expenditure took place in the past thirty to forty years with the dramatic rise in public subsidies and transfers (Table 2.4). To a small extent this was due to the emergence and extension of producer subsidies. Much more importantly, however, it reflects the increase in social spending for the expanding social or welfare activities of governments in industrialized countries. Political decisions to extend assistance programs to more and more people and to raise benefits levels were key to this spending growth, whereas technical factors, such as population aging, were of limited importance in this period.[6] It is also worthwhile noting that most of the spending increase took place over the 1960–80 period, the period of great faith in the beneficial effects of the government intervention in the economy and in policies aimed at guaranteeing and redistributing income.

In the late nineteenth century, the average level of subsidies and transfers was barely 1 percent of GDP in the countries for which data are available. At that time, the United Kingdom was the leader in this category with 2.2 percent of GDP, while France, Japan, and Norway hardly reached the 1 percent mark. Social insurance was virtually nonexistent and producer subsidies were very limited.[7]

By 1937, the Great Depression coupled with the emerging social security systems had resulted in an increase in the average expenditure on subsidies and transfers to 4.5 percent of GDP. France, Germany, and especially the United Kingdom incurred the largest transfers. While in the late nineteenth century, transfers and subsidies amounted to only about 10 percent of the much smaller public expenditure, by 1937 this share had risen to almost 20 percent.

Transfers and subsidies continued to increase, reaching 9.7 percent of GDP in 1960, or about one-third of total public expenditure. Austria was at the top of the list, but in Belgium, France, Germany, Italy, the Netherlands, and Norway spending on this category already exceeded 10 percent of GDP. Japan and the United States also expanded their transfer and subsidy provisions considerably in the

6. Technical factors such as the aging of the population are likely to become more important in future years.
7. See Lindert (1994), for a detailed discussion of welfare spending between 1880 and 1930 in various countries.

Table II.4. *Government Expenditure on Subsidies and Transfers,*
1870–95 (Percent of GDP)

	About 1870[a]	1937	1960	1970	1980	1995
Canada[b]	0.5	1.6	9.0	12.4	13.2	14.9
France[b]	1.1	7.2	11.4	21.0	24.6	29.9
Germany[b]	0.5	7.0	13.5	12.7	16.8	19.4
Japan	1.1	1.4	5.5	6.1	12.0	13.5
Norway[c]	1.1	4.3	12.1	24.4	27.0	27.0
Spain	. . .	2.5	1.0	6.7	12.9	25.7
United Kingdom	2.2	10.3	9.2	15.3	20.2	23.6
United States[c]	0.3	2.1	6.2	9.8	12.2	13.1
Average	**0.9**	**4.5**	**8.5**	**13.6**	**17.4**	**20.9**
Australia	. . .	. . .	6.6	10.5	16.7	19.0
Austria	. . .	. . .	17.0	16.6	22.4	24.5
Belgium[c]	0.2	. . .	12.7	20.7	30.0	28.8
Ireland	. . .	. . .	. . .	18.8	26.9	24.8
Italy	. . .	. . .	14.1	17.9	26.0	29.3
Netherlands[c]	0.3	. . .	11.5	29.0	38.5	35.9
New Zealand[c]	0.2	. . .	. . .	11.5	20.8	12.9
Sweden	0.7	. . .	9.3	16.2	30.4	35.7
Switzerland	. . .	. . .	6.8	7.5	12.8	16.8
Average	**. . .**	**. . .**	**11.1**	**16.5**	**24.9**	**25.3**
Total average	**1.1**	**4.5**	**9.7**	**15.1**	**21.4**	**23.2**

Sources: Compiled by Tanzi and Schuknecht based on Andic and Veverka (1964); Norway,
Statistisk Sentralbyrå (1969, 1978); Delorme and André (1983); Foster and Stewart (1969);
IMF, *Government Finance Statistics* (various years); Lindert (1994); Mitchell; IMF, *International Finance Statistics* (various years); OECD *National Accounts* (various years);
Peacock and Wiseman (1961).
[a] Or closest year available in all columns, central government for 1970–95, except Japan.
[b] Transfers only for historical data until 1937.
[c] Data for 1870 covers welfare spending on unemployment, pensions, health, and housing
only; see Lindert (1994).

1937–60 period, albeit from very low levels. Only Spain and to a lesser
extent the United Kingdom reduced expenditure in this category.

Between 1960 and 1980, the earlier limited social policies were progressively transformed into what in many countries came to be called
the welfare state. Subsidies and transfers as a share of GDP more
than doubled to over 20 percent of GDP, equivalent to 50 percent of
total government expenditure.[8] In Belgium, France, Ireland, Italy, the

8. Before World War II, social security was largely fragmented and decentralized, but the
postwar expansion of the welfare state coincided with a widespread nationalization and
the centralization of social security. (See Ashford and Kelly, 1986.)

Netherlands, Norway, and Sweden, expenditure in this category exceeded or approached one-quarter of GDP with a maximum share of 38.5 percent of GDP. The Netherlands. Japan, Spain, Switzerland, and the United States were the only countries where transfers and subsidies stayed near 10 percent of GDP. Although most of this increase was on account of household transfers, producer subsidies also increased rapidly in most countries over this period and in 1980 reached 7–8 percent of GDP in Ireland and Norway (see United Nations, *National Accounts*).

After 1980, the expansionary trend continued but at a much slower pace. Expenditure on transfers and subsidies increased from an average of 21.4 percent of GDP in 1980 to 23.2 percent of GDP in 1995, slightly more than half of total government expenditure. While transfers continued to grow, producer subsidies, however, started coming down in a majority of countries, with New Zealand eliminating such subsidies altogether. There were marked differences among countries regarding the growth of public transfers: some, such as Belgium, Ireland, the Netherlands, and New Zealand started to curtail state involvement, while others, especially Spain, continued expanding their welfare expenditures.

3. SOCIAL EXPENDITURE

The growing importance of transfers and subsidies is the result of increasing government obligations, or, seen from another side, of citizens' entitlements, in the social area. To understand fully the expenditure dynamics in social expenditure, it is worthwhile taking a closer look at some of the subcategories and the underlying policy decisions that resulted in their rapid expansion. These categories include education, health, pensions, unemployment benefits, and other transfer programs. In the European Union, social expenditure as a share of GDP more than doubled between 1960 and 1980, from 10 percent to over 20 percent of GDP, and continued to grow more slowly thereafter. In other countries of the Organization for Economic Cooperation and Development (OECD), expenditure growth in these categories was similar.[9]

---

9. Social expenditure consists mostly of cash transfers. However, they also contain some real expenditure.

Education

For over a century, the provision of a good educational system has been perceived by most people as one of the essential tasks of government. It has been frequently argued that education contributes to both economic growth and equity and thus to social stability and democratic values. Governments started providing primary education in the midnineteenth century. By 1900, the provision of fairly universal public primary education was the rule among today's industrialized countries, although in many countries the proportion of the relevant population that actually attended these schools was much lower than the potential number and many individuals remained illiterate. In the early 1900s, public expenditure on education exceeded 1 percent of GDP, with France, Germany, and Japan showing the highest expenditure levels (Table II.5). Education spending in Germany and Japan amounted to about one-fifth of total government spending.

Before World War II, public spending on education had almost doubled, to about 2 percent of GDP, as the average period of legally required school attendance continued to be raised. By 1960, secondary education up to some age was almost universally required and free in OECD countries and public spending had risen to 3.5 percent of GDP. Only Australia and Spain reported much lower spending levels. The post–World War II baby boom experienced by many countries, and the expansion of university systems resulted in a further rapid increase in public education expenditure in the period between 1960 and 1980. Since 1980, public expenditure on education has been almost constant.

In 1993–94, Canada, New Zealand, Norway, and Sweden reported the highest levels of public spending on education – between 7.3 percent of GDP and 9.2 percent of GDP. Germany, Japan, and Spain, however, spent less than 5 percent of GDP to finance schooling. One-fifth to one-sixth of educational spending, or about 1 percent of GDP was typically accounted for by tertiary education. This share was much higher for Canada. Japan reported by far the lowest public spending on *higher* education relative to GDP.

The growth of educational spending can explain some of the expenditure increases in the past. It reflects growing school enrollment especially at higher levels of education. But it also reflects gov-

Table II.5. *Public Expenditure on Education, 1870–93*
(Percent of GDP)

	Total public education[a]						Higher education	
	About 1870[b]	1913	1937	1960	1980	1993–94	1970–72	1993
Australia	...	...	0.7	1.4	5.5	6.0	1.5	1.2
Austria	...	...	2.5	2.9	5.6	5.5	0.7	1.1
Belgium	...	1.2	...	4.6	6.1	5.6	...	1.0
Canada	...	...	...	4.6	6.9	7.6	2.5	2.2
France	0.3	1.5	1.3	2.4	5.0	5.8	0.7	0.9
Germany	1.3	2.7	...	2.9	4.7	4.8	0.6	0.9
Ireland	...	...	3.3	3.2	6.6	6.4	0.8	1.1
Italy	...	0.6	1.6	3.6	4.4	5.2	0.5	0.8
Japan	1.0	1.6	2.1	4.1	5.8	4.7	0.5	0.4
Netherlands	...	...	1.5	4.9	7.6	5.5	2.1	1.4
New Zealand	...	...	2.3	3.2	5.8	7.3	1.3	1.5
Norway	0.5	1.4	1.9	4.2	7.2	9.2	0.9	1.5
Spain	...	0.4	1.6	1.3	2.6	4.7	...	0.8
Sweden	...	...	...	5.1	9.0	8.4	0.9	1.5
Switzerland	...	...	...	3.1	5.0	5.6	0.8	1.2
United Kingdom	0.1	1.1	4.0	4.3	5.6	5.4	1.4	0.9
United States	...	...	...	4.0	...	5.5	1.3	1.3
Average	**0.6**	**1.3**	**2.1**	**3.5**	**5.8**	**6.1**	**1.1**	**1.1**

Sources: Compiled by Tanzi and Schuknecht based on Fernández Acha (1976); Australian Bureau of Census and Statistics (1938); New Zealand Department of Statistics (1937); Japan Statistical Association (1987); League of Nations *Statistical Yearbook* (various years), Mitchell (1962); OECD, *Education at a Glance* (1996); [Italy] Istituto Nazionale di statistica (1951); UNESCO, *World Education Report* (1993); United Nations Development Programme, *Human Development Report* (1996); UN, *World Economics Survey* (various years).
[a] Expenditure by states only for Australia in 1937, central government for France for all years until 1937.
[b] Or closest year available for all columns.

ernments' decision to finance an increasing share of spending at all levels. Before World War II, student's tuition typically covered at least part of the costs of secondary education. Today, secondary education is mostly free. Even tertiary education is often predominantly financed by the government even though it has a large investment component for those who benefit from it because it often provides them with a professional qualification that increases their life income. Recent attempts by some governments (France, Italy) to begin to charge for part of the tertiary education has met stiff resistance from students. However, it is likely that financial pressures on governments will lead to an intensification of such attempts.

With universal secondary education and growing enrollment in largely publicly financed universities, education will continue absorbing a substantial share of public resources. However, declining birth rates have reduced the upward dynamic in education spending. Nevertheless, there will be pressure for reform in this sector to improve the quality and cost effectiveness of public education and to bring its often anachronistic output and organization more in line with the requirements of a modern economy. There will also be reforms attempting to give a larger role to the private sector, for example, through the use of school vouchers that allow students a choice of schools, including private schools, and force some competition in school bureaucracies.

Health

Major government involvement in the health sector is a relatively recent phenomenon. The lack of data for the pre–World War I period is symptomatic for this. The rapid progress in medicine and the realization that public health could contribute to individual well-being and economic productivity gave rise in this century, and especially in recent decades, to the rapid development of the health sector and with it to demands for government involvement in maintaining high health standards for the population. In health, as in education, the concept of externality and concerns for equity were used to justify governmental intervention in the provision of these services. The view that access to free health services is a basic right has been strongly promoted in some circles and in many countries.

In some countries, public health insurance was one of the first social insurance programs to become available. After Bismarck's introduction of health insurance in 1883, five other European countries followed suit before 1900 with compulsory or voluntary insurance schemes (Table II.6). Coverage was very limited, however, and in 1910 averaged only 22 percent of the labor force. Even in Germany, the pioneer of social insurance, only 44 percent of the labor force was covered by health insurance before World War I. In addition, benefit levels were very low, and costly technical innovations and the aging

Table II.6. *Social Insurance Coverage in Western Europe: Pension, Unemployment, and Health Insurance, 1910–75* (Percent of Labor Force)

	Pension Insurance					Health Insurance					Unemployment Insurance				
	Year of introduction		Percent of labor force covered			Year of introduction		Percent of labor force covered			Year of introduction		Percent of labor force covered		
	Voluntary[a]	Compulsory[a]	1910	1935	1975	Voluntary	Compulsory	1910	1935	1975	Voluntary	Compulsory	1910	1935	1975
Austria		1927	2	36	81		1888	24	49	88	(1920)	1920	NA	25	65
Belgium	(1900)	1924	29	44	100	(1894)	1944	12	31	96	(1920)	1944	NA	23	67
France	(1895)	1910	13	36	98	(1898)	1930	18	36	94	(1905)	1967	NA	1	65
Germany		1889	53	68	86		1883	44	52	72		1927	NA	35	76
Ireland	(1908)	1960	..	44	85		1911	..	38	71		1911	NA	30	71
Italy	(1898)	1919	2	38	94	(1886)	1928	6	22	91		1919	NA	31	52
Netherlands		1913	NA	56	100		1929	NA	42	74	(1916)	1949	NA	16	78
Norway		1936	NA	NA	100		1909	NA	56	100	(1906)	1938	NA	5	82
Sweden		1913	NA	NA	100	(1891)	1953	27	35	100	(1934)		NA	2	67
Switzerland		1946	NA	NA	100	(1911)		NA	69	100		1976	NA	28	29
United Kingdom	(1908)	1925	NA	79	80		1911	NA	82	100	(1924)	1911	NA	63	73
Average			**20**	**56**	**93**			**22**	**47**	**90**				**24**	**66**

Source: Flora et al. (1983).

NA = No public insurance program available.

[a] Voluntary = voluntary insurance (workman's compensation, or means-tested pension); year of introduction in brackets; Compulsory = compulsory insurance.

of the population had not yet driven up the costs of health services. By about 1930, average public spending still amounted to only 0.4 percent of GDP (Table II.7).

Between the 1920s and the 1960s, compulsory public health insurance became the predominant form of financing health services. By 1929, all the eleven European countries shown in Table II.6 had at least voluntary insurance schemes. By 1935, half the labor force was covered by health insurance, and by 1953, among the countries shown in Table II.6, only Switzerland did not have compulsory health insurance. By 1975, public health insurance covered between 71 and 100 percent of the total labor force in European countries. In addition, technical progress was driving up the costs of health. Benefits were extended especially in the 1960s and 1970s. Governments provided more and more generous insurance schemes, which reduced or even completely eliminated user charges on health services and with it the incentive to treat health services as a scarce and costly resource.[10]

By 1960, public expenditure on health had increased to 2.4 percent of GDP. By 1980, spending had again more than doubled to an average of 5.8 percent of GDP, with health expenditure exceeding 8 percent of GDP in Ireland and Sweden. Thereafter, public spending increased more slowly and reached 6.4 percent in 1994. The uniformity of public health expenditure across countries in the early 1990s is interesting: spending ranges between 5.5 percent of GDP in Japan and 7.6 percent in France. This picture masks considerable differences in total outlays on health, however, because it does not include private financing of health services. In fact, in some countries, as for example Italy, the relatively poor quality of public health in some parts of the country has stimulated the growth of privately provided health services. In the United States, private health care remains predominant for much of the population.

The slowing of health expenditure growth since 1980 reflects to some extent efforts to reform the health sector and to control its costs. However, the pressure on public health budgets is likely to grow. Technical progress will probably raise the costs of health services more strongly than in other sectors, and rising life expectancy

---

10. In Germany in the 1970s and early 1980s, for example, health insurance paid virtually 100 percent of all medical expenses including dental care and medication. The same was true for other countries.

Table II.7. *Public Expenditure on Health, 1913–94*
(Percent of GDP)

	About 1910[a]	About 1930	1960	1980	1994
Australia	0.4	0.6	2.4	4.7	5.8
Austria[b]	...	0.2	3.1	4.5	6.2
Belgium	0.2	0.1	2.1	5.1	7.2
Canada	...	...	2.3	5.4	7.0
France	0.3	0.3	2.5	6.1	7.6
Germany	0.5	0.7	3.2	6.5	7.0
Ireland	...	0.6	3.0	8.4	6.0
Italy	...	...	3.0	6.0	5.9
Japan	0.1	0.1	1.8	4.6	5.5
Netherlands	...	...	1.3	6.5	6.9
New Zealand	0.7	1.1	3.5	4.8	5.7
Norway	0.4	0.6	2.6	6.5	6.9
Spain	...	...	0.9	...	5.8
Sweden	0.3	0.9	3.4	8.8	6.4
Switzerland	...	0.3	2.0	5.4	6.9
United Kingdom	0.3	0.6	3.3	5.2	5.8
United States	0.3	0.3	1.3	4.1	6.3
Total average	**0.3**	**0.4**	**2.4**	**5.8**	**6.4**

Sources: Compiled by Tanzi and Schuknecht based on Fernández Acha (1976); Andic and Veverka (1964); Australia, Bureau of Census Statistics (1938); Norway, Statistisk Sentralbyrå. (1969, 1978); Census and Statistics Department, *New Zealand Official Yearbook* (1937); League of Nations, *Statistical Yearbook* (various years); Lindert (1994); Mitchell (1962); OECD, *Social Expenditure*, 1960–90; Okama et al. (1979); World Bank, *World Development Indicators* (1997).
[a] Or closest year available for all columns; governments subsidies for health care in all countries, except Austria (see Lindert (1994)).
[b] Central government only.

and population aging will make the use of public resources in a cost-effective manner even more urgent, if the attainment of good health standards is not to suffer. However, existing institutional arrangements in this sector do not provide strong incentives for keeping costs under control. There will be pressures on governments to introduce further cost-saving reforms and to reflect on the appropriate future role of the state in the health sector. In time, the state may become more of a regulator and less of a provider of health services except for the poorest sectors of the population.

Pensions

Government involvement in providing for old age started in the late nineteenth century when, in 1889, Germany introduced pension insurance (see Table II.6). France and Italy followed suit with voluntary schemes before the end of the century. By the mid-1920s, most of the eleven European countries for which data are available had rudimentary retirement insurance. Again, coverage was very limited and benefit levels were very low. By 1910, only in Germany half of the labor force was covered. In Italy or Austria coverage extended to only 2 percent of the labor force.

Public pension insurance developed along similar lines as public health insurance. It is not so easy to distinguish between developments before and after 1960, but the picture is similar: political pressures led to increased coverage and benefits; as a consequence, pension expenditure started to rise, especially after World War II. Between the 1920s and the 1960s, coverage increased from 20 percent of the labor force in 1910 to 56 percent in 1935 and to close to 100 percent of the labor force by 1975. Benefit levels also increased, but benefits increased most rapidly in the postwar period. The replacement ratio for pension – that is, the share of wages replaced by pension at retirement – increased from about 15 percent in 1939 to 51 percent in 1969 and to 62 percent in 1980 (Table II.8). Some increase in public spending also resulted from population aging: the share of the population over 60 in OECD countries increased from 8.7 percent in 1900 to 14.4 percent in 1960.

Public expenditure on pensions rose from 1.2 percent of GDP in 1920 to almost 2 percent in 1937 (Table II.9). By 1960, pension spending had reached an average of 4.5 percent of GDP, with Germany and Austria spending almost 10 percent of GDP on this category. By contrast, public pensions in Canada, Ireland, Japan, and Switzerland absorbed less than 3 percent of GDP.

As happened in other areas of social spending, pension spending "took off" during the 1960–80 period and, by 1980, it had almost doubled to 8.4 percent of GDP. In 1993, average spending on pensions had increased further and had reached 9.6 percent of GDP. In several countries, pension spending exceeded 10 percent of GDP, and it was close to 15 percent of GDP in Italy. Australia, Canada, Ireland,

Table II.8. *Development in Systems Generosity of Pension Benefits* (Percent of Average Wage)

	Pension benefits replacement ratio		
	1939	1969	1980
Australia[a]	19	. . .	. . .
Austria	. . .	67	68
Belgium	14	. . .	. . .
Canada[a]	17	41	49
France	. . .	56	75
Germany	19	55	49
Ireland	. . .	. . .	. . .
Italy	15	62	69
Japan	. . .	27	61
Netherlands	13	61	63
New Zealand[a]	. . .	. . .	. . .
Norway[a]	8	. . .	. . .
Spain	. . .	. . .	. . .
Sweden	10	56	83
Switzerland	. . .	45	55
United Kingdom	13	43	47
United States	21	44	66
Average	**15**	**51**	**62**

Sources: Compiled by Tanzi and Schuknecht based on Eurostat (1992); Palacios (1996).
[a] The main benefit is a universal flat or means-tested pension financed by general revenues.

and Japan were the countries with the lowest share of public spending on pensions, the share not exceeding 6 percent of GDP.

Holzmann (1988) has provided a detailed breakdown of the various factors that contributed to the rapid increase in public pension spending between 1960 and 1985. During this period, public pension expenditure as a share of total expenditure increased almost threefold in OECD countries. Increased eligibility for pensions and higher real benefits explain about three-quarters of this increase. Population aging was responsible for less than 20 percent, and growing unemployment for about 6 percent of the increase. The generosity of policymakers in distributing public money is reflected in the fact that, since 1970, the effective retirement age has declined in several indus-

Table II.9. *Public Expenditure on Pensions, 1913–93*
(Percent of GDP)

	About 1913[a]	1920[b]	1937[b]	1960	1980[c]	1990[c]	1993[c]
Australia	...	...	0.7	3.3	4.5	4.2	4.5
Austria	...	2.4	2.4	9.6	11.4	12.3	12.7
Belgium	...	0.3	3.7	4.3	11.2	11.2	10.9
Canada	...	...	...	2.8	3.4	4.8	5.5
France	...	1.6	...	6.0	10.5	11.3	12.3
Germany	...	2.1	...	9.7	12.8	11.3	12.4
Ireland	...	...	...	2.5	5.8	5.8	5.9
Italy	...	2.1	...	5.5	11.7	12.4	14.5
Japan	0.6	0.3	0.8	1.3	4.5	5.9	6.0
Netherlands	...	...	...	4.0	12.6	13.3	13.4
New Zealand	...	...	2.9	4.3	7.7	8.1	8.1
Norway	...	0.1	...	3.1	6.9	8.9	9.0
Spain	0.5	0.9	2.0	...	7.7	9.2	10.4
Sweden	...	0.5	...	4.4	9.9	10.8	12.8
Switzerland	...	...	...	2.3	8.5	8.9	10.2
United Kingdom	...	2.2	1.0	4.0	5.9	6.3	7.3
United States	...	0.7	...	4.1	7.0	7.0	7.5
Average	**0.4**	**1.2**	**1.9**	**4.5**	**8.4**	**8.9**	**9.6**

Sources: Compilation by Tanzi and Schuknecht based on Fernández Acha (1976); Australia, Bureau of Census and Statistics (1938); New Zealand Department of Statistics (1937); Institute National de Statistique, *Annuaire Statistique de la Belgique* (1952); Japan Statistical Association (1987); League of Nations *Statistical Yearbook* (various years); Mitchell, *International Historical Statistics* (1962); OECD, *Social Expenditure, 1960–1990* (1985); OECD, *Social Expenditure Statistics* (1996); Österreichisches Statistisches Zentralamt (1935); Palacios (1996); U.S. Social Security Administration, *Social Security Programs throughout the World* (1993).
[a] Or closest year available for all columns.
[b] Central government only.
[c] Old-age cash benefits, disability pensions, and survivors' pensions.

trial countries while life expectancy has increased significantly (World Bank, 1994a).

Governments gave generous benefits at a time when populations were still relatively young. Now, however, many countries face potentially explosive situations. The share of the population above the age of sixty is expected to increase to more than one-quarter of the total by the year 2020. This would be an increase of 50 percent over the current share of old-aged, and aging will be even faster in Canada and Japan. It will be shown later that past commitments by policymakers, coupled with an aging population, have resulted in considerable uncovered pension liabilities in many industrial countries (Chand and Jaeger, 1996). As with health, governments will be under pressure to reform pension systems to avoid causing major budgetary difficulties or sacrificing important achievements in preventing old-age poverty.

Unemployment

Unemployment insurance was a relative latecomer in the social security systems of industrialized countries and was only introduced in most of the European countries in the 1910s and 1920s (see Table II.6). France and Norway were the first to offer voluntary unemployment schemes, in 1905 and 1906 respectively. Compulsory insurance was first introduced in the United Kingdom and Ireland in 1911, but it was not before the 1960s and 1970s that compulsory unemployment insurance was required in France and Switzerland. By 1975, still only two-thirds of the labor force in Europe were covered by unemployment insurance.

Data on unemployment expenditure are not available for the period before the 1930s because there was probably not much unemployment compensation to speak of. The first test for the fledgling unemployment insurance systems, however, came quickly after their introduction with the onset of the Great Depression after 1929. In Norway, the United Kingdom, and the United States, public spending on the unemployed exceeded 2 percent of GDP in the mid-1930s (see Table II.10). In the postwar period, when full employment prevailed in much of the industrialized world, expenditure on the unemployed declined significantly. After the first oil crisis in 1974, unemployment in industrialized countries increased again and with it the budgetary costs of public unemployment programs. By 1996, the cost of unemployment compensation averaged 1.6 percent of GDP in the industrialized countries, with Belgium, Ireland, and the Netherlands spending around 3 percent of GDP. In 1996, expenditure on all labor market programs including retraining and public works averaged 2.7 percent of GDP. In Austria, Belgium, Ireland, and Sweden, it exceeded 4 percent of GDP. In the Netherlands, it almost reached 5 percent of GDP. Only Japan and the United States, both with relatively low unemployment rates, spent less than 1 percent of GDP for unemployment programs.

Table II.10. *Public Expenditure on Unemployment, 1937–96*
(Percent of GDP)

	Unemployment compensation				All labor market programs
	1937[a]	1960	1980	1996	1996
Australia	...	0.1	0.8	1.3	1.8
Austria	...	0.3	0.4	2.1	4.2
Belgium	0.9	0.7	2.6	2.9	4.3
Canada	...	1.5	2.3	1.3	1.9
France	...	0.2	1.5	1.4	3.1
Germany	...	0.1	0.9	2.4	3.8
Ireland	...	0.6	2.0	2.7	4.6
Italy	...	0.2	0.5	0.7	2.0
Japan	...	0.3	0.4	0.4	0.5
Netherlands	...	0.2	0.6	3.4	4.8
New Zealand	...	0.0	0.5	1.2	1.9
Norway	2.3	0.2	0.2	0.9	2.1
Spain	...	...	...	2.1	2.8
Sweden	0.2	0.2	0.4	2.3	4.5
Switzerland	0.6	0.0	0.1	1.3	1.9
United Kingdom	3.2	0.2	0.9	1.3	1.8
United States	2.2	0.6	0.6	0.3	0.5
Total average	**1.3**	**0.3**	**0.9**	**1.6**	**2.7**

Source: Compiled by Tanzi and Schuknecht based on Australia, Bureau of Census and Statistics (1938); League of Nations *Statistical Yearbook* (various years); OECD *Labor Market Policies for the 1990s* (1985); OECD, *Employment Outlook* (1997); OECD *Social Expenditure, 1960–90* (1985).
[a] Or latest available year for all columns.

Other Income Transfer Programs

A number of additional transfer programs has been implemented and extended significantly over the recent decades. While most individual programs are relatively small, together they now absorb an average of 5 percent of GDP (see Table II.11). This is a significant share of public resources and is on average comparable to the countries' education budget. These transfer programs include disability, sickness, maternity, early retirement, occupational injury and disease, family benefits, and a number of other contingencies including social assistance. In the Netherlands, in 1992, generous sickness and disability benefit systems and other contingencies absorbed over 10 percent of

Table II.11. *Public Expenditure on Other Income Transfer Programs, 1992 (Percent of GDP)*

	Total working-age related[a]	Disability	Sickness	Maternity	Occupational injury and disease	Early retirement	Other contingencies[b]	Housing	Family benefits
Australia	3.37	0.98	0.09	...	...	...	0.31	0.27	1.72
Austria	5.57	2.03	...	0.45	...	0.08	0.86	...	2.15
Belgium	6.32	1.55	1.02	0.17	0.55	0.74	0.30	...	1.99
Canada	4.32	0.80	0.06	0.18	0.28	...	2.70	...	0.30
France	5.39	0.96	0.52	0.21	0.56	0.40	0.19	0.77	1.78
Germany	6.31	1.51	1.66	0.10	0.76	0.49	0.48	0.16	1.15
Ireland	4.94	0.80	1.26	0.08	0.12	0.20	0.37	0.64	1.47
Italy[c]	2.99	1.40	0.18	0.13	0.55	0.27	...	0.00	0.46
Japan	0.91	0.30	0.06	0.08	0.21	...	0.14	...	0.12
Netherlands	10.25	4.64	2.92	0.09	...	0.46	0.79	0.34	1.01
New Zealand	3.13	0.71	0.32	...	...	...	0.09	0.44	1.57
Norway	9.63	3.18	2.42	0.50	0.02	...	1.14	0.24	2.13
Spain	3.31	1.39	1.10	0.05	0.49	...	0.05	0.10	0.13
Sweden	9.17	2.38	1.30	1.30	0.83	0.21	0.79	0.95	1.41
Switzerland	1.91	0.25	0.27	0.01	...	...	0.38	...	1.00
United Kingdom	7.84	1.83	1.03	0.07	0.09	0.05	1.60	1.49	1.68
United States	2.64	0.89	...	...	0.72	...	0.33	0.34	0.36
Total average	**5.18**	**1.51**	**0.95**	**0.24**	**0.43**	**0.32**	**0.66**	**0.48**	**1.20**

Source: OECD Social Expenditure database (SOCX).

[a] Except unemployment

[b] Includes social assistance in many countries.

[c] Disability data is 1991.

GDP, and in Sweden or Norway, these figures were not much smaller. Japan, Switzerland, and the United States were the only countries that had kept the costs for these programs well below 3 percent of GDP.

As we have seen, no single program is solely responsible for the dramatic increase in welfare expenditure in industrialized countries. Policymakers have granted generous benefits to most social groups.[11] Many of the main policies and programs that absorb one-quarter of country's resources were introduced earlier this century for highly selected groups, and when their cost appeared small, with the best of intentions to protect the beneficiaries from some catastrophic and life-threatening events. However, in recent decades these programs were often turned into almost universal benefits providing "cradle-to-grave" security and were made more generous. Health and pension expenditures, in particular, absorb the lion's share of social spending in most countries and, given demographic changes, have the most expansionary dynamics.

4. INTEREST ON PUBLIC DEBT

Since the early 1980s, interest payments have emerged as an important component of public expenditure. Historically, interest payments were high mainly during postwar periods, to service war-related debt.[12] Interest payments in Australia, France, Italy, or Spain were relatively high in the late nineteenth century, as governments had to service the debt incurred during earlier wars. After World War I, interest payments again increased as countries, especially European, had to service the new debt incurred during this war. The governments of Germany and Austria largely defaulted on their debt and, together with Switzerland and Sweden, which had stayed neutral during the war, had relatively small interest payments.

After World War II, rapid economic growth and balanced fiscal accounts in most industrialized countries brought about a

---

11. In some countries, such as Italy, these programs are largely tied to employment. Thus, they leave out groups that have not become part of the working population.
12. For a historical and international perspective on interest rates see Homer and Sylla (1991).

Table II.12. *Central Government Expenditure on Interest,*
1870–1995 (Percent of GDP)

	About 1870[a]	1913	1920	1937	1970	1980	1995
Australia[b]	3.6	2.8	5.4	5.8	1.7	1.8	1.8
Austria	...	...	1.0	1.5	0.8	2.5	4.0
Belgium	...	4.1	6.6	3.4	2.8	6.2	9.8
Canada[b]	...	...	4.8	5.8	1.2	2.5	4.3
France	5.2	...	4.5	5.4	0.5	1.5	3.2
Germany	0.3	0.3	...	0.9	0.4	1.0	2.5
Ireland	...	...	0.5	2.3	3.5	6.3	5.8
Italy	4.5	2.6	4.4	4.7	1.8	5.4	11.1
Japan	...	...	1.1	...	0.4	2.4	3.0
Netherlands	2.4	...	...	4.8	1.3	3.7	4.8
New Zealand	...	...	...	6.3	2.6	3.9	4.5
Norway	0.4	0.9	1.8	1.4	1.0	2.7	2.3
Spain	3.3	3.2	2.3	3.9	0.5	0.7	4.7
Sweden	...	...	1.0	0.9	1.0	4.1	6.6
Switzerland	...	...	...	1.1	0.3	0.5	0.9
United Kingdom[b]	1.7	1.7	5.7	5.3	2.7	4.7	3.7
United States[b]	1.4	...	1.3	1.0	1.3	2.3	3.2
Total average	**2.5**	**2.2**	**3.1**	**3.4**	**1.4**	**3.1**	**4.5**

Sources: Compiled by Tanzi and Schuknecht based on Fernández Acha (1976); Andic and
Veverka (1964); Butlin (1984); New Zealand Department of Statistics (1937); Norway,
Statistisk Sentralbyrå (1969, 1978); Delorme and André (1983); IMF, *Government Finance
Statistics* (1997); League of Nations *Statistical Yearbook* (various years); Mitchell (various
years); Mitchell, *Abstract of Historical Statistics* (1962); Peacock and Wiseman (1961).
[a] Or closest year available for all columns.
[b] Historical data 1870–1937, is general government.

considerable decline in the war-related public debt and interest
payments.[13] However, the rapid rise in public expenditure and the
subsequent public debt accumulation in most industrialized countries
since the 1960s has not been war-related. The government expenditure on interest increased rapidly from an average of 1.4 percent of
GDP in 1970 to 4.5 percent in 1995 (Table II.12). In Belgium and
Italy, interest payments in that year reached or exceeded 10 percent
of GDP or about 20 percent of total government expenditure – a

13. After World War II, in the United States, the share of public debt to GDP was about
    twice what it was in the mid-1990s. However, the level of real interest rate was very
    low or even negative, thus reducing the burden of the debt.

serious burden on the countries' government finances.[14] Only a few countries escaped this trend. For the majority, the ratio of public debt to GDP and public interest obligations continued its upward trend although at a reduced pace in recent years. The fall in inflation in the 1990s reduced nominal interest rates and in some countries (such as Italy) the share of interest payments in GDP.

Public Investment

Another interesting development in fiscal expenditure patterns is the decline in public investment in recent decades. In the European Union countries, for example, expenditure in this category declined from an average of 4.3 percent in 1970 to 3.2 percent in 1985 (Tanzi, 1986). For all industrialized countries in our sample, public investment in the mid-1990s is at its lowest level since the beginning of the century (Table II.13). The decline may be even larger in real terms, given that much of public investment in the early years of this century probably was on infrastructure that was relatively less costly than today's. There is a negative correlation between public expenditure for interest payment and expenditure for public investment. This might imply that the cost of servicing the public debt has been met at least in part with a lower expenditure on capital accumulation.

5. CONCLUDING REMARKS

The composition of public spending has changed considerably in industrialized countries over the past 125 years. Between 1870 and about 1960, expenditure growth largely resulted in an extension of government services and the formation of basic social security systems. Direct or real government expenditure was the guiding force until around 1960. Cash transfers were of marginal significance. Since the early 1960s, however, most spending growth has been absorbed by the expanding social programs and has often taken the form of cash transfers. For the most part, this growth was not induced by technical factors, such as declining government productivity or aging populations, but by political decisions that extended services, thus turning

---

14. Large interest payments can potentially lead to an explosive situation when they result in larger deficits and in growing debt-to-GDP ratios.

Table II.13. *General Government Expenditure on Public Investment, 1870–1995* (Percent of GDP)

	About 1870[a]	1913	1920	1937	1960	1980	1994–95
Australia	6.9	8.9	8.5	7.0	3.6	2.8	1.9
Canada	1.5	3.8	1.9	3.8	4.0	2.7	2.3
France	0.5	0.8	2.7	6.3	3.4	3.1	3.1
Japan	1.3	3.7	4.3	3.3	3.9	6.1	6.8
Netherlands	...	2.1	6.4	4.5	4.3	3.5	2.7
Norway	0.9	1.1	1.6	2.3	3.2	3.7	3.1
Spain	...	0.3	0.4	1.4	2.6	1.8	3.8
Sweden	...	...	...	0.6	3.2	3.3	2.4
United Kingdom	0.7	2.1	1.7	4.1	3.3	2.4	1.8
United States	2.2	2.7	3.5	5.1	2.3	1.7	1.7
Average	**2.0**	**2.8**	**3.4**	**3.8**	**3.4**	**3.1**	**3.0**
Austria	...	...	...	...	4.2	4.2	3.1
Belgium	...	...	...	...	2.2	3.6	1.5
Germany	...	...	...	...	3.2	3.6	2.5
Ireland	...	...	...	...	2.8	5.6	2.3
Italy	...	...	...	...	3.7	3.2	2.3
New Zealand	...	...	...	...	1.1	2.5	2.0
Switzerland	...	...	...	...	3.7	5.6	5.7
Average	**...**	**...**	**...**	**...**	**3.0**	**4.0**	**2.8**
Total average	**2.0**	**2.8**	**3.4**	**3.8**	**3.2**	**3.5**	**2.9**

Sources: Compiled by Tanzi and Schuknecht based on Fernández Acha (1976); Australia, Bureau of Census and Statistics (1938); Butlin (1984); New Zealand Department of Statistics (1937); Norway, Statistisk Sentralbyrå (1969, 1978); European Commission (1995); IMF, *Government Finance Statistics* (1995); OECD, *Economic Outlook* (1997); OECD, *Historical Statistics, 1960–1990* (1985); OECD, *National Accounts* (various years); Republica di Italiana Istituto Nazionale de Statistica (1951); Republique Française, Institut National de la Statistique et des Études Economiques (1961).
[a] Or closest year available for all columns. For historical data until 1937 central government data for France, Netherlands, Norway, Spain, and Sweden.

limited social safety nets into universal social benefits. Furthermore, the current policy commitments imply a considerable upward dynamics in some of the social expenditure categories and could become an important threat for future budgetary stability. In future years "technical" factors such as aging of the population will exert considerable pressure on public spending if current policies stay unchanged. This is one of the main reasons why current policies are not likely to remain unchanged.

Table AII.1. *Aging Population, Percentage of Population over Sixty Years Old*

	About 1900[a]	1930	1960	1990	2020 Proj.
Australia	6.2	9.9	12.3	15.0	22.8
Austria	...	...	...	20.2	28.9
Belgium	9.4	11.8	17.9	20.7	28.7
Canada	7.7	8.4	10.9	15.6	28.4
France	12.7	14.2	17.1	18.9	26.8
Germany	...	...	...	20.3	30.3
Ireland	...	...	...	15.2	20.1
Italy	9.6	10.8	13.9	20.6	30.6
Japan	...	7.4	8.9	17.3	31.4
Netherlands	...	...	...	17.8	28.4
New Zealand	7.2	10.4	12.2	15.2	22.7
Norway	...	...	...	21.2	26.0
Spain	8.0	9.5	16.5	18.5	25.6
Sweden	12.0	12.8	19.7	22.9	27.8
Switzerland	...	...	...	19.9	30.5
United Kingdom	7.4	9.4	15.9	20.8	25.5
United States	6.4	10.4	13.2	16.6	24.5
Total average	**8.7**	**10.5**	**14.4**	**18.6**	**27.0**

Source: Palacios (1996).
[a] Or closest year available.

III Revenue, Deficits, and Public Debt

The growth of public expenditure from 1870 to the present time had to be financed. For the first 100 years, until the 1960s, this was largely achieved through increased tax collection except during war periods. In recent decades, public revenue did not keep up with public expenditure despite the introduction of new taxes and significant increases in tax rates and in the share of tax revenue to GDP. Governments started recording fiscal deficits on a regular basis in the 1970s. These deficits accumulated to significant public debt burdens. Especially countries with high levels of public spending have been plagued by high tax burdens, fiscal deficits, and high public debt. In addition, governments have overcommitted themselves toward their retirees. Under current policies, the present value of the future deficits in the finances of the pension systems will dwarf the current explicit public debts in some industrialized countries. In recent years, these developments have led many governments and policy experts to worry about the high levels of public expenditure and about the implications of existing policies for future generations. Recently, fiscal consolidation has started to bear fruit in the form of lower deficits in most industrial countries and even surpluses in some. However, it remains to be seen whether this fiscal consolidation will continue in the future, especially if economic growth slows down.

1. REVENUE

Total Revenue

Until the early-1970s, in normal times, government revenue had largely kept pace with public expenditure. Sustained fiscal deficits were rare, except during wars or during the worst period of the Great Depression. Between 1870 and 1913, tax revenue (like expenditure) was around 10 percent of GDP (see Table III.1).[1] In 1870, the "biggest" governments of the time, Australia, France, and Italy, had also the highest level of tax revenues (between 12 and 18 percent of GDP) and showed virtually balanced budgets. It should be recalled though that at the time economists and tax experts in general considered such tax burdens to be excessive. For example, Leroy-Beaulieu, a prominent French economist, considered the level of taxation as "moderate" when the ratio of all taxes in national income is 5–6 percent. Taxes become "heavy" when the ratio rises to 10–12 percent. Beyond 12 percent, the level of taxation becomes exorbitant and such levels would have serious consequences for the growth of the country and the liberty of its citizens. (See Leroy-Beaulieu, 1888, pp. 127–8.) Furthermore, the Professor of Public Finance at Harvard in 1913 considered the *maximum* tax rate of 7 percent to be applied on personal incomes above US$500,000 to be "clearly excessive." (See Richard Goode, 1964, p. 3.) Finally, Cordell Hull, chairman of the Ways and Means Committee at the time, thought that the income tax rates of 1–6 percent being proposed "would produce more money than the mind of man would ever conceive to spend." (See Tanzi, 1988, p. 99.)

After World War I, many European countries struggled with war-related damages and public debts. Public revenue of about 14 percent of GDP in 1920 lagged somewhat behind public expenditure of about 18 percent of GDP. However, these figures are not fully comparable and overstate the average deficit.[2] In the non-European countries of Canada, Australia, New Zealand, and the United States, revenue con-

1. To a limited extent, revenue data from Table 3.1 can be compared with expenditure data in Table 1.1. However, data on general government revenue are more scarce than for expenditure. This limits the comparability of the data. In addition, the historical revenue and expenditure data under the same column are not always from the same year.
2. The average deficit is overstated for the period up to 1937, because general government revenue data are available for much fewer countries than general government expenditure data.

Table III.1. *General Government Revenue, 1870–1996 (Percent of GDP)*

	About 1870[a]	1913	1920	1937	1960	1980	1990	1996	1997
General government, all years									
Australia	17.8	16.7	19.4	14.9	24.4	29.7	35.5	35.0	35.1
France	15.3	13.7	17.9	20.5	37.3	46.1	48.3	50.3	50.6
Italy	12.5	14.7	24.2	31.1	24.8	36.9	42.4	46.2	47.9
Ireland	9.6	11.8	23.2	26.3	27.5	35.9	36.7	36.5	37.0
Japan	9.5	⋯	⋯	⋯	18.8	27.6	34.2	31.7	32.1
New Zealand	⋯	⋯	24.7	27.0	⋯	⋯	52.1	49.1	47.6
Norway	4.3	7.7	11.5	10.9	32.4	49.0	52.3	51.4	52.1
United Kingdom	8.7	11.2	20.1	22.6	29.9	39.6	38.7	37.2	37.8
United States	7.4	7.0	12.4	19.7	27.0	30.0	30.8	31.6	32.1
Average	**10.6**	**11.8**	**19.2**	**21.6**	**27.8**	**36.8**	**41.2**	**41.0**	**41.3**

Central government only, until 1937[b]

Austria	...	...	9.0	15.7	37.9	46.4	46.5	47.8	48.2
Belgium	11.6	17.0	...		30.3	49.0	48.1	49.8	50.1
Canada	4.1	5.5	16.6	22.6	26.0	36.1	41.9	42.7	43.5
Germany	1.4	3.2	8.6	15.9	35.2	45.0	43.0	45.3	45.0
Netherlands	...	6.4	11.8	11.9	33.9	51.6	49.0	47.3	47.7
Spain	9.4	10.3	5.8	11.9	18.7	30.0	38.2	39.0	39.5
Sweden	9.5	6.7	7.2	8.5	32.5	56.1	63.3	62.1	61.1
Switzerland	...	2.5	3.8	6.0	23.3	32.8	34.2	36.4	36.0
Average	**7.2**	**5.8**	**10.0**	**11.6**	**29.7**	**43.4**	**45.5**	**46.3**	**46.4**
Total average	**9.3**	**8.8**	**13.7**	**16.6**	**28.7**	**40.1**	**42.2**	**43.4**	**43.5**

Sources: Compiled by Tanzi and Schuknecht, based on Fernández Acha (1976); Australia Bureau of Census and Statistics, (1938); Butlin (1984); New Zealand Department of Statistics (1937); Norway, Statistisk Sentralbyrå (1969, 1978); IMF, *Government Finance Statistics* (1995); Mitchell (various years); Mitchell, *Abstract of British Historical Statistics* (1992); (OECD); *Economic Outlook* (June 1997); OECD, *Historical Statistics, 1960–1990* (1992); OECD, *National Accounts* (various years); Italy, Istituto Nazionale di Statistica (1951); Republique Française, Institut Nationale de la Statistique et des Études Economiques (1961).

[a] Or closest year available for all columns.

[b] Central government data, for Austria (1920); Belgium, Canada (1870, 1913); Germany, Netherlands, Spain, Sweden, and Switzerland.

tinued to match expenditure. Public revenue was lowest in the United States, with only 12 percent of GDP, and highest in New Zealand, with almost 25 percent of GDP. In Europe revenue was high in Italy and Ireland, at about 23–4 percent of GDP.

In the 1920s, the countries' fiscal position improved and, between 1920 and 1937, average revenue collection increased broadly in parallel with expenditure, from 15.6 percent of GDP to 19.5 percent of GDP. The Great Depression resulted in a temporary departure from balanced budgets in most industrialized countries, but by 1937 a number of countries not already engaged in war preparations showed balanced fiscal accounts again. In 1937 revenue amounted to 15 percent of GDP in Australia, 20 percent in the United States, and around 25 percent in Ireland and New Zealand. These levels were close to these countries' expenditure levels.

It is noteworthy that until the 1940s, many economists saw the limit for government involvement in the economy at levels that seem astonishingly low from the perspective of the 1990s. For example, in the 1940s, Colin Clark, an influential economist at that time, in a much discussed paper suggested that tax revenue of more than 25 percent of GDP would set in motion "forces of a political, economic, and psychological nature which inevitably, but with a lag of two or three years, [would] result in a general increase in costs and prices." Thus, 25 percent of GDP constituted a kind of ceiling on tax levels. In private correspondence with Clark, Keynes agreed that "25 percent as the maximum tolerable proportion of taxation may be exceedingly near the truth." (See Clark, 1964, p. 21.)

After, World War II, balanced budgets again became the rule for governments. Revenue grew slowly in line with expenditure until the 1960s.[3] In 1960, total government revenue averaged about 29 percent of GDP, in line with total expenditure of 28 percent. Balanced budgets predominated and the "big spenders" of that time – Austria, Belgium, Germany, the Netherlands, Sweden, and the United Kingdom – had also the highest revenue-to-GDP ratios. In these countries revenue exceeded 30 percent of GDP.

By 1970, revenue had increased to 32.4 percent of GDP, still

---

3. But, as reported in Chapter I, Keynesian economists were already chafing under this rule. In his critical account of this period, Tobin wrote that: "With respect to fiscal policy, balancing the budget and keeping it small became the touchstone of responsibility and respectability." (See Tobin, 1966, p. 38.)

roughly in balance with expenditure. The oil shock of 1973 caused the first major and general divergence between public expenditure and public revenue as governments attempted to maintain real household incomes and aggregate demand through increased public spending. The 1970s were the heydays of Keynesianism, and countercyclical policies were believed to be the "right" response to recessions, even when they might stimulate inflation. Unemployment was considered a greater problem than inflation and, it was believed policymakers could choose between unemployment and inflation. Helmut Schmidt, then German Chancellor, became famous for his saying that "it is better to have 5 percent inflation than 5 percent unemployment." Shortly thereafter Germany had both.

By 1980, the process of decoupling expenditure from revenue in most industrialized countries became evident. Expenditure increased on average by 15 percent of GDP between 1960 and 1980 to reach 42.6 percent of GDP, whereas revenue increased by "only" 11 percent of GDP to 40 percent of GDP. In Austria, Belgium, France, Germany, and Norway, revenue exceeded 45 percent of GDP. In the Netherlands and Sweden, it even exceeded 50 percent of GDP. But even these impressive figures for revenue collection, which must have made Colin Clark turn in his grave, were typically below the level of public expenditure in these countries.

By the 1990s, the situation had not changed much. Average revenue had increased by another 3 percent of GDP to 43 percent in 1996, but public expenditure had increased again as well. It is quite remarkable that governments in Belgium, Norway, and Sweden were able to collect revenue in excess of half of GDP. Australia, Japan, Switzerland, and the United States, however, reported revenue levels in the low to mid-30s, reflecting their lower public expenditure.

Revenue Composition

The revenue composition changed considerably over the past 125 years (see Table III.2). Initially, indirect taxes were the most important source of government revenue. Since World War II, however, income taxes and social security contributions have become the most important revenue categories and together account for almost two-thirds of total government revenue. However, the introduction of the

Table III.2. *Government Revenue Composition 1870–1994* (Percent of GDP)

	Indirect taxes: domestic							Indirect taxes: customs				
	1870[a]	1913	1920	1937	1960	1980	1994	1870	1913	1920	1937	1990[b]
Australia	4.7	1.9	2.6	3.1	10.9	12.3	13.7	4.1	1.6	1.8	2.1	1.2
Austria	..	6.3	5.0	7.0	14.7	16.4	16.7	..	2.3	1.6	2.2	1.1
Belgium	2.5	2.7	4.6	..	11.5	12.4	13.7	1.1	1.4	2.4	..	..
Canada	3.6	4.2	5.0	6.2	12.4	11.5	13.5	2.6	3.4	2.9	1.8	0.7
France	1.5	3.0	3.2	5.7	16.5	14.6	15.4	0.3	1.6	1.1	2.2	..
Germany	1.3	2.6	5.0	7.8	13.8	13.1	12.4	0.7	1.3	0.9	1.8	..
Ireland	..	..	9.1	10.3	15.3	15.0	17.0	..	..	4.5	6.4	..
Italy	0.8	1.2	0.5	0.9	11.2	8.6	14.2	0.8	1.2	0.5	0.9	..
Japan	1.9	3.8	1.7	2.3	8.5	7.4	7.5	0.4	1.5	0.4	0.8	0.2
Netherlands	..	3.0	2.8	4.3	..	12.0	13.8	..	0.6	0.8	1.7	..
New Zealand	..	..	..	..	..	..	14.8	..	..	..	..	0.8
Norway	3.0	3.2	2.0	5.6	12.7	15.7	16.9	2.2	2.7	1.7	2.5	0.2
Spain	2.9	2.8	1.4	2.7	7.5	6.6	11.9	1.6	1.7	0.9	0.4	..
Sweden	5.1	3.4	2.3	4.0	10.0	13.5	15.5	3.3	1.8	1.2	1.5	..
Switzerland	..	2.1	2.5	3.7	7.3	7.0	8.0	..	2.1	2.5	3.2	1.5
United Kingdom	4.0	3.1	5.6	7.1	13.0	15.7	15.7	1.9	1.4	2.2	4.7	..
United States	5.2	1.7	1.2	2.8	8.9	7.8	8.3	2.7	0.8	0.4	0.5	0.3
Average	**3.0**	**3.0**	**3.4**	**4.9**	**11.6**	**11.8**	**13.5**	**1.8**	**1.7**	**1.6**	**2.2**	**0.8**

	Direct taxes							Social security contributions			Other receipts		
	1870	1913	1920	1937	1960	1980	1994[c]	1960	1980	1994[c]	1960	1980	1994[c]
Australia	...	...	1.1	0.6	10.5	16.0	16.2	...	...	...	3.0	2.1	3.1
Austria	...	4.3	3.1	3.3	10.4	11.0	10.6	8.9	12.7	15.0	3.8	2.2	5.4
Belgium	1.2	4.5	4.3	...	7.9	18.2	17.5	7.7	13.5	15.5	3.3	4.8	4.2
Canada	...	...	0.8	2.3	9.0	14.7	16.0	1.7	3.3	6.1	2.8	6.9	6.3
France	1.4	1.3	1.1	2.0	5.5	7.6	7.8	11.8	17.8	19.1	...	3.5	6.5
Germany	...	...	3.6	6.4	9.3	13.4	11.5	10.3	13.1	15.4	1.8	2.4	7.2
Ireland	...	...	3.9	3.8	6.7	12.3	15.1	...	4.8	5.4	9.5	5.3	7.6
Italy	3.0	2.5	1.0	2.8	4.9	9.4	14.5	9.4	11.5	13.0	2.0	2.3	...
Japan	5.4	3.0	2.9	3.6	6.8	11.7	10.5	2.9	7.4	9.8	0.7	2.1	4.0
Netherlands	...	3.4	8.4	7.6	11.7	14.8	12.6	...	17.1	19.3	...	5.7	4.1
New Zealand	...	...	...	...	14.9	23.0	22.2	...	...	...	7.5	2.3	7.5
Norway	...	0.7	2.6	1.6	12.2	19.4	14.3	...	9.9	9.9	7.7	3.2	3.9
Spain	3.7	3.5	2.0	4.7	3.5	6.3	9.9	...	11.7	13.8	2.7	6.0	7.4
Sweden	1.4	1.0	2.5	2.1	14.9	21.2	21.6	4.9	14.1	13.9	4.1	5.1	0.4
Switzerland	...	...	0.5	0.6	8.6	12.7	13.4	8.9	9.5	12.4	5.8	4.4	2.4
United Kingdom	0.8	2.1	10.3	7.6	11.1	5.0	12.1	...	5.8	6.1	...	...	...
United States	...	...	...	2.5	13.9	13.4	12.3	4.3	5.9	7.0	...	...	...
Average	**2.4**	**2.6**	**3.2**	**3.4**	**9.5**	**13.5**	**14.0**	**7.1**	**10.5**	**12.1**	**3.4**	**3.6**	**4.4**

Sources: Compiled by Tanzi and Schuknecht based on Butlin (1984); OECD, *Economic Outlook* (various years); Mitchell, *International Historical Statistics* (various years).

[a] Or closest year available for all columns. Historical data until 1937 is central government only.

[b] 1988 data.

[c] Residual between total revenue (Table 3.1) and direct taxes, indirect taxes, and social security contributions.

value-added tax in many countries in the 1960s and 1970s has also played a major role in raising revenue from indirect taxes and in raising the total tax level.

Before World War I, indirect tax revenue was somewhat higher than direct tax revenue, but low tax rates and narrow tax bases prevented most countries from collecting more than 5 percent of GDP from either category. After World War I, however, a number of countries had significantly increased their revenue collection: Austria, Canada, Germany, and Ireland had expanded the collection of indirect taxes, whereas the Netherlands had considerably raised direct taxes. The United Kingdom showed very high revenue yields in both categories. Customs duties accounted for almost half of indirect taxes before World War II, and indirect tax revenue was on average still 20 percent higher than direct tax revenue.

By 1960, this ratio between indirect and direct tax revenue collection still prevailed. In addition, social security contributions had started to become an important revenue source. Indirect taxes and direct taxes yielded 40 percent and 33 percent of total revenue respectively. Social security contributions and other revenue contributed the remainder.

Over the next thirty years, revenue increases were largely on account of higher direct taxes and social security contributions. This was the period when personal income taxes came to be seen as the best and fairest taxes.[4] They became very popular.[5] Revenue as a share of GDP did not change much for indirect taxes and other revenue. By 1994, indirect tax revenue amounted to 13.5 percent of GDP or about 30 percent of total revenue and revenue from direct taxes had increased to 33 percent of total revenue, or 14 percent of GDP. Social security contributions increased from 22 percent of revenue in 1960 to almost 30 percent of revenue in the 1980s to finance the expanding social expenditures. By 1994, they averaged

4. See, for example, the annual surveys on "Changing Public Attitudes on Governments and Taxes," done by the U.S. Advisory Commission on Intergovernmental Relations.

5. In the environment of the 1960s and 1970s, personal income taxes were ideal instruments because they could be progressive and thus contribute to the objective of income distribution; could have high built-in flexibility and thus contribute to the objective of stabilization; and they could, presumably, reduce personal saving, thus contributing to aggregate demand. Furthermore, they lent themselves to social engineering through special treatment of favored groups.

about 12 percent of GDP and reached almost 20 percent in France and the Netherlands.

Tax Rates

The increase in total revenue collection over the past 125 years was achieved through a significant broadening of the tax base and rising tax rates. In fact, high tax and contribution rates are unavoidable in order to collect 40–50 percent of GDP in revenue. In particular, the increase in revenue from direct taxes and social security contributions suggest a considerable increase in tax rates and a broadening of the bases over the past decades. In addition, tax rate progressivity and the bracket creep associated with increases in nominal incomes caused by inflation provided governments with considerable revenue windfalls. In the 1970s and early 1980s, because income tax brackets were not fully indexed to inflation, tax revenue from personal income taxes rose. In recent years, however, increasing capital and labor mobility and growing concerns about distortions created by high tax rates have started to promote a decline in top marginal income and corporate tax rates (Owens, 1997; Tanzi, 1995).

The high marginal income tax and social security contribution rates are particularly noteworthy in industrial countries (Table 3.3). Top marginal income tax rates reach or exceed 50 percent in half the sample countries and only New Zealand levies top marginal rates in the low 30s. Corporate income tax rates have become much more uniform across industrialized countries since the late 1980s' tax reforms and in 1996 ranged between 28 percent in Sweden and 53 percent in Italy. Cumulative payroll taxes are also very high, especially in European countries and exceed 40 percent in Belgium, France, and Italy. They are lowest in Australia at only 7 percent. Sales tax or VAT rates average 17 percent and equal or exceed 20 percent in Australia, Austria, Belgium, France, Ireland, Norway, and Sweden. On the other hand, Japan, Switzerland, and Canada still have single-digit sales tax or VAT rates, and the United States still does not have a national sales tax.

It comes as no surprise that marginal tax rates are generally highest in countries with the highest revenue yield (and the highest public

Table III.3. *Tax Rates: VAT/Sales Tax, Income Tax, and Payroll Taxes*

| | Standard VAT or sales tax 1996 | Income tax | | Total payroll taxes[b] 1993 |
		Individual[a] 1997	Corporate 1997	
Australia[c]	32	20–47	36	0
Austria	20	10–50	34	41.8
Belgium	21	25–57	39	47.3
Canada	7	17–31	29	14.8
France	21	12–54	33	56.3
Germany	15	25.9–53[d]	45	38.2
Ireland	21	27–48	38	22.2
Italy	19	10–51	53	57.9
Japan	3[e]	10–50	38	31.5
Netherlands	18	6.35–60	35	54.7
New Zealand	13	24–33	33	2.7
Norway	23	37.5–23.5	21	24.5
Spain	16	30–56	35	38.7
Sweden	25	30–50	28	32.3
Switzerland	6.5	11.5	10	22.8
United Kingdom[c]	18	20–40	33	15.6
United States[f]	...	15–39.6	35	21.5

Source: Coopers & Lybrand (1997); Wunder and Crow (1997); Zee (1996).
[a] Federal tax only in selected cases.
[b] Employee and employer contribution; self-employed excluded.
[c] Social security provides pension, unemployment, and other benefits, all funded from consolidated revenues. Neither employees nor employers are required to make separate contributions.
[d] Excludes solidarity contribution.
[e] An accounts-based (substractive) VAT; 4.5 percent rate applies only to cars.
[f] State and local governments levy sales tax on goods and services that vary by jurisdiction, and can reach 10 percent.

expenditure levels). Marginal tax rates of 50 percent or more on income or 20 percent on sales are likely to cause significant distortions, including disincentives to work and to invest and incentives to evade taxes.[6] For example, Daveri and Tabellini (1997) have shown that a 9 percent increase in average tax rates on labor income between 1965–75 and 1976–1991 may have been responsible for a

6. There is an extensive literature that has identified these efficiency costs. For a recent survey of many of these tax-related issues, see OECD, *Making Work Pay: Taxation, Benefits, Employment, and Unemployment* (Paris: 1997).

permanent decline in the growth rate of $^1/_2$ percent and an increase in the unemployment rates of 4 percent. See also Zee (1996). In addition, the complexity and high administration costs of tax systems in industrial countries are frequently lamented. High tax rates are considered a growing disadvantage for competing in global capital and labor markets with new technological developments such as Internet commerce (Owens, 1997; Tanzi, 1998a). From the results of a survey, Brunetti, Kisunko, and Weder (1997a) have reported that tax regulations and/or high tax rates are perceived as the biggest obstacles to business in industrial countries.[7]

2. DEFICITS

The significant deterioration in the countries' overall fiscal positions identified in the previous section merits further discussion. We are not suggesting that balanced budgets are always the optimal fiscal stance for a country, and we agree that balanced budgets may be unrealistic or even unwise during wars and recessions. But as a rule of thumb, balanced budgets provide a useful benchmark for assessing countries' fiscal position during "normal" times.[8]

From the nineteenth century until the 1960s, institutional constraints, together with strong moral and intellectual beliefs, encouraged governments to balance budgets or even to generate budget surpluses during peacetime. Balanced-budget rules emerged as a response to fiscal irresponsibility by many monarchs and governments in earlier times. As Galbraith put it, "the spendthrift tendencies of princes and republics were curbed by the rule that they must unfailingly take in as much as they paid out" (1958, p. 15). The increase of public expenditure and public debt incurred during war periods was typically rolled back in the interwar years (Buchanan, 1985). In 1960, most industrialized countries had balanced budgets or

---

7. For an empirical study on New Zealand, see Caragata (1998).
8. Some caution should be applied in assessing the fiscal position of countries solely on the basis of deficits. A small deficit during a recession may be a sign of better fiscal "health" than a balanced budget after an extended boom. The definition of the deficit, and the inclusion or exclusion of implicit liabilities from the pension or financial systems and public debt can provide a very different picture. Also, Barro (1979) has shown that a fiscal policy that maintains relatively constant tax rates, and thus allows surpluses and deficits to occur when particular circumstances arise, is more efficient than one that allows the rates to be moved up or down.

Table III.4. *General Government Fiscal Balance, 1960–96*
(Percent of GDP)

	1960	1980	1990	1996	1997
Australia	3.2	−1.7	0.6	−0.9	−0.3
Austria	2.2	−1.7	−2.2	−3.9	−2.5
Belgium	0.0	−8.8	−5.8	−3.2	−2.1
Canada	−2.6	−2.8	−4.1	−2.0	+0.9
France	2.7	0.0	−1.6	−4.0	−3.0
Germany	2.8	−2.9	−2.1	−3.4	−2.6
Ireland	−0.5	−12.3	−2.3	−0.9	+0.9
Italy	−5.3	−8.6	−11.0	−6.7	−2.7
Japan	1.3	−4.4	2.9	−4.3	−3.1
Netherlands	0.2	−4.2	−5.1	−2.3	−1.4
New Zealand	. . .	. . .	−1.6	+3.0	+1.6
Norway	2.5	5.2	2.6	+5.8	+7.3
Spain	−0.1	−2.0	−3.8	−4.7	−2.6
Sweden	1.5	−4.0	4.2	−3.5	−0.8
Switzerland	6.1	0.0	0.7	−2.2	−2.0
United Kingdom	−2.3	−3.4	−1.2	−4.7	−1.7
United States	0.0	−1.4	−2.7	−1.1	0.0
Average	**0.7**	**−3.3**	**−2.3**	**−2.3**	**−0.8**

Sources: OECD, *Economic Outlook* (various years).

even small surpluses. Only Canada, Italy, and the United Kingdom reported deficits of more than 2 percent of GDP, whereas eleven of the seventeen countries reported surpluses (Table III.4).

By 1980, the situation had changed fundamentally. Fiscal deficits on average exceeded 3 percent of GDP. Ireland had a deficit of over 12 percent of GDP and Belgium and Italy were close to double digits as well. Only Switzerland, France, and Norway managed to maintain a balanced budget or to have a surplus. The economic boom of the late 1980s helped to improve the countries' fiscal balances, and in 1990, Australia, Japan, Norway, Sweden, and Switzerland had a surplus. The average deficit, however, still exceeded 2 percent of GDP, with Italy now at the top of the list. After a period of further fiscal deterioration in the early 1990s, the run up to the European Monetary Union (with its 3 percent deficit limit), reforms in New Zealand and in other countries, and the positive economic environment coupled with some reforms in the United States and the United Kingdom resulted in 1996 in average fiscal deficits similar to those of

1990. New Zealand and Norway had achieved significant surpluses, but most other countries continued to report deficits. The fiscal situation continued to improve in 1997 and 1998 when a number of countries achieved fiscal balances or even surpluses.

One of the main differences between the period before and after the 1960s is the chronic nature of fiscal deficits even during times of "normal" economic growth. Many industrialized countries have had fiscal deficits almost continuously since the early 1970s. As we have seen, even prolonged economic booms like the one of the second half of the 1980s only pushed a few countries into fiscal surplus. The extent of deficits was unprecedented for peacetime. The earlier revenue and expenditure tables show that even during the mid-1930s, no country experienced double-digit deficits.

Structural Deficits

Another way of looking at the soundness of countries' fiscal policies is through the so-called structural balances. Compared to unadjusted fiscal balances, structural balances attempt to take into account the countries' position in the business cycle. A country in deep recession, but with only a relatively small actual deficit, may in fact have a structural surplus. The reason is that in an economic downturn, public revenue is typically depressed while public expenditure obligations do not decline or may even grow (e.g., through growing unemployment compensation). Hence the fiscal deficit becomes larger than it would be if the country were not in recession. Fiscal surpluses during economic booms, on the other hand, may hide structural deficits, because revenue may be artificially inflated by the boom. However, the calculation of structural deficits requires several questionable assumptions and may even have basic problems.

Structural deficits do not reveal a much different picture than the unadjusted figures.[9] Until 1970, most industrialized countries were not in deficit. Expansionary policies in the 1970s, however, pushed structural deficits to an average of 4.7 percent by 1980, and the structural deficits of Belgium and Ireland exceeded 10 percent. Structural deficits averaged between 3 and 4 percent in the early 1990s but came down to 2.3 percent in 1996 and 1.1 percent in 1997 as fiscal consolidation efforts began to bear fruit.

9. For data on structural deficits, see OECD, *Economic Outlook* (annual).

Between countries, however, there are considerable differences. Belgium and Ireland were able to significantly reduce their structural deficits after 1980, and the Netherlands and Italy have consolidated their fiscal positions as well in recent years. New Zealand and Canada also had a significant turnaround. However, some countries (e.g., Japan) have experienced major deteriorations in their structural deficits.

3. PUBLIC DEBT AND IMPLICIT LIABILITIES

Public Debt

The damage associated with high fiscal deficits is not limited to the immediate crowding out of private sector activities and investments but may extend to the long run. High chronic deficits can generate considerable debt burdens especially when the country's growth rate is low and the real rate of interest on government borrowing is high. We have mentioned above the potentially explosive nature of growing debt when the resulting interest obligations in turn raise the deficit further and default risk pushes up real interest rates. The growth of public debt in industrial countries over the past twenty-five years is a good barometer of the cumulative effect of government fiscal profligacy in recent decades. Table III.5 shows the impact of fiscal deficits on public debt in the past 125 years.

Public debt is not a new phenomenon.[10] In the 1870s, Australia, France, Italy, the United Kingdom, and the United States had public debt between 40 percent and 100 percent of GDP, all caused by major wars. Until World War I, all of these countries, except for France, significantly reduced their public debt burden as a consequence of the fiscal policies they followed during this period. During World War I, public debt rose rapidly again. Some countries such as Germany and Austria got rid of their debts through hyperinflation. Still, average public debt stood at 60 percent of GDP in 1920 with debt levels in Australia, Belgium, France, New Zealand, and the United Kingdom exceeding 100 percent of GDP.

Because of the impact of the Great Depression, no country

10. Leroy-Beaulieu (1888) dedicated hundreds of pages of his two-volume treatise to public debt.

Table III.5. *Gross Public Debt from a Historical Perspective,*
1870–1996 (Percent of GDP)

	About 1870[a]	1913	1920	1937	1970	1980	1990	1997
Australia	100.1	75.1	122.4	153.0	...	...	21.3	38.7
Austria	...	...	22.5	40.5	19.4	37.3	58.3	65.9
Belgium	...	128.4	132.9	117.2	67.5	78.2	129.7	122.4
Canada	...	...	40.6	74.1	51.9	44.0	72.5	93.8
France	51.4	66.5	136.8	137.2	53.1	30.9	40.2	64.6
Germany[c]	...	...	4.2	17.4	18.4	31.1	45.5	65.0
Ireland	...	...	9.6	31.4	67.4	72.7	96.3	68.3
Italy	92.0	70.6	91.3	95.7	41.7	58.1	104.5	121.7
Japan	0.6	53.6	25.6	57.0	12.1	51.2	65.1	87.1
Netherlands	...	...	...	71.9	50.6	46.9	78.8	71.4
New Zealand	...	...	158.3	154.8	...	44.8	60.9	47.0[b]
Norway	6.8	27.9	28.4	28.0	47.0	47.6	32.5	40.6[b]
Spain	...	77.7	37.7	57.4	14.2	18.3	50.3	73.5
Sweden	...	...	21.5	26.5	30.5	44.3	44.3	77.1
Switzerland	...	...	...	33.4	...	...	31.9	48.2[b]
United Kingdom	40.2	30.4	132.0	188.1	81.8	54.0	39.3	60.3
United States	43.9	2.5	31.0	43.7	45.4	37.0	55.5	61.5
Average	**47.9**	**59.2**	**66.3**	**78.1**	**42.9**	**46.4**	**60.4**	**71.0**

Sources: Compiled by Tanzi and Schuknecht based on Fernández Acha (1976); Butlin (1984); Norway, Statistisk Sentralbyrå (1978); Dornbusch and Draghi (1990); Field (1934); Japan Statistical Association (1987); Kindleberger (1993); League of Nations, *Statistical Yearbook* (various years); Mitchell (1962); IMF, *New Zealand: Selected Issues and Statistical Appendix* (1996k); OECD, *Economic Outlook* (1997); Republique Française, Institut National de la Statistique et des Études Economiques (1961); United Nations, *World Economics Survey* (various years).
[a] Or closest year available for all columns. Since 1970 data includes all financial liabilities as defined by the System of National Accounts and covers the general government sector which is a consolidation of central government, state and local government, and the social security sector. Definition differs from the Maastricht Treaty.
[b] 1996.
[c] Includes the debt of the German Railways Fund in 1995. Assets held by one subsector of general government that constitute liabilities for another subsector of general government have not been fully consolidated.

managed to reduce its public debt burden significantly between 1920 and 1937. However, debt levels did not creep up much despite the unprecedented economic decline and the unemployment experienced during the early 1930s. In 1937, the average debt stood at only about 10 percentage points of GDP above the 1920 level.

After World War II and until the middle of the 1970s, public debt declined as balanced budgets, rapid economic growth, and relatively low real interest rates, reduced the share of debt into GDP. By 1970, average public debt had declined to about 40 percent of GDP, while real interest rates were at a historic low. At that time, the United Kingdom reported the highest level of debt at over 80 percent of GDP. In Austria, Germany, Japan, and Spain, government liabilities stood at less than 20 percent. Twenty-five years later, the average public debt had gone up by more than 30 percentage points of GDP. Belgium, Canada, and Italy were reporting public debt exceeding their nominal GDP. Only Norway and the United Kingdom were able to reduce their level of indebtedness between 1970 and 1997. Austria, Belgium, Canada, Italy, Japan, and Spain reported the largest increase from 10–20 percent to 70–80 percent of GDP over this period. Once again in 1997 and 1998 several countries reduced the level of public debt as a share of GDP, but the reductions were marginal.

It is not only the high level of public debt that is a cause for concern. Some countries may have lost their ability to run high deficits during severe economic crises without risking macroeconomic destabilization.[11] Sweden may illustrate the dramatic effect of a crisis on public debt. Sweden experienced a fiscal surplus in 1990 and a double-digit deficit three years later. Within only five years, public debt doubled to 81 percent of GDP. Japan has been experiencing a similar increase in the share of debt into its GDP. Italy or Belgium, which owe more than 100 percent, would find it much more difficult to get through a similar sudden economic deterioration. In the 1970s and in the early 1980s, unanticipated inflation reduced the increase in the real value of public debt despite high deficits by keeping low or even negative the real rates of interest.[12] More recently, however, very low inflation has reduced nominal GDP growth and, combined with low real growth and high real interest rates has accelerated the growth in public debt as a share of GDP even though fiscal deficits have been more contained. In fact, in the absence of inflation or high growth and in the presence of high real interest rates, significant fiscal surpluses would be necessary to bring down the debt levels.

11. Japan may well be one of these countries because of its high fiscal deficit and large and growing public debt.
12. At that time, the distorting effect of inflation on the fiscal deficit and on public debt made some economists such as Eisner question whether there really was a fiscal problem.

Implicit Government Liabilities

In recent years, other types of government liability have been attracting considerable attention. It was previously mentioned that, over past decades, governments in industrialized countries have extended benefits and eligibility for pensions. Until recently, a favorable, or fiscally friendly, demographic structure, with relatively few recipients of benefits and a lot of contributors to the financing of the pension systems, had kept pension systems in good financial condition. In most countries, pay-as-you-go schemes have been used to finance relatively high pensions for the still relatively few retirees. However, increasing life expectancy and declining birth rates will raise the share of people in the retirement age by almost 50 percent over the next twenty-five years assuming that the retirement age is not changed. By 2020, over one-quarter of the population will be older than sixty years. At the same time, the number of workers to finance the pensions of these retirees will shrink because of longer stays in school, because of high unemployment especially among younger people, because of a trend to early retirement especially among men, but mostly because of demography. As most pension systems have not used the period of more favorable demographics to build up reserves for "bad" times, this demographic shift will have dramatic effects on the financeability of future pension obligations.[13] A large difference has been created, under current policies, between the present value of the future pensions obligations and the present value of future contributions by workers.

Several studies have estimated the net government liabilities that arise from current pension policies under certain assumptions about life expectancy, interest rates, and productivity growth. The long time horizons of these studies can give rise to significantly different results if the underlying assumptions differ only slightly. However, the basic point of these exercises is not to determine the exact amount of these liabilities over future years, but to show that, in principle, governments face significant uncovered liabilities. The magnitudes of these liabilities can be enormous under current policies.

The average net pension liabilities for the main industrialized countries are estimated at between 66 percent of GDP (Chand and

13. For the OECD countries the share of the population aged 65 and older in the population aged 25 to 64 will rise from 22.8 percent in 1990 to 26.9 percent in 2010; 39.6 percent in 2030; and 52.4 percent in 2050. See *Group of Ten* (April 1998, p. 3).

Table III.6. *Estimated Net Pension Liabilities of Selected Industrialized Countries* (Percent of GDP)

	Chand and Jaeger	Masson and Mussa	Van den Noord and Herd
Canada	68	99	250
France[a]	114	98	216
Germany[b]	111	139	160
Italy	76	113	233
Japan	107	110	200
United Kingdom	5	19	186
United States	26	31	43
Sweden	20	. . .	. . .
Average	**66**	**87**	**184**

Sources: Chand and Jaeger (1996); Masson and Mussa (1995); Van den Noord and Herd (1993).
[a] Excludes "fictive" contributions.
[b] Excludes statutory transfers from the federal government.

Jaeger, 1996) and 184 percent of GDP (Van Den Noord and Herd, 1993) (Table III.6). Even if only the lower two estimates in Table III.6 are considered, it can be seen that important implicit liabilities exist in some countries that far exceed the explicit obligations of government debt. The studies agree that uncovered liabilities are highest in Canada, France, Germany, Italy, and Japan. The magnitude of liabilities in the more optimistic studies lies between 68 and 139 percent of GDP. Only in the United Kingdom, the United States, and Sweden is the net present value of future implicit pension liabilities relatively small, amounting to less than 30 percent of GDP. These countries have also relatively high reserves in pension funds in anticipation of future obligations: the United Kingdom, the Netherlands, and Switzerland have reported pension fund assets of 75 to 117 percent of GDP in 1996. The United States has reported 58 percent and Japan 42 percent. Germany, Italy, France, and other countries with high implicit liabilities, on the other hand, have no or only very small pension fund assets.

Chand and Jaeger (1996) estimated that industrial countries would have to raise their annual pension contributions on average by 1.8

percent of GDP to cover future liabilities. In Japan, Germany, and France this so-called contribution gap exceeds 3 percent of GDP; in Canada and Italy it is 2 percent. If current policies were continued for another five years and the reform of pension systems were post-poned until then, the contribution gap would rise by 0.3 percent of GDP. A 15-year delay would almost double the necessary increase in pension contribution. This adds considerable urgency to pension reform, an issue we will discuss again in a later chapter.

4. CONCLUDING REMARKS

After the 1960s, government revenue did not keep up with increas-ing public expenditure. In the process, chronic fiscal deficits in the past twenty-five years resulted in significant government debt accu-mulation in most industrial countries. In some of these countries, the increase in debt to GDP ratios has been very large.[14] In addition, gov-ernments have incurred pension commitments that constitute con-siderable implicit financial liabilities. These results have to be placed in a context in which tax burdens have become so large in most coun-tries that it will be difficult to increase them even more. In fact, there are now intense pressures in several countries, including Germany, Italy, and the United States, to lower these countries' tax burdens. Thus, much of the inevitable adjustment must somehow come from a reduction in public spending. Regardless of the benefits derived from higher public spending (an issue to be discussed in Part Two of this book), these findings make a strong case for fiscal reform.

14. As already mentioned, in 1997 and 1998 the share of public debt into GDP did not rise or even declined in several industrial countries. It remains to be seen if this represents a new trend.

Gains from the Growth of Public Expenditure

The first part of this study reported on the growth of public expenditure in the past century and the reasons for that growth. It was shown that the growth was particularly pronounced after about 1960. In this period many countries expanded their previously limited social protection systems and some converted them into the welfare states of today. The period 1960–80 was especially the time when government was most trusted to be able to solve many social and economic problems.

In the second part of this study, comprising three chapters, the important question of what benefits accrued to the populations of the industrial countries as a consequence of the growth of public spending will be addressed. Presumably, governments tax their citizens to be able to carry out public programs that should increase the well-being of their citizens. Unless this occurs, there seems to be little point in reducing individual economic freedom through higher taxes in order to raise public spending. We will discuss the evidence available that bears on the question of whether the growth in public spending did in fact bring about a higher level of social welfare.

IV Historical Evidence on Government Performance

1. A NOTE ON THE METHODOLOGY FOLLOWED

Between 1870 and 1996 the share of public spending in gross domestic product (GDP) for the group of industrial countries for which data are available rose by a factor of more than 4. In the first part of this study we have shown that this growth was promoted by the interaction of particular events (wars, depressions) with changing views that came to assume that many social or economic problems could be solved by greater governmental intervention, especially through higher public spending. Higher public spending was believed to bring higher social welfare.

As a consequence of these events and views, there was an expansion of the government role in: (a) education, with the result that in most countries free or at least inexpensive public schools at all educational levels, became the norm; (b) health; (c) the provision of public pensions, which eventually created a situation where most aged individuals were receiving or expected to receive government-provided pensions; (d) public assistance to the unemployed and to various other groups; (e) subsidies to enterprises; and so on. The expansion in public spending may have promoted greater public welfare in many ways. For example: it increased the literacy rate and human capital in general; it reduced infant mortality and increased general health, thus leading to higher life expectancy; and it provided an important safety net for those who became unemployed, incapacitated, or indigent. There is no question that in this century the growth in public spending and in the role of government in the economy contributed to an increase in the quality of life mainly by reducing some risks that affect the daily life of most citizens.

An important question that we will be asking is whether there is a continuous, positive relationship between higher public spending and higher social welfare. In other words, does more public spending *always* or necessarily imply more social welfare? Or are there diminishing returns in terms of welfare gains to such spending? This is a difficult question for which no clear methodology exists to provide a definitive and uncontroversial answer. The reason is that while economists have talked a lot about social welfare and similar concepts, especially for large groups or whole nations, they have not been able to measure it empirically in any objective and broadly acceptable way. (See Slesnick, 1998.) As Slesnick puts it:

The measurement of welfare forms the foundation of public policy analysis. A full consideration of taxes, subsidies, transfer programs, health care reform, regulation, environmental policy, the social security system, and educational reform must ultimately address the question of how these policies affect the well-being of individuals." (p. 2108)

In this study, we follow a new, modest, and understandably controversial, approach, which allows us to reach some interesting, and we believe useful, conclusions.

Assume that social welfare, W, depends on the values of various socioeconomic indicators such as $X_1, X_2, \ldots X_n$. For example, X_1 could be life expectancy; X_2 infant mortality; X_3 the literacy rate; X_4 the amount of schooling that the population has received; and so on. Thus:

$$W = f(X_1, X_2, \ldots X_n)$$

Improvements in social welfare will depend on improvement in the values of the relevant indicators. Thus:

$$\Delta W = \sum_{i=1}^{n} \frac{\delta f}{\delta x_i} \Delta x_i$$

Assume that through public spending and perhaps through other policies, such as tax policies, regulations, and so on, governments attempt to influence social welfare by bringing about desirable changes to these indicators. We assume that there is no controversy about the change in an indicator that is considered desirable. For example, longer life expectancy, lower infant mortality, lower inflation, higher literacy, and so on are unquestionably desirable changes. As a consequence, the greater the desirable or positive impact of public spending on these indicators, the greater the improvement in social welfare will be assumed to be. Thus, changes in socioeconomic indicators will be taken as proxies for changes in social welfare.

There are obvious limitations to this approach. For example, more *public* spending often implies less immediate or future *private* spending. Higher (present or future) taxes to finance higher public spending generate an opportunity cost for that spending in terms of forgone private spending. This opportunity cost could be high. It is ignored by the approach followed here, which registers only the positive impact of public spending on the indicators and ignores the cost of that spending.

Another problem is that it is difficult or even impossible to consider all the social and economic objectives (and, thus, all the socioeconomic indicators) that the governments might want to influence with this spending. By necessity, the analysis will include fewer indicators than might have been desirable to include. Still another problem is that the impact of different socioeconomic indicators on social welfare is not the same. Some may have a significant impact, others much less so. Therefore, it would have been useful to assign weights to these indicators. We have not done so because we were unable to determine such weights. Of course, the readers will be able to evaluate the impact on social welfare of the socioeconomic indicators provided, according to their own social preference function.

In conclusion, we will be following an approach that, to the best of our knowledge, has not been followed before. It is an approach that, with all its shortcomings, provides some answers to the important question of what benefits the populations of the industrial countries have derived from the increase in public spending in recent decades. The approach will also allow us to speculate on whether higher public spending necessarily means higher public welfare.

To shed some light on the main questions raised above, we will look at a broad array of social and economic indicators which tend to be affected by government spending. In particular, we will look at how these socioeconomic indicators have changed over time. To anticipate an important conclusion, we will argue that in this century considerable gains in social and economic welfare were achieved with the help of government spending. However, the rapid and considerable growth in public spending in more recent decades does not seem to have resulted in significant *additional* gains in socioeconomic objectives. Or, putting it differently, the productivity of additional public sector spending in terms of improvements in social and economic objectives has been low in recent decades.

In subsequent chapters, we will argue that, in terms of many of these socioeconomic indicators, countries with relatively small governments performed as well or even better than their counterparts with relatively big governments. We will also show that today's newly industrialized countries have achieved almost comparable levels of social and economic welfare with much lower levels of public spending. This analysis will lead us to conclude that governments could probably be much smaller and more efficient than they are today without reducing the benefits that are often claimed to justify high government spending.

Governments influence the functioning of markets by enforcing contracts and preventing coercion. Consequently, economic growth and per capita income are, in a way, indicative of the quality of government policies over time. Other economic variables that governments influence include inflation, savings and investment, and unemployment. The future economic potential of a society is also affected by the government's financial liabilities, by real interest rates, and by a number of social indicators in health and education. Most people would also agree that a certain degree of income equality and social stability are indicative of a society's well-being, and government policies can exert an influence on these indicators as well. Administrative and regulatory efficiency, environmental protection, and "economic freedom" could also usefully be seen as indicators for the quality of government policies.

Governments cannot be assumed to be responsible for all the differences in countries' performance as represented by these indicators. In fact, differences between countries and changes over time often have a lot to do with technical progress or cultural differences between countries. It is, therefore, not useful to compare countries on the basis of only one particular indicator or a set of indicators, but one should look at a comprehensive picture. From a multitude of indicators, we will conclude that much improvement was achieved until around 1960. Since then, however, improvements in the achievement of social and economic objectives have been relatively limited in most industrialized countries. As mentioned earlier, this may be taken to imply that the role of government, as played through higher public expenditure, has not given us as high returns as in earlier years.[1]

2. ECONOMIC INDICATORS

Growth and Per-Capita Income

Real economic growth was high in the first part of our observation period. Between 1870 and 1913, when the industrial revolution combined with laissez-faire policies was still in full swing, real growth averaged 3 percent per year (Table IV.1). Australia and the United States even reported real growth rates of around 5 percent. Most other countries for which we have data for that period experienced growth rates between 2 and 3 percent (Maddison, 1995). After World War I, during the relatively short so-called golden years of the 1920s, growth accelerated to almost 4 percent. The Great Depression brought considerable harm to the world economy, as beggar-thy-neighbor policies and protectionism spread, and resulted in negative growth in many countries during the early to mid-1930s. As mentioned earlier, much of the skepticism toward laissez-faire gained momentum during the Great Depression, when unemployment and poverty reached levels that had not been thought possible before.

Economic growth accelerated again after World War II when governments and newly created international institutions provided a more stable and market-friendly economic climate during the postwar reconstruction. Growth averaged almost 4 percent during the 1960s. Japan, the Netherlands, and Spain grew at a rate of over 5 percent, and no country reported real growth of less than 2 percent per year in this period.

1. An econometric analysis looking at public spending and other variables as determinants of social and economic indicators is not attempted in this study. However, in Tanzi and Schuknecht (1998b), we provide some first evidence in this regard that supports the findings of this and the following chapters.

Table IV.1. *Economic Indicators from a Historical Perspective: Real Economic Growth* (Percent of GDP)

	1870–1913	1920–29	1930–37	1960–68	1986–94
Australia	5.3	3.4	1.6	2.6	2.9
Austria	...	5.2	–1.8	3.9	2.5
Belgium	...	...	2.2	3.2	2.2
Canada	3.8	10.0	–0.3	2.8	2.3
France	1.7	4.9	–0.4	4.0	2.2
Germany	3.3	2.5	4.4^a	3.2	2.9
Ireland	...	1.5	–0.4	4.5	4.3
Italy	1.5	3.4	0.6	4.3	2.0
Japan	2.6	2.1	6.7^a	5.4	3.1
Netherlands	...	4.3	–0.0	5.0	2.5
New Zealand	...	...	...	2.8	1.0
Norway	2.2	3.1	2.6	4.0	2.4
Spain	...	2.9	1.1	6.5	2.9
Sweden	2.8	4.8	2.2	4.2	1.0
Switzerland	...	5.2	0.5	4.5	1.6
United Kingdom	1.7	1.7	1.7	3.6	2.3
United States	4.7	4.2	–0.0	2.5	2.5
Average	**3.0**	**3.9**	**1.3**	**3.9**	**2.4**

Sources: Compiled by Tanzi and Schuknecht based on Mitchell (various years); OECD, *Historical Statistics* (1992, 1996).
^{a} Rapid expansion toward end of period starting war preparations.

Since the early seventies, however, average growth has been declining. Initially, two oil crises contributed to the economic disturbance. In the past decade, however, growth continued to slow down without any major external shocks. For the 1986–94 period real growth averaged only 2.4 percent, with Ireland alone showing more than 4 percent real growth per year. Furthermore, the standard deviation of the GDP growth rate has increased compared to the 1960s, although Keynesian-type intervention was supposed to achieve the opposite result. Many economists now argue that Keynesian stabilization policies have been a failure, and big and inefficient governments, regulations and high taxes are taking their toll on growth.

Table IV.2 illustrates how real per capita income evolved over the past 125 years.[2] In 1870, per capita GDP averaged about US$2,000 in

2. The table provides estimates of per capita GDP in 1990 prices. Comparing real incomes over such long period of time is nevertheless problematic as consumption bundles have changed considerably. The numbers should, therefore, serve only illustrative purposes.

Table IV.2. *Economic Indicators from a
Historical Perspective: Per Capita GDP*
(1990 US$ prices)

	1870	1913	1960	1990
Australia	3,801	5,505	8,793	17,260
Austria	1,875	3,488	8,022	20,527
Belgium	2,640	4,130	7,817	19,264
Canada	1,620	4,213	9,244	20,441
France	1,858	3,452	8,857	21,070
Germany	1,913	3,833	9,008	20,665
Ireland	. . .	. . .	4,699	12,837
Italy	1,467	2,507	6,948	19,302
Japan	741	1,135	5,005	23,734
Netherlands	2,640	3,950	9,108	18,973
New Zealand	3,115	5,178	8,720	12,943
Norway	1,303	2,275	10,580	27,199
Spain	1,376	2,255	4,141	12,662
Sweden	1,664	3,096	13,180	26,822
Switzerland	2,172	4,207	19,100	33,674
United Kingdom	3,263	5,032	8,928	16,977
United States	2,457	5,307	12,259	21,966
Average	**2,119**	**3,723**	**9,083**	**20,372**

Sources: Maddison (1995); OECD, *National Accounts* (1995).

1990 prices. Australia, New Zealand, and the United Kingdom were the richest countries with per capita GDP exceeding US$3,000. Japan was the poorest country, with per capita income of less than US$1,000, about half the average of the sixteen countries for which we compiled data. By today's standards and according to the categorization of the World Bank's *World Development Report*, the then newly industrialized countries would be considered as lower-middle-income countries.

In the following forty years until World War I, per capita GDP almost doubled to near US$4,000. This is perhaps comparable to today's upper-middle-income countries of Brazil, Malaysia, Hungary, or Mexico. The United States had joined the group of the richest countries with the equivalent of over US$5,000.

It took another fifty years to double per capita income again. By 1960, per capita GDP reached US$9,000 on average, equivalent to the per capita GDP of Korea or Portugal in the early 1990s. Switzerland was by far the richest country with per capita GDP of US$19,000, followed by Sweden and the United States. Ireland, Japan, and Spain reported little more than half the average income level.

During the period 1960–90, per capita income doubled again. However, half of the increase had in fact taken place by 1970 and no wars or deep crisis had reduced economic activity over this period. Per capita growth in the past twenty-five years reverted back to the growth rates of the late nineteenth century. This reflects the slow-down in real growth that started in the early 1970s and continued until the 1990s.

Unemployment

Unemployment is one of the most important indicators of people's well-being, not only from an economic but also from a social perspective. The unemployed are not only materially worse off, but many studies have shown that over time they suffer from low self-esteem and other psychological problems and find it increasingly difficult to participate fully in the society around them. Although labor market and employment policies can reduce or increase the rate of unemployment, government spending policies are relatively ineffective in addressing structural unemployment.

Between 1870 and World War I, most countries had near full employment. The assumption of classical economics seemed to be realistic as markets cleared through changing prices and wages and with relatively little governmental intervention. Unemployment averaged 3.6 percent, and all countries, except for France, experienced unemployment of 4 percent or less (Table IV.3).

The second column in Table IV.3 shows unemployment between the peak of the Great Depression in the early 1930s and World War II. The Great Depression still had not been overcome fully by most countries. Average unemployment exceeded 10 percent, and it reached or exceeded 20 percent in Norway and the Netherlands. Germany, Italy, and Japan had much lower unemployment because of large public works programs and especially because of military spending.

The post–World War II economic boom resulted again in full employment. By 1960, Germany, Japan, the Netherlands, Sweden, and

Table IV.3. *Economic Indicators from a Historical Perspective: Unemployment Rate* (Percent)

	About 1870[a]	About 1937	1960	1980	1996
Australia	3.9	8.8	2.4	6.0	8.5
Austria	...	...	3.5	1.0	6.2
Belgium	...	13.8	5.4	8.0	12.9
Canada	...	9.1	7.0	7.5	9.7
France	7.0	...	...	6.2	12.4
Germany	0.2	4.6	1.3	3.2	10.3
Ireland	...	...	6.7	7.3	11.3
Italy	...	4.6	4.2	5.6	12.1
Japan	...	3.7	1.1	2.0	3.3
Netherlands	2.5	26.9	1.2	4.0	6.7
New Zealand	...	5.4	...	2.5	6.1
Norway	3.9	20.0	2.5	1.7	4.9
Spain	...	...	...	11.5	22.7
Sweden	...	10.8	1.4	2.0	8.0
Switzerland	...	10.0	...	0.2	4.7
United Kingdom	3.7	7.8	1.7	5.3	7.4
United States	4.0	14.3	5.5	7.2	5.4
Average	**3.6**	**10.8**	**3.4**	**4.8**	**9.0**

Sources: Compiled by Tanzi and Schuknecht based on Mitchell, *International Historical Statistics* (various years) OECD, *Economic Outlook* (1997); OECD, *Historical Statistics, 1960–90* (1992).
[a] Or earliest before 1913.

the United Kingdom reported unemployment below 2 percent. In those days, only Canada and Ireland had high unemployment rates of close to 7 percent. Over the following decades, however, the situation changed dramatically. In the early 1990s, many industrialized countries would have been happy to report unemployment of "only" 7 percent, a figure that most countries would have found unacceptable thirty years earlier. Only one-third of the countries listed in the table reported unemployment below this level in 1996. In that year, the average for industrialized countries had reached 9 percent, almost three times the average rate in 1960. In several European industrial countries the unemployment rate is now around 12 percent.

High unemployment is perceived as perhaps the major economic challenge for most of today's industrialized economies. It is certainly a major concern for many governments. Social assistance cushions some of the material hardship from unemployment, but crime, alcoholism, and family strains are often attributed to growing unemployment. Although there is no full consensus on the reasons for the growth in unemployment, many experts have argued that the rapid increase in unemployment in industrialized countries in the past thirty years is partly a consequence of the growing burden of taxes and social security contributions that reduce labor demand, and of the disincentives to work that result from generous government-financed benefits in many countries. (See OECD, 1997.) Labor market rigidities such as work-time regulations and job security, introduced with the best intentions during times of full employment, have also contributed to unemployment. In some countries, unemployment has become an insider-outsider problem, where those who have jobs expect high wages and other benefits such as pensions, at the expense of those who do not have jobs, especially in the low-income categories. Unemployment is also becoming a problem between generations because of its large concentration among the young. The dilemma of high unemployment coupled with the emergence of a new class of so-called working poor, has created resistance in high-unemployment countries to attempt to liberalize the labor markets (for a survey, see Lindbeck, 1996, and Siebert, 1998).

Inflation

Inflation is another important economic variable traditionally influenced by governments. Low inflation rates and low variability in inflation are perceived as important economic objectives. Low inflation is also desirable from a distributional perspective because inflation affects more strongly the poor who often hold much of their assets in cash and who therefore cannot protect themselves against inflation.

In the late nineteenth century, under widespread use of the gold standard, inflation was very low (Table IV.4). Only France and the United Kingdom experienced inflation of slightly above 2 percent. Most other countries reported rates between 0 and 2 percent, which today many people perceive as the optimal degree of price stabil-

Table IV.4. *Economic Indicators from a Historical Perspective:*
Inflation (Percent)

	1870[a]	1920[b]	1937	1960–68	1986–94	1997
Australia	1.4	1.7	2.0	2.2	5.3	0.3
Austria	. . .	104.7	1.1	3.5	2.8	1.3
Belgium	2.0	2.3	3.6	2.8	2.4	1.6
Canada	. . .	−1.6	1.6	2.4	3.5	1.6
France	2.2	5.0	8.3	3.6	2.8	1.2
Germany	1.4	231.1	1.2	2.7	2.3	1.8
Ireland	. . .	0.6	1.0	4.0	2.9	1.4
Italy	1.2	15.7	6.6	4.0	5.4	1.8
Japan	. . .	. . .	8.7	5.7	1.5	1.7
Netherlands	. . .	−2.1	3.8	3.6	1.7	2.2
New Zealand	. . .	2.8	3.1	3.3	6.0	1.2
Norway	. . .	−1.4	3.0	3.9	4.5	2.6
Spain	. . .	1.4	. . .	6.6	5.9	2.0
Sweden	0.8	−3.6	2.1	3.8	5.5	0.9
Switzerland	1.2	−3.1	1.2	3.4	3.0	0.5
United Kingdom	2.6	−2.4	1.1	3.6	4.8	3.1
United States	−2.7	0.3	1.0	2.0	3.6	2.3
Average	**1.0**	**22.0**	**3.1**	**3.6**	**3.8**	**1.6**

Sources: Compiled by Tanzi and Schuknecht based on Mitchell, *International Historical Statistics* (various years); OECD, *Economic Outlook* (1998); OECD, *Historical Statistics, 1960–90* (1992).
[a] Or earliest before 1913.
[b] About three-year average around 1920, price movements typically very volatile. Austria and Germany experienced hyperinflation in the early 1920s.

ity.[3] By contrast, the post–World War I period shows very volatile price developments in almost all countries caused by the war efforts. Austria, Germany, and, to a lesser extent, Italy inflated out of their war-related debts. Others pursued disinflation policies and reported decreasing price levels. In the following years, prices stabilized again, and after a period of deflation in the early-1930s, price increases between 1 and 3 percent per year were the rule. In 1937, only France, Italy, and Japan experienced inflation rates in excess of 6 percent.

3. See, for example, New Zealand's inflation target policies and the European Central Bank's difinition of price stability.

The early post–World War II period was again characterized by relative price stability. The system of fixed-exchange rates and the convertibility of the dollar, the anchor currency, for the industrialized countries, to gold at a fixed price probably contributed significantly to this development. The average growth in the price level during the 1960s was 3.6 percent, a little higher though than during most of the previous century. However, considerable differences in the development of overall price levels started emerging, and Japan and Spain reported average inflation of over 5 percent for the 1960–68 period.

After the collapse of the Bretton Woods fixed exchange rate system and the first oil crisis in the early 1970s, industrialized countries experienced a phase of much more rapid inflation. This coincided with the period of fastest growth in public spending. In response to this in the early 1980s, countries began tightening monetary policies. Based on the perception that policymakers' hands need to be tied to prevent opportunistic short-term oriented inflationary policies, the independence of central banks and monetary policies from political interference was strengthened in many countries. As a result, the inflation rate fell again. For the 1986–94 period, it has been close to the level prevailing in the early 1960s and after 1994 it has been even lower. In a large number of countries inflation is now less than 3 percent per year. On balance, and unlike what has happened to growth and employment, governments have been relatively successful in improving their policy record on monetary policy over the past fifteen years. This success has been largely due to the political decision to take monetary policy discretion away from politicians (for a survey, see Eijffinger and de Haan, 1996).

Interest on Public Debt

The interest rate on public debt, if not artificially lowered through financial repression or tax concessions to the holders of this debt, is a very important variable to assess the government financial position and the risk premium that the government has to pay on its debt. High real interest rates, especially on long-term liabilities, can reflect people's fear that governments might default or inflate out of their debt. High real interest rates on international bond issues can illustrate the perceived default risk, independent of inflationary expectations. Government borrowing and debt may also affect the real

Table IV.5. *Real Interest Rates on Public Debt, 1960–90*

	1960–67	1968–73	1974–79	1980–90
Australia	...	...	-1.9	5.5
Austria	...	2.3	2.6	4.2
Belgium	2.9	2.1	0.8	6.0
Canada	2.8	2.2	...	5.9
Frnace	1.9	1.6	-0.4	5.0
Germany	2.9	2.1	3.0	4.5
Ireland	...	...	0.1	4.9
Italy	0.9	0.2	-4.2	2.8
Japan	...	0.4	...	4.6
Netherlands	...	0.3	1.3	5.4
New Zealand	3.6	-2.5	-3.9	3.1
Norway	...	-1.0	-0.4	5.0
Spain	...	...	...	4.3
Sweden	1.2	1.7	-1.1	3.7
Switzerland	-1.0	-1.0	1.1	0.8
United Kingdom	2.7	2.0	-2.0	3.5
United States	2.2	0.6	-0.6	5.4
Average	**2.0**	**0.8**	**-0.4**	**4.4**

Source: OECD, *Historical Statistics, 1960–90* (1992).

interest rate in the economy as a whole and thereby affect economic growth. Since the 1980s, indications are that real interest rates have risen significantly as governments have incurred chronically high fiscal deficits and accumulated large public debt burdens.

Historical data on real interest rates are scarce but by comparing nominal interest rates and inflation, as well as public debt and interest bills, we can see that nominal and real interest rates before World War I and World War II were typically much lower than in the 1990s (see Homer and Sylla, 1991). We have easily comparable data on real interest rates only for the period after 1960. In the 1960s, real interest rates on public debt in industrialized countries averaged 2 percent and only New Zealand reported rates over 3 percent (Table IV.5). The inflationary environment of the 1970s, coming after a long period of price stability, resulted in a surprisingly long period of very low or even negative real interest rates. More than half of the sample countries reported negative interest rates for at least part of the 1970s.

Only Austria and Germany show real interest rates of more than 2 percent for the total period.

As inflationary expectations eventually caught up with price developments, the experience of the 1970s resulted in very high real interest rates in the 1980s as the tight monetary policy came at a time when the inflation experience of the 1970s had created high inflationary expectations on the part of creditors. Some of the countries with negative interest rates in the 1970s, such as Australia, France, Norway, and the United States, experienced real interest rates of 5 percent or more on government debt in the 1980s. Interest premiums in Austria and Germany, however, increased comparatively little, probably a reward for Germany's more stable monetary policies and the Bundesbank's independence, and Austrian monetary policies closely following those of Germany.

Real interest rates on public debt in the 1980s averaged 4.4 percent, 2.4 percent more than in the 1960s. This increase is consistent with the literature that has estimated the effect of rising public debt on interest rates (e.g. Tanzi and Fanizza, 1995; Ford and Laxton, 1995; or Helbling and Wescott, 1995). This literature has estimated that the increase in public debt from the 1970s to the 1990s may have increased real interest rates by anywhere between 1.5 and 4.0 percentage points.

Although the findings in these studies illustrate the upward trend in real interest rates, they do not adjust for inflationary expectations, differential tax treatment, and financial repressions that make the real cost of borrowing difficult to compare between countries. Another way of comparing real interest rates on public borrowing between countries without such noise in the data is to look at interest rates on Eurobond issues. By comparing issues between different countries in the same (nondomestic) currency and with the same maturity, one can estimate the default premiums governments have to pay. Table IV.6 shows the launch spread over the benchmark rate for a number of countries on five- to ten-year Eurobond issues in U.S. dollar, yen, deutsche mark, or pound sterling.

During the 1991–95 period, risk premiums were particularly high for countries with high and growing government debt such as Greece or Italy. Greece, for example, had to pay between 100 and 175 basis points more in interest on five- to ten-year public debt than the country in whose currency the bond was issued. A simple regression

Table IV.6. *Risk Premiums on Public Debt, Selected OECD Countries, 1991–5*

Currency Years to maturity	Selected Eurobond issues (US$, Yen, DM, STG)[a]		Percent of GDP	
	5–7	10	Public debt (gross) 1995	Fiscal balance 1995
Public debt under 60 percent of GDP				
Norway	12–28	...	43.5	–0.7
Germany	0	0	51.5	–2.6
New Zealand	60	...	55.2	3.0
United Kingdom	0–10	0–22	54.5	–6.9
Average	**21**	...	**51.2**	**–1.8**
Public debt under 100 percent of GDP				
Finland	25–82	55–60	62.7	–5.8
United States	0	0	64.3	–2.0
Austria	9	18–25	65.7	–4.5
Spain	25–55	13–31	68.2	–6.6
Denmark	10–28	...	68.7	–3.8
Portugal	20–75	28–45	70.4	–5.8
Japan	0	0	75.6	–3.5
Sweden	35–65	42	79.5	–10.4
Canada	25	36	95.6	–5.3
Average	**33**	**27**	**72.3**	**–5.3**
Public debt over 100 percent of GDP				
Greece	100–140	175	119.8	–11.4
Italy	47–65	29–75	123.9	–9.0
Belgium	13–27	16–56	135.0	–5.3
Average	**65**	**88**	**126.2**	**–8.6**

Sources: Compiled by Tanzi and Schuknecht from Euromoney Bondware, OECD; *Economic Outlook* (1996).
[a] Launch spread over benchmark rate in basis points.

between public debt and the interest premiums on Eurobond issues shows that a 10 percent increase in public debt raises the interest premium by 6 basis points.[4] This regression implies that, for example, a country with public debt of 100 percent of GDP pays

4. This simple regression should only be seen as illustrative. More thorough regressions with more observations controlling for different currencies and years of issue would yield more reliable estimates.

0.6 percent higher real interest rates than a country without public debt. The interest premium alone would translate into 0.6 percent of GDP more in interest payments, which is not a negligible amount.

The table does not show that risk premiums increase considerably during national or international crisis periods and periods of nervousness in international financial markets. After the European Exchange Rate Mechanism (ERM) in its old form broke down in 1992, for example, risk premiums increased considerably also for countries outside ERM. Mexico's premiums on Eurobond issues increased considerably shortly before the peso crisis in late 1994. The peso crisis in turn increased Eurobond premiums on other Latin American countries as well. This illustrates the "early-warning" effect that interest premiums on Eurobond issues can have. It also shows that deficits and debt levels that seem to be quite manageable during "normal" times can develop dangerous dynamics during times of crisis.

Savings

Ricardo's equivalence theorem would predict that people increase their private savings in anticipation of future tax obligations arising from public debt. If public deficits are financed with increased private savings, private investment should remain relatively unchanged. Tanzi and Fanizza (1995) show that in G7 countries, public deficits, and debt increased considerably between 1970 and the early 1990s, but private savings stagnated or even declined (Table IV.7).[5] In the early 1990s, the financing of deficits absorbed over 15 percent of private savings instead of less than 5 percent as it did around 1970. This and the reduction in overall savings over the period are indicative of some crowding out of private sector investment by public borrowing, which in turn may explain some of the weakening in economic growth. Incidentally, as we mentioned earlier, public investment has also declined considerably over the past two decades.

---

5. In a recent paper, Tanzi and Zee (1998), have shown that increases in the tax levels in OECD countries have led to falls in saving rates.

Table IV.7. *Fiscal Deficits, Public Debt, and Savings of G-7 Countries, 1970–94*

	General government deficit[a]	Gross private saving	General government deficit[b]	Public debt
	As percentage of G-7	Group GDP	As percentage of G-7 gross private saving	As percentage of G-7 Group GDP
Average				
1970–74	−0.7	20.4	3.4	40.5
1975–79	−2.7	21.5	12.5	40.1
1980–84	−3.4	21.0	16.4	46.6
1985–89	−2.5	19.5	12.7	57.2
1990–94	−3.3	19.5	16.9	63.8

Sources: OECD, *National Accounts* (various years); OECD, *World Economic Outlook* (various years); and Tanzi and Fanizza (1995).
[a] Figures are PPP-weighted averages of national figures, as percentage of GDP.
[b] Excludes Italy 1970–9.

3. SOCIAL INDICATORS

Historical data on social indicators are very limited. Only a few health and education indicators date back to the nineteenth century, and data on income distribution are even scarcer. However, from the limited evidence available, we can conclude that significant progress in achieving social objectives was reported especially until about 1960. After 1960, social progress seems to have slowed down significantly, repeating in some sense the findings on economic indicators.

Health Indicators

In the late nineteenth century, in many newly industrialized countries of the time, every fourth or fifth child died before reaching the first anniversary. Austria, France, Germany, Italy, the Netherlands, Spain, and Switzerland all had infant mortality rates exceeding 200 per 1,000 births (Table IV.8). Not even today's poorest developing countries show higher infant-mortality rates. Similarly, life expectancy at birth

Table IV.8. *Social Indicators from a Historical Perspective: Infant Mortality and Life Expectancy*

	Infant mortality (per 1,000/births)				Life expectancy			
	About 1870	About 1937	1960	1995	About 1870–1900	About 1937	About 1960	1995
Australia	111	38	20	6	49	66	71	77
Austria	253	92	38	6	...	...	69	77
Belgium	145	83	31	8	...	59	71	77
Canada	187	77	27	6	...	65	71	79
France	201	70	27	6	47	...	71	78
Germany	298	64	34	6	47	...	70	76
Ireland	95	73	29	6	...	60	70	77
Italy	230	109	44	7	...	...	70	78
Japan	...	106	31	4	44	49	69	80
Netherlands	211	38	18	6	52	65	73	78
New Zealand	93	39	23	7	...	67	71	76
Norway	101	42	19	5	50	...	73	78
Spain	203	130	36	7	35	50	70	77
Sweden	132	45	17	4	56	67	74	79
Switzerland	222	47	21	6	...	65	72	78
United Kingdom	160	58	22	6	51	62	71	77
United States	...	50	23	8	47	64	70	77
Total average	**176**	**68**	**27**	**6**	**48**	**62**	**71**	**78**

Sources: Compiled by Tanzi and Schuknecht based on Easterlin (1980); Lancaster (1990); Maddison (1995); Mitchell, *International Historical Statistics* (various years); World Bank, *Social Indicators of Development* (1995); World Bank, *World Development Report* (1997).

was only between forty and fifty years, which is less than in many of today's poorest countries.

In the nineteenth-century primary health care began to be established in many countries, and some programs such as smallpox vaccinations became mandatory with government financial support. Important discoveries about the causes of diseases, vaccinations, technical developments like X-rays, and the importance of hygiene slowly began to influence people's behavior and improve the quality and effectiveness of health care. Although most health care was still provided privately or by churches, and although exact data on the share of government spending in total health spending are not available, the role of governments in health provision expanded considerably since the turn of the century.[6] Health indicators improved significantly as well. By World War II, in industrialized countries, infant mortality had declined by 60 percent to an average of 68 per thousand births. Australia, the Netherlands, and New Zealand even reduced infant mortality to below 40, similar to today's infant mortality in Mexico, Thailand, or Colombia. Life expectancy also increased considerably between 1870 and 1937. In Spain life expectancy increased from 35 to 50 years, and in Australia, the Netherlands and Sweden it increased from about 50 to over 65 years.

Public health expenditure increased considerably after World War II (see Part I, Chapter II). In addition, technical progress, especially in curing diseases, was very rapid. Antibiotics and other new treatments made many previously fatal diseases and infections curable. Consequently by 1960, infant mortality had declined to an average of 27. The deviation between countries had also declined over this period. In 1937, Spain's infant mortality of 130 was almost 4 times as high as Australia's 38. By 1960, Italy's infant mortality rate of 44 was only 2.5 times as high as Sweden's 17. On average, life expectancy in 1960 exceeded 70 years. The variance between countries had become relatively small with 69 being the lowest and 74 the highest average life expectancy.

Since 1960, infant mortality and life expectancy have improved further. However, it seems that countries with a large share of

---

6. Especially at the beginning of the public sector intervention in the health area, the increase in public spending may have led to a decrease in private spending.

public provision and financing of health care, such as the United Kingdom, do not show better indicators than countries with a relatively smaller role for government in health, such as Switzerland. It is therefore questionable as to how far growing public expenditure is still contributing to these improvements. Progress in health indicators seems to be more correlated with technical progress and access to health care does not seem to differ much between countries any more.[7]

Education

We have discussed earlier the important role that governments have played in providing education. They have contributed to the growing human capital stock which, in today's world, is generally assumed to be much more important for a country's economic well-being than natural resources or a favorable geographical location. Table 4.9 illustrates the remarkable improvements in education in all industrialized countries in the past 125 years. Charlotte Brönte's Jane Eyre reported that in mid nineteenth-century England, schooling was far from universally available and was highly dependent on the initiative of local clergymen. By the late nineteenth century, however, primary schooling must have already been available to a large share of children. West (1970, p. 113) estimates that literacy in England may have reached 90 percent of the adult population. At that time, however, education was still largely financed privately, especially by the parents. This only changed during the course of the 1880s, when England started government funding of education in 1883.[8] Average primary schooling amounted to 5.4 years for our sample of countries. Canada, France, Switzerland, and the United States were particularly advanced in the provision of education and, for them, average years of schooling exceeded 7 years. On the other hand, Ireland, Italy, and the United Kingdom averaged less than 3 years of schooling. In the following decades, the average length of school enrollment increased rapidly, and reached 7.4 years in 1937. By 1937, no country reports less than 5 years of primary schooling, and Australia, Canada, and

7. The United States may be an exception in that rapidly rising public and private health expenditure hardly benefit the very poor who often do not have access to insurance or to high-quality health facilities.
8. We mentioned before that by 1900, universal, public, primary education was common in most of today's industrialized countries.

Table IV.9. *Social Indicators from a Historical Perspective: Education*

	Years of schooling (average)			Secondary school enrollment	
	About 1870	About 1937	1992[a]	About 1960	1994
Australia	6.2	9.2	...	51	96
Austria	3.6	7.3	...	50	92
Belgium	5.0	8.0	15.2	69	100
Canada	7.5	10.0	...	46	94
France	7.2	7.9	16.0	46	96
Germany	...	7.4	12.2	87	96
Ireland	2.9	7.3	...	35	93
Italy	2.9	5.7	11.2	34	81
Japan	4.3	7.1	14.7	74	96
Netherlands	4.7	7.1	13.3	58	98
New Zealand	6.4	9.3	...	73	94
Norway	5.9	6.3	...	57	94
Spain	5.5	5.0	11.5	23	82
Sweden	6.3	5.7	14.2	55	96
Switzerland	8.0	7.0	...	26	87
United Kingdom	2.6	6.8	14.1	66	87
United States	7.9	8.4	18.0	86	95
Average	**5.4**	**7.4**	**14.0**	**55**	**93**

Sources: Compiled by Tanzi and Schuknecht based on Maddison (1995); Mitchell, *International Historical Statistics* (various years); United Nations, *Human Development Report* (various years).
[a] Includes all types of formal education.

New Zealand report more than 9 years. By this time illiteracy rates had become very low.

Years of schooling have increased further since the 1930s, and all countries in our sample report an average of over 10 years of formal education. Secondary school enrollment is perhaps a better indicator of progress in educational objectives since World War II. By 1960, secondary school enrollment on average already exceeded 50 percent. Germany, Japan, New Zealand, and the United States reported secondary school enrollment of around 75 percent or higher. Only Ireland, Italy, Spain, and Switzerland showed enrollment rates significantly below 50 percent.

By 1994, secondary school enrollment approached 100 percent in most countries. Education is therefore an area in which public provision and financing of services has been very successful, even beyond

1960.[9] However, in some countries, the quality of public secondary education, especially for the poor, is reported to be of low quality. School enrollment in public universities has also increased considerably since 1960. Public universities have contributed significantly to the extension of the human capital base. However, as has happened with secondary education, the quality and costs of public tertiary education are being scrutinized with increasing frequency. Tertiary education contains a large component of investment in skills that directly raise the future incomes of those who graduate. It is thus a valid question whether it necessitates as much public intervention as, for example, primary or secondary education, for which externalities create a much stronger justification for public sector intervention.

Income Distribution

Historical data on income distribution are also scarce and difficult to compare internationally. However, Flora, Kraus, and Pfennig (1983) show for a number of European countries that income distribution improved significantly between the early twentieth century and 1975. Since 1960 (and for a few countries since the 1930s), more complete data are available (see Table IV.10). Data on the income share of the poorest 40 percent of the households show that for many non-Anglo-Saxon countries – such as France, Germany, Italy, Japan, the Netherlands, Norway, Spain, and Sweden – that share grew significantly between 1960 and 1980. By contrast, the share of income going to the poorest 40 percent of households fell in Australia, Canada, New Zealand, the United Kingdom, and the United States. For the whole group, the share of income going to the poorest 40 percent of households grew from 16.7 percent in 1960 to 18.6 percent in 1980. The difference between the two groups of countries indicates that cultural or social factors are possibly at work in the determination of income distribution. These factors may be more important than public expenditure in determining income distribution. See Brandolino and Rossi (1998) and Tanzi (1998d).[10]

Income distribution can be improved mainly via two types of

9. For the fifteen countries of the European Union there was an increase of 27.6 percent in the number of students in secondary schools between 1975–76 and 1991–92. The increase was particularly large in Portugal, Spain, and Ireland.
10. Tanzi (1998d) elaborates on how social norms and "positional rents" play a large role in determining Gini coefficients in some societies.

Table IV.10. *Social Indicators from a Historical Perspective: Income Distribution*

	Income share of lowest 40 percent of households		
	1930s	1960s	1980s
Australia	. . .	20.1	15.5
Austria	19.2	19.7	. . .
Belgium	. . .	. . .	21.6
Canada	. . .	19.7	17.5
France	. . .	10.0	18.4
Germany	. . .	14.8	19.5
Ireland	. . .	. . .	. . .
Italy	. . .	15.6	18.8
Japan	. . .	15.3	21.9
Netherlands	. . .	14.5	20.1
New Zealand	. . .	20.9	15.9
Norway	10.3	17.1	19.0
Spain	. . .	16.5	19.4
Sweden	10.8[a]	15.1	21.2
Switzerland	. . .	. . .	16.9
United Kingdom	19.2	18.1	17.3
United States	. . .	15.9	15.7
Average	**14.9**	**16.7**	**18.6**

Sources: Flora et al. (1983), United Nations, *Human Development Report* (various years).
[a] 1920 data.

public policies. The first is expenditure policies that increase the productive potential of the poorer elements of the population. Primary health and primary education expenditure and basic infrastructure such as rural roads typically fall under this category. The beneficial effect of efficient government policies in these areas is widely acknowledged. The second type of policies attempts to improve income distribution via direct redistribution of income. Taxation and transfers could, theoretically, achieve this objective, but the suitability of tax policies for income redistribution is normally quite limited (Tanzi, 1996a).[11]

11. Tanzi's 1996a paper provides a detailed discussion of some of the problems in human capital oriented public expenditure policies, especially in Latin American countries. These problems, however, may be less severe in industrial countries. See also Harberger (1998). For a discussion of OECD countries, see OECD *Economic Outlook*, 62 (December 1997), pp. 49–59.

Table IV.11. *Targeting of Transfers versus Universal Benefits, Mid–1980s*

	Share of transfers by quintile		
	Poorest	"Middle classes"[a]	Richest
Australia	40.1	50.7	9.2
Switzerland	38.5	48.2	13.3
Norway	34.0	50.9	15.1
Ireland	32.0	58.4	9.6
Canada	29.5	58.4	12.1
United States	29.2	55.7	15.1
United Kingdom	26.7	61.4	11.9
Netherlands	24.9	55.9	19.2
Germany	21.8	59.9	18.3
Belgium	21.5	59.8	18.7
France	17.5	57.8	24.7
Italy	15.6	56.8	27.6
Sweden	15.2	67.4	17.4
Average	**26.7**	**57.0**	**16.3**

Sources: OECD, *Income Distribution in OECD Countries* (1995).
[a] Share of transfers to second, third, and fourth quintile.

Relatively little improvement in income distribution is actually caused by taxation and by transfer programs, even though the latter expenditure category accounts for about 50 percent of total public spending and tax revenues are a large share of GDP. The main reasons are that when the total tax burden becomes a large share of a country's GDP, it is no longer very progressive and, equally, when public transfers become very large, they tend to be poorly targeted. According to available information, only four of the thirteen countries for which data are available – Australia, Switzerland, Norway, and Ireland – spend more than 30 percent of their transfer budget on the poorest 20 percent of the population (see Table IV.11). Three of these four countries have among the smallest levels of public spending among industrialized countries. In some countries, on the other hand, transfers are even regressive. In France, Italy, and Sweden, for example, the poorest quintile of the population receives less than 20 percent of total transfers. In several countries the "middle classes" (second to fourth quintile) receive about 60 percent of the share of

Table IV.12. *Equalization of Income Distribution through Taxation and Transfers, Mid-1980s* (Percent of GDP)

	Income share of bottom 40% of households		Improvement in income distribution due to taxation and transfers
	Gross income	Disposable income	
Australia	15.1	17.7	2.6
Canada	16.1	17.8	1.7
France[a]	14.8	16.8	2.0
Germany[a]	18.7	21.7	3.0
Netherlands	19.7	22.6	2.9
Sweden	19.9	22.4	2.5
Switzerland	17.4	18.9	1.5
United Kingdom	15.8	17.5	1.7
United States[a]	13.9	16.3	2.4
Average	**16.8**	**19.1**	**2.3**

Source: Zandvakili (1994).
[a] Only households with positive incomes have been selected. Some inequality measures are not defined for income values of zero. The German data set excludes some 8 percent of households with foreign national heads of households. The United States' data set has a top coding of US$50,000. The noted problems with data sets alter the true inequality.

transfers. This means that basically they get as much as they pay. Given the efficiency losses from redistribution, which are probably very high,[12] there cannot be many *net* winners in this group. Palda (1997) has called this "fiscal churning" and has shown that much public spending could be eliminated and taxes could be lowered correspondingly. This change would make everybody better off but would require major reforms that will be discussed in Part Three of this book.

Given the poor targeting of transfers and the many loopholes for high-income taxpayers in industrial countries, the leveling of income via taxation and public transfers is relatively small. According to a recent study, in the mid-1980s, this leveling-off averaged only 2.3 percent of GDP for the bottom 40 percent of households (see Table

12. Citing OECD (December 1997, p. 59): "Expenditures on redistributive policies have risen considerably in most OECD countries in the past quarter century and such expenditures, and the taxes needed to pay for them, can reduce overall economic prosperity by distorting economic decisions."

IV.12). Countries with lower but better-targeted public spending on transfers sometimes report better results toward improving income distribution than countries with large but not well-targeted transfer programs. Australia and the United States, for example, report public expenditure on subsidies and transfers of less than 20 percent of GDP in the early 1990s. However, improvements in income distribution via taxes and transfers in these countries, according to this study, are greater than in Sweden with subsidies and transfers of 35 percent of GDP. Although this finding does not apply to all countries in the sample, the question should be asked whether one could justify a 20 percent higher level of public spending (and the corresponding higher taxes, and disincentives to invest and work) to have such a small effect on income distribution.

4. CONCLUDING REMARKS

In the period between the 1870s and World War I, economic and social indicators reflected the predominance of laissez-faire and the limited government involvement in public education, health, pensions, and other programs. Perhaps reflecting the growing government role, by 1937, social indicators had improved significantly, except for unemployment, since most countries were still suffering from the effects of the Depression. By 1960, economic and social indicators had again improved considerably, and it seems that by this year, several basic social problems had been successfully reduced in intensity. For the period up to 1960, a reasonable claim can be made that the increased public sector spending (on education, health, training, basic social security, and so on) had led to measurable improvements in economic and social indicators. After 1960, however, progress in improving the social and economic objectives slowed down considerably or even reversed in spite of a continuous large expansion in public spending in many countries. The social returns to this additional spending will be the subject of the next chapter.

V The Size of Government and Its Performance

1. INTRODUCTION

The 1960s was a period of great optimism in the ability of governments to solve economic and social problems, especially through higher public spending. As a consequence, governments were continually asked to take additional responsibilities. In the previous chapter, we found that progress in the achievement of various social and economic objectives has been relatively limited since 1960 despite the considerable increase in public expenditure in all industrialized countries. Progress had been much greater before 1960. In some sense, it could be argued that the growth in public spending after 1960 was less socially and economically productive than before. With the benefit of hindsight, many would now say that the optimism of the 1960s about the benefits that could be derived from higher public spending was a bit naive. Some would go as far as to decry the rise in tax levels and in public spending and argue that much of the public spending in recent decades has been a waste.

This chapter will argue that countries which contained the growth of that spending performed equally well or even better, in most of the areas that governmental action attempts to influence, than countries with relatively big governments. To pursue this analysis, the countries in the sample will be divided in three groups, depending on the level of public expenditure in 1990.[1] Belgium, Italy, the Nether-

---

1. Since then expenditure levels, expenditure composition, and expenditure patterns across countries have not changed much with the exception of New Zealand.

lands, Norway, and Sweden, where public spending exceeds 50 percent of GDP, constitute the group of "big governments" or big spenders. Austria, Canada, France, Germany, Ireland, New Zealand, and Spain, with public spending between 40 and 50 percent of GDP, constitute the group of "medium-sized governments." Australia, Japan, Switzerland, the United Kingdom, and the United States, with public spending below 40 percent of GDP in 1990, constitute the group of "small governments."

In the following pages, we will first look at differences in expenditure patterns between these country groups. We will then compare for these groups many socioeconomic indicators related to economic and labor market performance, to health, education, the environment, income distribution, and social stability, and finally to governance.

2. PUBLIC EXPENDITURE PATTERNS

Between 1960 and the early 1990s public expenditure by today's big governments grew much faster than that of the small and medium-sized governments. In 1990, public expenditure in countries with big governments averaged 55 percent, up from 31 percent in 1960 (Table V.1). In medium-sized governments it grew from 29 percent to 45 percent of GDP. In small governments it grew about half as fast as in big governments for this group; average spending increased from 23 percent of GDP to 35 percent of GDP. Big governments on average spend 60 percent more than small governments or about 20 percent of GDP more. In 1960, the difference was only 35 percent or 8 percent of GDP.

The difference in public expenditure levels is almost completely due to differences in spending on transfers and subsidies and on interest on public debt. The levels of public consumption and public investment do not differ much between the country groups.

In 1960, the differences in spending on subsidies and transfers were relatively small. At that time, big governments spent about 12 percent of GDP on this category, or 1.5 percent of GDP more than the medium-sized governments and 5 percent of GDP more than the small governments. By 1990, in the big-government countries, subsidies and transfers had increased to almost 31 percent of GDP. Sub-

Table V.1. *Size of Government and Public Expenditure Composition, about 1960 and 1990* (Percent of GDP)

	Industrialized countries						Newly industrialized countries[d]
	Big governments[a]		Medium-sized governments[b]		Small governments[c]		
	1960	1990	1960	1990	1960	1990	1990
Total expenditure[e]	31.0	55.1	29.3	44.9	23.0	34.6	18.6
Consumption	13.2	18.9	12.2	17.4	12.2	15.5	9.1
Transfers and subsidies[f]	11.9	30.6	10.4	21.5	6.9	14.0	5.7
Interest[f]	1.5	6.4	1.3	4.2	1.3	2.9	1.5
Investment[f]	3.1	2.4	3.2	2.0	2.2	2.2	2.7
Expenditure by function[e]							
Health	2.6	6.6	3.0	5.9	2.3	5.2	1.8
Education	4.5	6.4	2.9	5.6	3.4	5.0	3.3
Social security	13.5	19.5	9.6	13.9	6.2	7.9	1.0
Research and development	...	2.0	...	1.6	...	2.0	...
Environment	...	0.6	...	0.8	...	0.7	...

Sources: Compiled by Tanzi and Schuknecht from previous tables.
[a] Belgium, Italy, the Netherlands, Norway, Sweden (public expenditure more than 50 percent of GDP in 1990).
[b] Austria, Canada, France, Germany, Ireland, New Zealand, Spain (public expenditure between 40–50 percent of GDP in 1990).
[c] Australia, Japan, Switzerland, United Kingdom, United States (public expenditure less than 40 percent in GDP in 1990).
[d] Chile, Hong Kong, Korea, Singapore, early 1990s.
[e] Please note that the components of total do not add to the totals because some expenditures are not netted out from the subcategories.
[f] Central government, 1972 instead of 1960 for interest and investment. Transfers and subsidies for 1960 is mostly general government.

sidies and transfers had doubled to 14 percent of GDP in countries with small governments and had grown to 21.5 percent in the medium-sized governments. Small governments had been better able to limit the growth in spending; still, public spending had increased considerably in all countries.

Average expenditure on interest payments in the 1960s was similar among the country groups. However, the larger accumulation of public debt by big and medium-sized governments after 1960 increased their interest payments. For big government countries, as percentages of GDP these payments increased fourfold after 1960 and in 1995, they averaged 6.4 percent of GDP. This is more than 10 percent of total spending. The increase for medium-sized governments was somewhat smaller, but the share of interest payments in GDP still more than tripled. Small governments did not avoid completely the curse of rising debts and interest bills and ended up in the 1990s with average expenditures on interest of about 3 percent of GDP.

Looking at public expenditure developments from a functional perspective, we can see that the spending patterns do not differ significantly between the country groups in several categories. Educational spending by big governments in 1990 absorbed 6.6 percent of GDP or, as a share of GDP, about 25 percent more than in the small governments. The spending pattern across country groups in the health sector is similar. For both health and education spending, the difference across countries is much smaller than the difference in overall spending levels. Medium-sized governments have the smallest share of spending in research and development and the highest share in spending on the environment. However, public spending on research and development or the environment is similar between the country groups.

By far the main difference in functional expenditure patterns lies in spending for social security broadly defined. Big governments increased their spending on this category from 13.5 percent of GDP in 1972 (the earliest year for which we have comprehensive data) to almost 20 percent of GDP by 1990. Small governments increased social security spending by less than 2 percent to about 8 percent of GDP in 1990. In the 1990s, social security related expenditure in big-government countries was two and one-half times as high as in small-government countries.

In the following, we will examine whether such considerable differences in the evolution of public expenditure levels and in spending patterns have resulted in different results in terms of economic and social objectives in the countries under consideration.

3. ECONOMIC PERFORMANCE, PUBLIC DEBT, AND LABOR MARKET INDICATORS

We will show that economic performance, public debt, and the functioning of labor markets are, to some extent, inversely related to the size of government. The surprising result is that small governments have performed better than the large ones in many of the areas we compare.

Economic Growth and Per Capita GDP

Economic growth has slowed down in all country groups from about 4 percent in the 1960s to around 2.5 percent for the 1986–94 period (Table V.2). The decline in economic growth has been most pronounced, however, in countries with big governments, where growth rates fell from 4.1 to only 2 percent. Small and medium-sized governments both report average growth rates of about 2.5 percent, but the decline in growth was smallest in the small-government countries.[2] However, growth rates were higher in big and medium-sized government countries in the 1960s.

Variability in Output

The standard deviation in economic growth increased slightly in absolute terms in countries with medium-sized and big governments between 1960 and the early 1990s, despite attempts to use Keynesian stabilization policies to reduce the variability of output and the intensity of business cycles. The standard deviation of growth rates was lowest in countries with big governments in the 1960s. However, it increased slightly to 1.6 percent for the period around 1990. Medium-sized governments post the highest standard deviation in economic growth after an increase from 1.7 percent in the 1960s to 2.1 percent around 1990. The standard deviation of GDP growth in countries with small governments stayed constant at 1.9 percent and falls between the other two country groups in 1980.

Investment

Gross fixed capital formation averaged 21 percent of GDP in 1960 and was highest in countries with large governments and lowest in the small-government group. By 1990, the average investment rate

2. The literature on the relation between overall spending and economic growth is not always conclusive. Commander, Davoodi, and Lee (1997) report a significant negative relation between government *consumption* spending and economic growth. Please note that our work relates mostly to total spending rather than to public consumption. For a general analysis of the relationship between fiscal variables and long-run growth, see Tanzi and Zee (1997).

Table V.2. *Size of Government, Economic Performance, Financial Indicators, and Labor Market Indicators in Different Country Groups, about 1960 and 1990*

| | Industrialized countries | | | | | | Newly industrialized countries[d] |
| | Big governments[a] | | Medium-sized governments[b] | | Small governments[c] | | |
	1960	1990	1960	1990	1960	1990	1990
Economic performance indicators							
Real GDP growth (in percent, 1960–68, 1986–94)	4.1	2.0	4.0	2.6	3.7	2.5	6.2
Standard deviation of GDP growth (1961–68, 1986–94)	1.5	1.6	1.7	2.1	1.9	1.9	...
PPP-based per capita GNP (US$)[e]	3,291	18,280	2,977	17,297	3,928	20,448	16,673
Gross fixed capital formation (in percent of GDP)	23.4	20.5	21.1	21.3	19.6	20.7	31.2
Inflation (in percent, 1960–68, 1986–94)	3.6	3.9	3.7	3.7	3.4	3.7	15.3
Government financial liabilities and interest indicators							
Public debt[f]	47.5	79.0	37.4	59.9	46.4	53.3	13.5
Implicit pension liabilities (in percent of GDP)	...	113.0[g]	...	112.0	...	53.3	...
Real interest rates[h]	1.7	3.9	2.8	4.6	1.3	4.0	...
Risk premium on government debt[i]	...	37.0	...	27.0	...	2.0	...

Labor market indicators

Unemployment rate (in percent, 1996)	2.9	...	8.5	4.6	11.9	2.7	6.6	2.9
Youth unemployment rate, age 15–24 (in percent)	...	16.0	...	19.0	...	13.0	...
Women in administrative and managerial positions[j]	...	38.0	...	33.0	...	49.0	17.0

Sources: Compiled by Tanzi and Schuknecht based on OECD, *Economic Outlook* (1994, 1995, 1996); OECD, *Historical Statistics, 1960–90* (1991); OECD, *National Accounts* (1995); United Nations, *Human Development Report* (various years); and previous tables.

[a] Belgium, Italy, Netherlands, Norway, Sweden (public expenditure more than 50 percent of GDP in 1990).

[b] Austria, Canada, France, Germany, Ireland, New Zealand, Spain (public expenditure between 40–50 percent of GDP in 1990).

[c] Australia, Japan, Switzerland, United Kingdom, United States (public expenditure less than 40 percent of GDP in 1990).

[d] Chile, Hong Kong, Korea, Singapore.

[e] 1970 data for 1960 column and early 1990s for 1990 column.

[f] 1970 data for 1960 columns.

[g] Only data for Italy available.

[h] 1960 column is an average of 1960–7 and 1990 column is an average of 1980–90.

[i] Launch spread over benchmark rate on basis points for selected five- to seven-year Eurobond issues in nondomestic currency, 1991–5.

[j] In percent as compared to men working in these positions.

across all countries had not changed much from the previous level. However, in 1990 all three groups had similar levels of gross fixed capital formation. A small share of the decline in investment in countries with big governments can be explained by a decline in their public investment (see Table V.1). However, much of the decline must have been on account of private investment. This could be indicative of large public sector deficits crowding out private investment in these countries.

Inflation

Inflation was similar among country groups in both the 1960s and around 1990.

Public Debt and Implicit Financial Liabilities

The indicators on public debt and implicit pension liabilities show very clearly the result of government profligacy and higher deficits in countries with relatively large public sectors. Big governments increased the level of public debt by about 30 percent of GDP in the past three decades, whereas this increase amounted to less than 10 percent for small governments. In the 1960s, public debt levels of around 40 percent of GDP were quite similar between country groups. By 1990, public debt of big governments had increased to almost 80 percent of GDP, compared with 53 percent of GDP for small governments.

Explicit debt, however, is not the only financial liability that governments will have to face in the future. On the basis of current policy commitments, future pension contributions will not cover expected obligations, and many governments, as a consequence, will face considerable implicit liabilities.[3] As with explicit debt, we find that big governments and medium-sized governments show much larger net

3. As mentioned, the net present value of the sum of future deficits in the pension system approximates such liabilities. The measurement of these liabilities is, of course, very difficult because some underlying assumptions on growth and discount rates are somewhat arbitrary. Also governments can change their policy commitment. However, it is important to acknowledge such commitments and the potentially large magnitude of them. These magnitudes will either create major future problems or require difficult policy changes.

liabilities from their pension systems than small governments. In a number of countries from these groups, implicit pension liabilities exceed the value of explicit debt or even the value of GDP. In fact, the adding of public debt and implicit pension liabilities generates some rather worrisome totals.

Real Interest Rates

The development of real interest rates on public debt reflects the increase in government financial liabilities over the past decades. In the 1980s and early 1990s, all governments have had to pay much higher real rates than in the 1960s or 1970s. Real interest rates also became more similar across countries probably as a consequence of greater capital mobility and less intervention into domestic capital markets. In other words, a world capital market came into existence. However, deviations in real interest rates between countries cannot be easily explained because of the role played by different tax treatment and inflation expectations. In the previous chapter, it was argued that the differences in the financial positions of countries can be appreciated much better by looking at the risk premiums paid by countries in international bond markets. Of interest to our analysis is that countries with big governments as a group pay the largest interest premium on public debt. This premium averaged 37 basis points in 1990. Medium-sized governments faced a risk premium of one-quarter of 1 percent This may not seem much but, as mentioned earlier, on high levels of public debt it can add significantly to the interest bill of a country. Should public debt continue to grow and should a crisis occur, these risk premiums could quickly reach much higher dimensions.

Unemployment

Unemployment has become *the* major policy challenge for industrialized countries. In the 1960s, unemployment was not much of an issue and was independent of the size of government, and country groups reported unemployment rates between only 2.7 percent and 4.6 percent. By the 1990s, however, big and medium-sized governments had almost tripled their unemployment rates. Unemployment not only increased after the oil crises in the mid-1970s, but it increased further in the first half of the 1990s, especially in countries with relatively large public sectors. This occurred without any serious recession or exogenous shock boosting unemployment. Interestingly, countries with small governments experienced unemployment rates much lower than either of the other two groups. Average rates above 10 percent for medium-sized governments in particular show problems in the functioning of labor markets and in the incentives that public expenditure policies create.

High youth unemployment rates are of particular concern in this context. Youth unemployment is on average almost twice as high as overall unemployment in all country groups. This reflects labor rigidities, but it also reflects the poorly functioning professional education systems in a number of countries that may continue to produce graduates with anachronistic skills. However, if the youths do not get a useful professional education and do not gain work experience, the human capital base of a country is reduced. In addition, social problems with the frustrated and the unoccupied youths are bound to increase. Again, the data show that high public expenditure is associated with higher rather than with lower youth unemployment. Incidentally, Table V.2 shows that the situation of women in the labor markets is not much affected by the size of government. The share of women in more qualified jobs such as managerial or administrative jobs is highest in countries with small governments. However, cultural factors may play an important role here.

4. SOCIAL INDICATORS

Social indicators have been and are still very similar between country groups, showing that higher public spending did not have a significant effect on these indicators. Judging from the UN human development index, which is a composite index of life expectancy, education, and per capita income, countries with small governments are even somewhat better off. All the countries in our sample rank among the top twenty countries in the world. However, the small-government countries come on the average in the sixth place, while the other two groups come in the eleventh and thirteenth places (Table V.3).

Table V.3. *Size of Government, Health, Education, and Environment Indicators in Different Country Groups, about 1960 and 1990*

| | Industrialized countries[a] | | | | | | Newly industrialized countries[a] |
| | Big governments | | Medium-sized governments | | Small governments | | |
	1960	1990	1960	1990	1960	1990	1990
Rank in UN Human Development	...	11	...	13	...	6	31
Health							
Government expenditure	2.6	6.6	3.0	5.9	2.3	5.2	3.3
Life expectancy	72.0	77.0	70.0	77.0	71.0	77.0	75.0
Infant mortality/1,000 births	23.0	6.7	29.0	7.1	22.4	6.4	8.6
Education							
Government expenditure	4.5	6.4	2.9	5.6	3.4	5.0	3.4
Illiterate population as percent of population age 15+	9.3	1.2	13.3	1.2	2.2	1.0	5.9
Secondary school enrollment (in percent)	55.0	96.0	51.0	100.0	61.0	92.0	85.0
Mathematical ability of secondary school students[b]	...	515.0	...	523.0	...	533.0[c]	607.0[c]
Female tertiary enrollment ratio, 18–23 years (male = 100)	63.0	101.0	63.0	79.0	58.0	100.0	76.0
Environment indicators							
GDP (US dollars) per energy unit[d]	0.7	4.8	0.7	4.7	0.6	5.9	4.5
Greenhouse gas emissions per capita (world median = 1)	...	4.7	...	4.6	...	5.9	...
Waste recycling (as percent of consumption)[e]	...	42.2	...	33.2	...	36.8	...

Sources: Compiled by Tanzi and Schuknecht based on Bottani (1996); Kanbur (1991); United Nations, *Human Development Report* (various years); World Bank, *World Development Report* (various years); World Bank, *Social Indicators of Development* (1996).
[a] Country groups are identical to Table V.1.
[b] International median is 500.
[c] Only United States and Switzerland have data for "small" governments and only Korea for newly industrialized countries.
[d] Kg oil equivalent is energy unit.
[e] Glass, paper, and cardboard.

Health and Mortality Indicators

As mentioned, public health expenditure at 6 percent of GDP is about 20 percent higher in countries with big governments than in those with small governments for which the share of GDP is 5.2 percent. Life expectancy across country groups is identical, however, and infant mortality does not deviate much either. The latter is, in fact, lower in small government countries. This suggests that higher public expenditure in big government countries have not changed health standards significantly. The quality of public programs, per capita income, and technical progress have probably been more important in achieving good health and longer life expectance than higher public spending.

Education

Public expenditure on education by big-government countries is also somewhat higher than that by small-government countries. This difference again does not seem to have much of an effect on the countries education indicators. Literacy is close to 100 percent in all countries. Secondary school enrollment is highest in the medium-sized government group, but enrollment is almost universal in the other groups as well. International indicators that compare the quality of education are very scarce and we could only find one. An international test of mathematical abilities conducted by the OECD for secondary school students shows that the scores for the sample countries on average are above the international median but that the countries with small governments outperformed the others. Female tertiary school enrollment, an indicator of women's education and emancipation in different societies, shows that women attend universities equally frequently as men in most countries. However, they lag behind among the countries with medium-sized governments.

5. ENVIRONMENTAL INDICATORS

Environmental protection is becoming an important issue for industrialized countries. Pollution within and across countries has caused significant concerns among populations and has given rise to "green" movements in many countries. In response to this, governments have increasingly put environmental protection on their policy agenda. Environmental cleanup programs, emission standards, the sale of pollution rights, or tax incentives feature prominently among policy responses to promote a cleaner environment. The nonrenewable character of some natural resources and the pollution caused by the use of resources has given a quasi-moral dimension to the objective of lowering energy consumption and increasing recycling. In light of these developments, the environmental indicators presented in Table V.3 may provide a rudimentary picture of how environmental protection may be related to the size of government.

Environmental expenditure does not differ much between country groups, and public expenditure is only one policy variable that affects environmental indicators. Environmental indicators are slightly better in countries with bigger public sectors. Countries with small governments produce more greenhouse gas per capita than the other two groups (about six times the world average compared to almost five times the world average for the other two groups). However, the amount of income (dollars/GDP) produced with one energy unit is higher in countries with small public sectors indicating a more efficient use of energy. One energy unit produces almost US$6 worth of GDP in the small government countries compared with about US$5 in the other two country groups.

Recycling is another interesting indicator of environmental protection. In some European countries, households have several cans for the various types of garbage, and recycling has become a sophisticated industry. In many countries, governments set rules or targets for recycling, but the recycling itself is privately organized. Public expenditure, therefore, is relatively small, but environmental protection can still be quite effective. In our sample countries, on average almost 40 percent of glass, paper, and cardboard is recycled, but this ratio exceeds 60 percent in some European countries. Countries with big governments together show the best record.

Among small governments, there is considerable variation in environmental indicators, and the slightly poorer performance of this country group is largely due to the performance of thinly populated countries such as the United States and Australia. The relative scarcity of environmental resources and differences in energy prices as resulting from taxation and government regulations are probably much more important for these results than public expenditure policies.[4] Switzerland and Japan, for example, show some of the best records on greenhouse gas emissions, efficient energy use, and recycling; Australia and the United States show two of the worst records.

6. DISTRIBUTIONAL AND SOCIAL STABILITY INDICATORS

Income Distribution

We would expect that high levels of public spending, especially if a large share is related to the welfare state, should have their strongest impact on income distribution. Income distribution is indeed more equal in the big-government countries and it improved the most in these countries between 1960 and 1990 (Table V.4). In 1960, the group of countries with small governments had the most equal income distributions and the bottom 40 percent of households received over 17 percent of GDP. The income share for the same group of households in big government countries was about 2 percentage points lower. By 1990, this situation had reversed. Income distribution as measured by this indicator had become more equal in all income groups. However, the income share of the poorest 40 percent of households in countries with high public spending at 20.1 percent of the total was about 3 percentage points higher than in countries with small governments. Gini coefficients show a similar picture. They range in the 30s for all three country groups, which is a sign of relatively equal income distribution by international standards. However, Gini coefficients in the low 30s in countries with big governments show even more equal income distribution for this group.

Although income distribution is an area where big governments achieved somewhat better results than their small counterparts, it is noteworthy how little the income distributions indexes differ among the groups given the enormous differences in the size of public transfer programs. The explanation for this, on average, lies in the poor targeting of transfer programs in countries with large public sectors. The share of transfers to the poorest 20 percent of households is

---

4. In some instance, however, significant public expenditure on the environment are probably unavoidable, e.g., for the costs of the cleanup of Germany's highly polluted industrial areas in former East Germany or the Chernobyl related pollution.

Table V.4. *Size of Government and Distributional and Social Stability Indicators in Different Country Groups, about 1960 and 1990*

| | Industrialized countries[a] | | | | | | Newly industrialized countries[a] |
| | Big governments | | Medium-sized governments | | Small governments | | |
	1960	1990	1960	1990	1960	1990	1990
Income distribution and equalization							
Income share of lowest 40 percent of households	15.6	20.1	16.9	18.7	17.1	17.3	15.3
Gini coefficients[b]	33.7	32.1	34.4	33.4	32.4	37.6	42.1
Share of transfers to poorest 20 percent of households (in percent of total transfers)	...	22.2	...	25.2	...	33.6	...
Income equalization via taxation and transfers[c]	...	2.7	...	2.2	...	2.1	...
Social stability indicators							
Prisoners/100,000 people[d]	...	23.0	...	58.0	...	123.0	...
Juveniles (in percent of total prisoners)	...	6.0	...	5.0	...	2.0	...
Divorces (in percent of marriages contracted, 1987–91)	...	33.0	...	29.0	...	36.0	...
Suicides by men (per 100,000 people)	...	21.0	...	23.0	...	22.0	...
Emigration (in percent of total population)	0.6	0.2	0.3	0.8	0.2	0.1	0.1

Sources: Compiled by Tanzi and Schuknecht based on Bruno, Ravallion, and Squire (1996); Gwartney, Lawson, and Block (1996); OECD, *Trends in International Migration* (1994); United Nations, *Human Development Report* (various years); and previous tables.

[a] Country groups are identical to those in Table 5.1. Averages of 1960 may contain in-between years from 1962–75 mostly for big government, averages for 1990 may contain data for the years 1988–92.

[b] Income share of bottom 40 percent of households. Data available for 1979–81 instead of 1960.

[c] Increase in income share of lowest 40 percent of households. Average from 1980–6 in 1990 column.

[d] Excluding United States, average is 64.

hardly more than 20 percent in the big-government group. The poorest quintile in countries with medium-sized governments receives about one-quarter of all transfers. Countries with small governments target their transfers the best: about one-third of all public transfers reaches the poorest quintile. Public transfers by some of the big-government countries are even regressive, and in a number of countries, the middle classes are benefiting the most.

Taxation and transfers in big-government countries improve the share of disposable income for the poorest 40 percent of households by 2.7 percent on average. Recall that transfers and subsidies exceed 30 percent of GDP in this country group. The improvement in disposable income, however, is only 0.6 percent of GDP higher than in countries with small governments which spend "only" 14 percent of GDP on subsidies and transfers. Given the relatively poor quality of transfer programs (in terms of reaching vulnerable groups disproportionately), and the relative equality of income even in countries with small governments, it is questionable whether it is worthwhile to have 20 percent of GDP more in public spending and taxation and the subsequent distortions caused by such policies to achieve a marginally more equal income distribution.

These findings suggest that public transfers do not aim mainly at improving the lot of the poor but probably at gaining political support from the middle classes or certain important social groups. Transfer programs in many countries therefore seem to be a huge redistribution program that redistributes in circles without much benefiting those for whom they were originally intended. They also create a very nontransparent picture on the costs of those programs and on the likely winners.

Social Stability Indicators

The following indicators can only be influenced to a very limited extent by government policies, but it is nevertheless interesting to examine whether there are any systematic differences between country groups. Crime has become one of the prime concerns of citizens in many industrialized countries. The United States especially has been reporting high levels of violent crimes, although in the most recent years the crime wave has started to fall significantly. A high share of prisoners in the population may, therefore, reflect to some extent the perceived threat from crime, and indirectly reflect on social stability and welfare. Countries with big governments show the best record in this category, whereas the small government group fares the worst. However, these results are strongly affected by the United States, which, in relative terms, has ten to twenty times more people in prison than most other industrialized countries. However, a large proportion of these people is in jail for drug-related crimes. Leaving out the United States, small and medium-sized governments show similar shares of prison population.

Divorce rates are typically more related to cultural developments and divorce laws than to differences in public expenditure. Nevertheless they are also a sign of social stability. Those who argue that the welfare state promotes social stability by reducing the stress experienced by families would believe that small-government countries have higher divorce rates. Some people argue, however, that extensive welfare benefits make divorce more affordable. They would expect a higher divorce rate in countries with big governments. We observe that big and small government countries report relatively high divorce rates while medium-sized governments show the lowest average divorce rate. The very low divorce rate of Spain and the very high divorce rate of the United States, however, significantly affect the average divorce rate in their country groups. Similarly, low suicide rates could be a sign of social stability. However, all country groups report similar rates.

Emigration, an indicator for the hope of a better life in another country, and indirectly also of the hope of better government policies, has declined, except for countries with medium-sized governments. This shows that on the whole people are not perceiving their economic circumstances as unfavorable or their rulers as oppressive enough to warrant emigration. The decline in emigration is probably also related to the fact that per capita GDP became relatively equal among industrial countries and country groups over the past decades. Nevertheless, we find that emigration was and still is lowest in countries with small governments.

7. GOVERNANCE-RELATED INDICATORS

A final group of indicators compares governance-related issues between country groups. Only in recent years have attempts been made to "quantify" governance-related performance by countries.

These "quantifications" essentially reflect perceptions by those who respond to the relevant questions. They may thus be subject to wide margins of error. On average, all three country groups seem to show reasonable indicators in most categories by international standards. However, there can be sizable differences between countries, and the countries with small governments typically fare better in most of these categories. Especially the relatively large and growing share of the informal sector in countries with big governments should be some source of concern.

Economic and Political Freedom Indicators

Political rights, civil liberties, and economic freedom are considered by many observers to be among the most important qualities of modern pluralist societies and economies. Recent studies have concluded that economic activity suffers when governments are not accountable to the people, or when economic freedom is restricted. Although there is no unambiguous relationship between economic growth and the political regime of countries in the developing world (Borner, Brunetti, and Weder, 1995), all modern industrialized economies reflect some common characteristics such as democracy, the rule of law, and a market-oriented economy. Consequently, political rights and civil liberties have received perfect scores in almost all of our sample countries. Scores on economic freedom are also quite favorable but nevertheless show a moderate difference between country groups. Small governments received on average 7.6 out of 10 points and thereby fared somewhat better than medium-sized governments, which received 7.2 and, especially, big governments, which scored 6.6 (Table V.5).

Administrative Efficiency

The rule of law and the freedom of markets require a functioning government whose institutions are conducive to maintaining these basic principles for modern market economies. An efficient judiciary is essential because it secures the rule of law by enforcing and interpreting it, if necessary even against policymakers. The judiciary thereby is a crucial element in a country's system of checks and balances and ensures that no individuals place themselves above the law.

Table V.5. *Size of Government and Governance-Related Indicators, about 1990* (Percent of GDP)

	Industrialized countries[a]			Newly industrialized countries[a]
	Big governments	Medium-sized governments	Small governments	
Economic and political freedom indicators[b]				
Political rights	10.0	10.0	10.0	7.5
Civil liberties	10.0	9.9	10.0	7.5
Economic freedom	6.6	7.2	7.6	7.5
Administrative efficiency indicator[b]				
Efficiency of judiciary system (1994)	9.3	8.6	10.0	8.3
Red tape (1994)	8.1	7.8	9.0	8.9
Corruption	8.2	8.2	8.1	7.2
Regulatory efficiency indicators				
Size of shadow economy	17.7	12.0	9.4	...
Patents/10,000 population (inventiveness coefficient, 1990)	2.0	2.3	8.6	...

Sources: Compiled by Tanzi and Schuknecht based on Gwartney et al. (1996); Mauro (1995); OECD, *Main Science and Technology Indicators* (1995, 1996); Transparency International (1996); Schneider (1997); United Nations, *Human Development Report* (various years), Weck-Hannemann, Pommerehne, and Frey (1984).

[a] Country groups are identical to Table 5.1.

[b] Ranking between 0 = worst and 10 = best.

The absence of corruption suggests that laws and the implementation of the law by bureaucrats cannot be "bought." It thus also guarantees a level playing field in the economy. Bureaucratic red tape can undermine market economies by raising the costs of law abidance. This provokes corruption and drives people into the underground economy.

Again, in all these areas, scores are relatively high for all country groups. Small governments, however, show better scores than big governments. Medium-sized governments show the poorest scores, albeit by a small margin. The efficiency of the judiciary received the maximum score in all small governments. Small government countries also seem to be least affected by red tape, whereas corruption scores are almost identical for all country groups.[5]

Regulatory Efficiency

The final set of indicators tries to assess indirectly the quality of government policies and regulation by looking at the size of the shadow economy and the inventiveness of an economy. Bad policies and regulations, as mentioned, induce economic agents to go into the informal economy. They also discourage people from being innovative if they produce an environment that does not protect the property rights in innovations and does not provide hopes for a reasonable return.

Developments in the size of the shadow economy should give rise to concern. According to some studies, between the 1960s and the 1990s, the share of the shadow economy more than doubled, and increased particularly strongly in countries with large public sectors. In this group, the shadow economy has been estimated to comprise more than 17 percent of the total economy, almost twice the size in small government countries. The number of patents per 100,000 people, a proxy for the inventiveness of an economy, is also much higher in countries with small governments (although the magnitude of the difference is exacerbated by the figure for Japan). These results suggest that the size of government may provide incentives to leave

5. For a more detailed discussion of governance see Gwartney, Lawson, and Block (1996) on economic and political freedom, Mauro (1995) on administrative efficiency, and Transparency International on corruption. Brunetti, Kisunko, and Weder (1997a) confirm the relatively favorable business climate in most industrialized compared to many developing countries.

the formal economy, and it may also reduce the innovative potential of economies.

8. CONCLUDING REMARKS

Our review of the many indicators discussed above indicates that the evidence available, while tentative and limited, suggests that, on balance, small governments did not "produce" less desirable socioeconomic indicators than big governments. In areas such as economic performance, labor markets, government financial liabilities, governance, and the regulatory environment, small government countries seem to produce better results than the other country groups. Furthermore, there are indications that stabilization policies have failed to achieve their objective of reducing the variation of output while growing deficits have crowded out the private sector and have depressed growth. Progress in terms of economic and social objectives that could arise from additional public spending seems therefore unlikely. The findings also suggest that, *with intelligent policies*, governments can achieve the same social and economic objectives with much lower levels of public spending. Of course, this conclusion ignores possible transition costs from high to lower public spending.

This conclusion is not necessarily a backing for laissez-faire policies or for policies where the government plays no role or a very limited role in the economy. After all, in all the countries considered, including the small- government countries, the government was important and had achieved a level in terms of public spending much larger than in the early part of this century. Rather, the conclusion is that public spending may not necessarily be an answer to many socioeconomic problems and that with intelligent policies public spending may be reduced.

VI The Experience of the Newly Industrialized Economies

In this chapter, we examine the spending patterns and government performance indicators for some of today's newly industrialized economies. These countries had been growing very fast until they ran into the financial and economic crisis of 1997–8. We find that levels of social and economic indicators almost similar to those of the industrialized countries had been achieved by these countries with much lower levels of public spending. The discussion in this chapter refers to the precrisis period. It remains to be seen how much permanent effect the crisis will have on the social and economic indicators of these countries. The best guess is that the effect will be marginal.

Newly industrialized countries have, so far, not created extensive welfare programs and, therefore, have not experienced the effects of the latter policies on growth, labor markets, and other areas.[1] Although these countries differ in many ways from industrialized countries (their population structure is different, and perhaps strong vested interests dependent on support programs have not yet formed), there may be some lessons to learn from them. We restrict our analysis to three newly industrialized countries – Chile, Korea, and Singapore – and to Hong Kong, China.

---

1. Because of the lack of such programs, the short-run impact of the 1997–8 crisis on some of the sectors of the populations of these countries may have been harder. Korea, for example, had to develop quickly a system of limited unemployment compensation.

120

1. PUBLIC EXPENDITURE PATTERNS IN THE NEWLY INDUSTRIALIZED ECONOMIES

The level of public spending in the newly industrialized economies has been much lower than in the industrialized countries. Average total public expenditure in these countries in 1990 amounted to only 18.2 percent of GDP (see Table V.1 above), less than half the level in the industrialized countries. However, their expenditure levels in 1990 were broadly comparable to those prevailing in 1960 in the industrialized countries with "small" governments. At that time, Switzerland and Japan had public spending of less than 20 percent of GDP and Australia had public spending marginally above 20 percent of GDP.

These figures have to be seen in light of a different attitude toward the role of the state in the newly industrialized countries. This attitude was not influenced by the pro-spending thinking that became fashionable in Western countries in the 1960s and early 1970s. While many industrialized countries were experimenting with Keynesianism and were creating welfare states, the newly industrialized countries were pushing growth and were pursuing policies that (with some exceptions that became very visible during the Asian crisis) relied on market and economic incentives and kept government spending small and lean. In Chile, these policies came after a failed economic experiment in the early 1970s that favored a large public sector.

Among this group, Korea has had the most interventionist approach to development but has still kept public spending under tight control.[2] Hong Kong has represented the noninterventionist extreme.[3] Philip Haddon-Cave, Hong Kong's financial secretary in the 1970s, coined the term "positive non-interventionism" to define the role of government in the economy. As he put it: "In the majority of circumstances it is futile and damaging to the growth rate of the economy for attempts to be made to plan the allocation of resources available to the private sector and to frustrate the operation of

2. In Korea, the government intervened heavily in directing credits in order to pursue its industrial policy aimed at promoting growth through fast industrialization.
3. During the Asian crisis, the Government of Hong Kong abandoned this extreme non-interventionist policy by intervening in the stock markets through the purchase of shares.

market forces which, in an open economy, are difficult enough to predict, let alone to control" (Haddon-Cave, 1984, quoted from Chau, 1993). As a result, companies could enjoy the full rewards of their successful activities, but they had to pay for mistakes and mismanagement.

In Singapore, Lee Kuan Yew, architect of the postcolonial success, believed that policies should focus on a few key principles of good governance promoted by many political philosophers, including Adam Smith or David Hume, such as: "maintaining the rule of law and the sanctity of property rights, fair commercial practices, a level playing field between all players whether they be well-connected insiders or unconnected outsiders, and transparency and accountability in decision making."[4] The application of these principles has made Singapore one of the freest economic areas in the world today.

In Hong Kong, governments did not reject public intervention as a matter of principle but believed that: "The primary role of government is to provide public services and economic infrastructure which only the government can sensibly provide" (Haddon-Cave, 1984). In this, Haddon-Cave is essentially restating Adam Smith's views on the proper role of government. The provision of services was often transferred to the private sector, and consumers had to pay for the full costs of services.

In the newly industrialized countries much emphasis has been placed on human capital formation with governments taking a leading role in providing and financing much of the primary and secondary education and some tertiary education. Health and education for the poor was promoted by targeted government support, but user fees remained important. "Social responsibility to the needy is accepted, but the work ethic must not be weakened by social policies and redistributive fiscal policies" (Haddon-Cave, 1984). Similar concerns also kept welfare benefits limited in the emerging social security system in Korea (*Financial Times*, June 26, 1995). In some of these countries, for example, until the Asian crisis there had not been any program that supported the incomes of the unemployed.[5]

---

4. *Financial Times*, February 12, 1997. It should be clear that philosophically Singapore and Hong Kong were very different from Korea, where the government believed in positive intervention.
5. There has been a lot of soul searching on whether to abandon the old principles in the face of the Asian crisis.

The composition of public expenditure in the newly industrialized economies has to be seen in light of the limited government role. About one-third of the expenditure has been on government consumption, one-third on subsidies and transfers, and the remaining third on interest payments and public investment. These proportions refer of course to the much lower levels of total public spending as a share of GDP. The main difference compared with the industrialized countries was to be found in the much lower level of subsidies and transfers. These amounted to only 5.7 percent of GDP, or about one-quarter of the average expenditure on this category in the industrialized economies. In fact, the expenditure composition is similar to the one prevailing in 1960 in some of the small governments in industrialized countries. Public investment of 3.4 percent of GDP is higher than the average for industrialized countries, as infrastructure development was given high priority.[6]

Until the Asian crisis, this country group reported virtually no budget deficits over the years. Hong Kong, for example, experienced only seven budget deficits since 1946. Thus, its government accumulated significant financial assets. The same is true for Singapore. Since the mid-1980s, Chile also experienced budget surpluses. As a consequence, these countries did not have a large public debt to service. In Korea the banking crisis and the deep 1998 recession created a sizable fiscal deficit and a potentially large public debt because of government guarantees.

From a functional perspective, spending on health and education in the newly industrialized economies has been relatively high in comparison with the spending on these categories in industrialized countries in the 1960s. This reflects the high priority put on universal, high-quality education and on human capital in these newly industrialized countries. In 1990 Korea, for example, spent 6 percent of GDP on education, exactly the same as the average for industrialized countries and was rapidly creating one of the most formally educated populations in the world. In fact, in some ways it was over-investing in education, which was leading to rapidly falling rates of return especially to higher education. Although Hong Kong has sometimes been called the last bastion of laissez-faire and has been

---

6. Weak infrastructure was seen as one of the main shortcomings in several rapidly developing Asian economies (Brunetti, Kisunko, and Weder, 1997).

admired for this by conservative economists such as Milton Friedman, in the 1970s it introduced free, compulsory secondary education up to the age of fifteen. This reflected the view of its administrators that a high level of education for the population is a valid objective for the government.

Social security spending of 1 percent of GDP by the newly industrialized countries is only a small fraction of what the industrialized countries spend for social security. These figures reflect the strong role of traditional family networks for providing safety nets, and the aversion toward welfare dependency. However, it also reflects significant private sector participation in health, education, and social security in some of these countries. Singapore's Central Provident Fund or Chile's privatization of retirement insurance have become important examples for other countries that are interested in government reform aimed at reducing public spending over the long-run (see Bercuson, 1995 on Singapore; Bosworth, Dornbush, and Laban, 1994 on the Chilean experience; and later chapters in this study).

2. ECONOMIC AND LABOR MARKET INDICATORS

The long-run economic performance of the newly industrialized countries has been impressive. That performance is not invalidated by the Asian crisis. Real economic growth averaged 6.2 percent over the last decade (see Table V.2). This was almost three times as high as the average growth in the industrialized countries. Political uncertainty in Hong Kong over the 1980s lowered its economic growth to 6 percent, after an average of 9–10 percent in the previous three decades (Chau, 1993). Over many years, Korea experienced the most impressive growth record with almost 10 percent per annum in the first half of the 1990s (Table VI.1). One should recall that, after the Korean War in the early 1950s, Korea was not seen as a country with good growth and development prospects. There is a story often told of a World Bank mission to Korea in the early 1960s that concluded that the country had no possibility of development. The problems that have appeared recently on the economic front do not change the extraordinary past achievements. Once the crisis is over, it is likely that Korea will return to a strong economic performance.

Table VI.1. *Government Performance Indicators, Selected "Small" Governments, and Newly Industrialized Countries, Early 1990s* (Percent of GDP)

	Industrialized countries			Newly industrialized countries		
	United States	Japan	Switzerland	Chile	Korea	Singapore
Economic indicators						
Economic growth (percent, 1991–5)	2.3	1.3	1.6	7.4	9.5	8.8
PPP-based per capita GNP (US$, 1995)	26.980	22,110	25,860	9,520	11,450	22,770
Inflation (1991–5)	3.2	1.4	3.2	13.9	6.2	2.5
Gross public debt (1994–5)	64.3	81.3	48.2	17.4[a]	8.0	15.2
Labor market indicators						
Unemployment (mid-1990s)	5.4	3.3	4.7	4.6	2.4	2.7
Social and distributional indicators						
Life expectancy (1995)	77	80	78	76	72	77
Infant mortality (per 1,000 live births)	9	4	6	12	10	4
Secondary school enrollment ratio	97	96	91	70	93	84
Educational attainment (mathematics scores, eighth grade students, 1994)	500	605	545	...	607	...
Income share of lowest 40 percent of households (about 1990)	15.4	17.7	18.1	10.5	19.7	17.3
Economic and political freedom indicators[b]						
Political rights	10.0	10.0	10.0	7.0	9.0	7.0
Civil liberties	10.0	10.0	10.0	8.0	8.0	7.0
Economic freedom	8.0	7.3	7.9	6.2	6.7	8.2
Administrative efficiency indicators[b]						
Efficiency of judiciary system	10.0	10.0	10.0	7.3	6.0	10.0
Red tape	9.3	8.5	10.0	9.3	6.5	10.0
Corruption	7.8	6.7	8.8	7.9	4.3	9.3

Sources: Tables 2.10–2.12.a.
[a] External debt only.
[b] Ranking between 0 = worst and 10 = best.

As a result of this rapid growth, per capita GDP on the basis of purchasing power parity (PPP), had recently reached over US$14,000 for the four newly industrialized economies of Chile, Hong Kong/ China, Korea, and Singapore. On average, this is about 70 percent of the current per capita income in the industrialized countries and is comparable to the level in these countries in the late 1960s. In Hong Kong and Singapore, the per capita GDP on a PPP basis has caught up with Japan and even exceeds the per capita income in a number of other industrialized economies. In Chile and Korea, the PPP-based per capita income of more than US$9,000 is lower but nevertheless reaches already two-thirds of the level in Spain, Ireland, or New Zealand. If data were available and Taiwan was added, equally impressive results would be shown.

The impressive growth rates in the newly industrialized economies have been attributed to several factors, of which an important one is the high rate of gross fixed capital formation. Investment in excess of 30 percent of GDP exceeds by a wide margin the investment levels in industrialized countries. High savings rates have been key to the high investment, and Korea, for example, has reported savings rates of around 35 percent of GDP. With public investment of about 3 percent of GDP, or only 10 percent of total investment, private investment has clearly been driving economic growth in these countries. In fact, the fast rate of growth has generated various bottlenecks, suggesting that the building of infrastructures should be accelerated.

Some of the other macroeconomic variables have also looked quite good. Inflation has been low and declining, and in the first half of the 1990s, it has averaged only 2.5 percent in Singapore. In Chile, the country with the least favorable historical inflation record, inflation was down to 4 percent in 1998 and was being reduced gradually. The interest bill on government debt in newly industrialized economies is very low because of the very low level of public debt which, for this country group, has amounted to only about 13 percent of GDP.[7] In addition, these countries (except possibly Korea) do not have significant implicit pensions liabilities, as is the case for the industrialized countries. Singapore and Chile, for example, have fully funded

---

7. As already mentioned, interest payments are likely to go up in Korea in future years because of the debt accumulated during the Asian financial and economic crisis.

schemes, while the Korean public basic pension scheme has accumulated some reserves to cover future liabilities.

The newly industrialized economies had also reported good employment performances. Until the 1997–8, financial crisis, unemployment averaged about 3 percent, with a maximum of 4.6 percent for Chile. These rates compare favorably even with respect to the lowest rates in the industrialized countries and were probably the result of the newly industrialized countries' very limited social assistance programs and relatively limited interventions in labor markets. In Korea, however, the recent crisis led to higher unemployment and the lack of programs to insure the unemployed created social difficulties, thus leading to the introduction of a limited unemployment insurance.[8]

The role of women has also become an important indicator of social and economic progress. Growth and emancipation resulted in increased female labor force participation. Equal-opportunity programs for women should also result in a growing share of women in professional and managerial ranks. In these countries, the economic emancipation of women defined in this way has progressed considerably over the past decades although it still lags somewhat behind the industrialized countries (see Table V.2). The share of women in administrative and managerial positions is still only 17 percent, or about half the share in industrialized countries (United Nations Development Programme (UNDP), 1995).

3. SOCIAL AND DISTRIBUTIONAL INDICATORS

In the area of social indicators, newly industrialized economies have also largely caught up with industrialized countries. All countries rank very high in the UN Human Development Indicator. Given that the first twenty slots in that indicator are taken by industrialized countries, the twenty-fourth rank for Hong Kong, and ranks of around thirty for the other three countries are not bad (see Table V.3).[9]

8. Until the crisis, Korean workers in the large conglomerates had life guarantee on their employment.
9. In the *Human Development Report* (1998) in which the Human Development Index refers to 1995, the rankings of the newly industrialized countries were, respectively: Hong Kong, China (25); Singapore (28); Korea (30); and Chile (31).

In the areas of health and mortality, differences between the two country groups have become very small. Life expectancy averages 74 years (only three to four years less than in industrialized countries) and exceeds 70 in all four countries. Hong Kong's and Singapore's life expectancy is even higher than in a number of industrial countries. Infant mortality rates are also similar between industrialized and newly industrialized countries. Hong Kong's infant mortality rate has come down by 80 percent in recent decades and is now as low as in any industrialized country. Only Chile reports somewhat higher infant mortality. However, it is still among the lowest of nonindustrialized countries, and its rate is similar to that in Hungary and Poland, countries that spend more than twice the Chilean share of public spending in GDP.

Educational standards in the newly industrialized economies have improved significantly over the past decades, and are close to those in industrialized countries. This reflects the high priority put on education, and the universal access to free basic education. Adult literacy is 94 percent of the population, and secondary school enrollment averages 88 percent of the potential. In Chile secondary school enrollment is lowest with 74 percent, Korea reports over 90 percent, and in Hong Kong, secondary school attendance is compulsory.

Regarding women's role in society and in the economy, female tertiary school enrollment relative to men is another key indicator. Women's educational opportunities have increased considerably since 1970 when their share among students was much smaller than today. Chile and Singapore report almost equal shares of male and female university students, while Hong Kong and Korea have some catching up to do (UNDP, 1995).

The income share of the poorest 40 percent of the households is on average somewhat smaller than in the industrialized countries. It ranges from little over 10 percent of GDP in Chile to almost 20 percent in Korea. The average for the group is 15.3 percent of GDP, similar to the United States' average (Table VI.1). Korea, in particular, has an income distribution similar to that of a number of industrialized countries. The income distribution in newly industrialized countries has improved considerably in recent decades. In Korea, high economic growth and the introduction of some basic social security had rapidly reduced the number of poor;[10] similar trends toward

10. However, this progress is likely to have been stopped or even (temporarily?) reversed during the Asian crisis.

a better income distribution have been reported by Hong Kong for the period after 1970 (Kwon, 1993; and Chau, 1993). These results would also indicate that high public spending is not essential for improving the distribution of income.

Although there is not much information on the targeting of social expenditure in newly industrialized countries, the limited evidence available suggests that social spending is relatively efficient and well targeted, despite considerable differences between countries in the institutional setup of support systems. In Chile, for example, only pensions below a minimum income threshold are topped up with government assistance. In 1993, almost one-third of education expenditure and one-quarter of health expenditure in Chile benefited the poorest quintile, a share much higher than in most other Latin American countries. In Korea, a contribution-based public pension scheme provides a basic safety net for the elderly (first tier) which is complemented by company-based retirement insurance. Health-service provision is private, but public health insurance provides universal, though very limited, coverage. User fees are still a very important element to prevent waste. The poor can receive additional public support (Kwon, 1993).

4. GOVERNANCE-RELATED INDICATORS

Regarding economic freedom and administrative efficiency (which are often considered as very important prerequisites for economic growth, prosperity, and equal opportunity) newly industrialized countries compare well with the industrialized countries. Economic freedom in newly industrialized countries matches the average ranking of even the top-scoring small-government group among the industrialized countries. Hong Kong and Singapore show the highest score in this category, and the average for newly industrialized countries of 7.5 (out of 10) is higher than the average for all industrialized countries in our sample.

Administrative efficiency in newly industrialized economies also compares favorably with the industrialized countries. Hong Kong, Singapore, and Chile report low corruption indexes, little red tape, and a relatively efficient judiciary. Korea, however, lags behind in these aspects of governance. Singapore reports the highest score in all three categories, closely followed by Hong Kong. It is interesting to note that Japan, Switzerland, and the United States with relatively small governments report similar scores in these categories. Earlier it was reported that big governments have the most red tape. Despite this favorable record the less than "sterling" scores on political rights and civil liberties should not be forgotten. This, and the role of crony capitalism in some newly industrialized countries, illustrates that their "model" role shouldn't be overstated. While they may provide some lessons in keeping public spending low and efficient, they may learn from industrialized countries about reforming their political systems. But this is a different point and goes beyond the scope of this study (see Table V.5).

5. CONCLUDING REMARKS

Our brief survey leads us to conclude that newly industrialized countries have generated almost similar levels of socioeconomic indicators as industrialized countries and are rapidly catching up in areas where they are still lagging behind. These results have been achieved with public spending levels much lower than those prevailing in industrialized countries, and even lower than those in the industrialized countries with small governments. This favorable picture is explained not so much by different goals on the part of the governments of these countries but by a different role given to the state. Governments intervene to provide essential services or to set incentives in a market-friendly manner. The question of the "proper" future role of the state will be the theme of the next three chapters in this study.

PART THREE

The Role of the State and Government Reform

In previous chapters, we showed that the growth in public spending over the past century resulted from a considerable expansion of relatively new activities in which governments became involved. During this period, citizens requested a larger role of the government in the economy, while institutional constraints and intellectual resistances on public spending were progressively weakened. For some time, the growth in public spending from a very low level generated significant gains in social and economic welfare. For the period after 1960, however, when the rapid increase in public spending became largely of a redistributive kind, the earlier link between the growth in government spending and improvements in social and economic objectives seems to have been broken. In our analysis, we have found that the industrial countries with small governments and, to some extent, the newly industrialized countries with low public spending, were able to achieve levels of socioeconomic indicators similar to those achieved by countries with much higher levels of public spending. This has led us to the conclusion that there must be considerable scope for redefining the role of the state in industrialized countries so as to *decrease public spending without sacrificing much in terms of social and economic objectives*. In other words, we believe that it is possible to reduce public spending without necessarily changing the fundamental objectives of the government.

In the following chapters we will argue that there is considerable scope for government reform and, borrowing from countries experiences, we will outline a rough blueprint for such reforms. To become smaller and more efficient, governments will need to refocus their role toward setting the "rules of the game" to provide an appropriate framework for market forces to stimulate both growth and social welfare. It will be necessary to both improve the rules and strengthen the institutions that promote good, fiscal policymaking. Despite the increasing awareness of the need for reform, and despite the pressure arising from increasing globalization, the implementation of reform will not be easy because of the resistance of those who, in the short run, will be, or think that they will be, the losers. Reform will, therefore, be a lengthy and politically arduous task, but in the end, it could significantly lower the levels of public spending without much cost, or even with gains, in economic and social well-being.

In Part Three of this book, Chapters VII–IX, we shall outline the many reforms that have been introduced in countries around the world with the specific motive of reducing public spending while increasing efficiency in the delivery of particular services. We present these reforms to illustrate the scope for possible action without necessarily endorsing all of them.

VII Rethinking the Role of the State

1. THE SCOPE FOR REFORM

We have suggested in the preceding text that, by around 1960, when public spending was, on average, below 30 percent of GDP, most industrialized countries had reached adequate levels of social welfare. Public spending on essential services in health and education or in infrastructure and basic social security systems provided the most basic public services. The contribution that public spending had made to the achievement of high levels of socioeconomic indicators was very significant.[1] However, we could not find much evidence that the large growth of government spending over the post-1960 years contributed much to the further achievement of identifiable social and economic objectives. In fact, some of these objectives seemed to change in the wrong direction. At the same time, today's newly industrialized countries show relatively high levels of desirable economic and social indicators even though their public spending is only about 20 percent of GDP. The governments of these countries may not be doing everything that the governments of the industrial countries do, but they carry out the essential tasks quite effectively and leave it to the private sector to fill the gap. In other words, they focus their attention more on the "core activities" of the government and less on the more recent, redistributive activities. They assume that to a large

1. It is true that in this period high defense spending was claiming resources that could have been spent more productively in other areas.

133

extent what they do not do is either nonessential or it will be done by the private sector.

If one accepts the conclusions from the previous chapters – that reasonable social security and prosperity can be achieved with lower levels of public spending – there may be considerable scope for reducing the size of public spending especially in the "big-government" countries. The reduction in public spending and conse-quently in the level of taxation would leave more resources in the hands of the citizens and allow them to use these resources in ways that more directly improve their welfare. With these resources they should be able to buy, perhaps more cheaply, some of the same goods and services now provided by the government. If the private sector provides these same services more cheaply, as it often does, then society would gain from the change. Obviously in this process the reg-ulatory role of the state will need to become more important, better directed, and more efficient.[2]

A convenient benchmark to assess the scope for reducing the current size of government is the level of public spending reached in 1960 by the industrialized countries. A more ambitious but less real-istic goal would be to aim for the current level of public spending in the newly industrial countries or for the level in industrialized coun-tries in the years before 1960. In Japan and Switzerland, for example, in 1960, the level of public expenditure was less than 20 percent of GDP, almost identical to the level in the newly industrialized countries today. Expenditure by most other governments did not exceed 30 percent of GDP. Therefore, over the long run, total public expenditure could be reduced to, perhaps, under 30 percent of GDP without sacri-ficing the essential or core activities of the public sector and without affecting negatively the relevant social and economic indicators.

It is important to consider how the composition of govern-ment expenditure should change to permit the decline in total expenditure. Because a large proportion of the increase in public expenditure over this century originated from subsidies and transfers, substantial expenditure reduction would have to take place in this category. Subsidies and transfers amounted to less than 4 percent of GDP in Japan in 1960, and, by 1995, they were a little over 10 percent

---

2. Governments have often regulated the wrong activities and in the wrong manner, thus increasing the distortions in the economy.

in Japan, New Zealand, or the United States.[3] This is only half of the average for all industrialized countries. Cutting back on subsidies and transfers could thus yield significant budgetary savings and tax reduction.

Public consumption must also be closely scrutinized. In Japan or Switzerland in 1960, public consumption absorbed less than 10 percent of GDP, and some of today's newly industrialized countries spend even less. This is much less than the *average* expenditure on public consumption of almost 18 percent of GDP for the industrialized countries in 1995 and much higher percentages in some of them. But even in 1995, Japan's public consumption was still below 10 percent of GDP, even though that country was spending more than any other industrial country on public investment. Many countries could probably reduce public spending to around this level by scaling down the public provision of goods and services to essential levels, including military spending, and privatizing others.

A reduction in spending on public consumption would, in many countries, require extensive privatization of enterprises and services. This could yield considerable savings in other expenditure categories such as producer subsidies if privatization included public enterprises that had been kept alive through public support. The example of airlines is an interesting and instructive one. In today's world it is difficult to think of valid reasons why national airlines should continue to exist. The objective of providing air transportation is surely satisfied by private companies. Privatization has greatly improved the performance of previously public airlines, as for example with British Airways, while large subsidies have been keeping alive loss-making airlines. The experience of some countries has also shown that the private provision and financing of traditionally public investment projects can significantly reduce public investment budgets while improving the quality of the services. However, care must be taken not to create excessive contingent public liabilities.[4]

3. It should be mentioned that many conservative thinkers in the United States, including the politicians in the Republican Party, consider the current level of spending in the United States excessive. They would not agree with our classification of the United States as a "small-government" country. For a conservative, philosophical discussion of the "minimal" and "ultra minimal" state, see Nozick (1974).

4. This occurs when private investors in infrastructure projects (such as roads) require and obtain public guarantees on the rate of returns to the projects. (See Irwin, et al., editors, 1997.)

A major rethinking of public expenditure policies and the role of the state is therefore desirable. The idea that the government can be reinvented, to use Vice President Gore's expression, should not just be a political slogan. (See Osborne and Gaebler, 1992.) Fundamental and radical reforms will be needed if the objective of substantially reducing public spending while making it more efficient, is to be achieved (Tanzi and Schuknecht, 1997b, 1998; Bismut and Jacquet, 1997). This objective should be seen as achievable and not just a mirage.

2. CHANGING THE POLICY REGIME

Reform of government and reduction in public expenditure can generate considerable long-term benefits if they result in higher economic growth. Reforms will stimulate growth mainly when they reduce marginal tax rates and alter expectations on the part of the private sector about the future investment climate for both real and human capital and for new activities. When the expectations are good, individuals will be willing to commit themselves to undertake the necessary changes in their behavior.[5] Such a change in expectations, however, is more likely to occur when the policy regime of a country or its basic rules of the game change. The more important, promising, and permanent the reforms are assumed to be, the stronger the change in expectations.

Fiscal policies have often accommodated the desire by policy makers to redistribute rents to politically powerful interest and social groups instead of providing essential services and a framework conducive to market-based growth and social welfare.[6] This redistribution was facilitated by fiscal policy rules that allowed expansionary and inefficient expenditure policies and the accumulation of deficits and public debt. It was also facilitated by the political and intellectual climate that favored a larger public sector.[7] However, if existing

---

5. For example, the present value of investment in education must be influenced by the level of taxes at which the return to human capital will be taxed.
6. For example, educational reforms have often had more to do with the compensation or the hiring of teachers than with attempts to bring the curriculum closer to the needs of the economy.
7. A lack of transparency in fiscal policy rules and processes also prevented the pursuit of a more efficient policy.

rules resulted in excessive government growth in past years, a reversal of that trend may not happen automatically even if the political and intellectual climate changes. (See Forte and Peacock, 1986.) A change in the policy regime that had permitted such policies to be enacted may be necessary. Putting it differently, the rules of the game have to change so that policymakers' incentives for fiscal policymaking also change. (See Brennan and Buchanan, 1985; Solimano, Sunkel, and Blejer 1994; and Kopits and Craig, 1997.)

It is worthwhile discussing briefly the analogy between rules of the game in society and in sports. In most sports, the rules do not allow use of brute force and unfair tactics on the field. This code of behavior is translated into detailed definitions on what constitutes a foul and how it is penalized. Rules reduce the uncertainty for players and introduce a level playing field. They give players an incentive to play well, which in turn makes the game more fun for them and for the spectators. But rules do not determine the outcome of the game, and everybody would be outraged if goals in soccer, for example, were awarded on grounds other than merit. This distinction between influencing outcomes and processes is confused in much of the current debate over the role of state. A change in the rules for fiscal policymaking should aim at improving the process of policymaking rather than at determining the outcome of such policies. [8]

In many countries, over past years, the inadequacy of the existing rules of the game in fiscal policymaking has promoted the growth of inefficient spending and high fiscal deficits. Therefore, a fundamental shift in the fiscal policy regime is warranted.[9] There is no precise road map to reform, but the introduction of appropriate budgetary institutions and, possibly, fiscal rules that harden government budget

---

8. The important next question is why policymakers should agree to a rules change that may curtail their own discretionary power even if different rules increase the overall welfare of society. Buchanan (1985) has argued that if there is sufficient uncertainty about the future relative position of individuals in society, policymakers will make the choice of rules behind a "veil of uncertainty" and choose the policy regime with the best rules that maximizes overall welfare. Additionally, the change in political and intellectual climate may facilitate these changes in rules. For example, the now popular attitude vis-à-vis the political independence of central banks could not have occurred without that change in climates. See also Breton (1984) on the role of the constitution in an economy, the difficulties surrounding constitutional change, and a case study of constitutional change in Canada.
9. The current attention paid to transparency in fiscal policy and the development by the International Monetary Fund of a Code for Fiscal Transparency is an indication that such a shift may be on the way.

constraints and improve the quality of expenditure programs is essential. Budgetary institutions that strengthen incentives for prudent fiscal policies by limiting expansionary interventions in the preparation, approval, and execution of budgets have been identified as important prerequisites for efficient expenditure programs and for the control of fiscal deficits. (See, inter alia, Milesi-Ferretti, 1996, and Alesina and Perotti 1995a.) Furthermore, fiscal transparency in processes, institutions, and reporting of outcomes is now considered of great importance as compared to the past when fiscal illusion was often seen as a virtue. (See Kopits and Craig, 1998.)[10]

If complemented by appropriate budgetary institutions, fiscal rules may help constrain expansionary fiscal policies. These rules can take the form of constitutional rules, legal statutes, administrative guidelines, or other controls on deficits and public debt in many countries. Some authors have argued that constitutional rules can play a particularly prominent role. They may be able to tie a government's hand more firmly than simple legislation because, in most countries, they are more difficult to reverse. In some countries, constitutional rules now guarantee the independence of their central banks, rendering the monetization of fiscal deficits more difficult. It has also been argued that direct democracy as a constitutional principle has slowed down the expansion of public expenditure in Switzerland (Pommerehne and Schneider, 1982). However, constitutional rules are no panacea for fiscal problems, because they require strong implementation and enforcement mechanisms. In some countries where they exist, they have been disregarded or circumvented.[11] This is particularly the case when lack of fiscal transparency makes it difficult to decide whether the constitutional rule is being observed in both the spirit and the form of the law – as for example when extrabudgetary accounts are allowed.

The need for a strong monitoring agency for fiscal policies is also widely acknowledged. Following the success of many independent central banks in controlling monetary expansion and the failure of many national ministries to monitor spending and the overall fiscal

10. At its April 1998 meeting in Washington, D.C., the Interim Committee, made up of ministers of finance representing all the 182 member countries of the IMF, approved a Code of Conduct for Fiscal Transparency.
11. For example, the spirit of Article 81 of the Italian constitution, that would seem to require the balancing of the budget, has been ignored through the reinterpretation of that article.

position of countries, the idea of an independent body overseeing fiscal policies that would take away discretion from politicians has recently been promoted. It could be located within the country or at a supranational level (as for example in the European Union for the stability and growth pact under European Monetary Union). (See also Alesina, Housemann, Hommes, and Stein, 1995.) A proxy for such an institution vis-à-vis many developing countries has been provided by the International Monetary Fund, which has often constrained fiscal expansion by countries where an IMF-supported program was in existence.

Other elements, which can strengthen the institutional framework for fiscal policy making include adequate accounting practices that facilitate the monitoring of fiscal performance. This is part of the new movement toward fiscal transparency pioneered by New Zealand, Australia, and the United Kingdom. A reorientation of expenditure management systems toward managerial structures similar to those within corporations with task-oriented agencies, performance-oriented compensation, decentralized decision-making, and strong accountability can in many cases increase the cost effectiveness of service provision and help central agencies, such as the ministry of finance, focus on strategic policy decisions. A qualified and well-motivated civil service is essential to improve expenditure management and the quality of government policies. Such a civil service would minimize principal–agent problems within the bureaucracy which can distort policies. The next chapter will discuss in more detail how reforms of fiscal rules and institutions can contribute to expenditure efficiency and fiscal discipline. We will argue that this is crucial for effective takeover of government functions by the private sector.

3. REDUCING THE ROLE OF THE STATE

When considering the traditional normative role of the state as identified, for example, by Musgrave (1959), the basic functions such as allocation of resources, redistribution of income, and stabilization of the economy, need to be revisited in a fundamental way. Government provision often seems much too expensive, especially when intelligent regulation of private sector activities could address market failures while leaving the activity in private hands. Similarly, the way in which attempts at redistributing income are practiced in most industrialized countries are much too expensive when the full costs are compared with the benefits.[12] Over the years, some of the greatest crimes in economy policy, in terms of resource waste and welfare costs, have been committed and justified in the name of income redistribution. Many so-called redistributive policies do not benefit those in real need but, rather, benefit politically important groups or tax and subsidize the same families at the same time (tax churning). Often the net impact of redistributive policies on income distribution is unknown and cannot be determined. However, the costs to the economy are real.

Palda (1997), for example, has argued that Canadian public spending could be reduced by several percentage points of GDP *without making anybody worse off*, and, in fact, making many better off, if, *for the same households*, spending cuts were matched by tax cuts, thereby avoiding "fiscal churning" and related waste. The OECD has estimated the extent of "tax churning" for eleven industrial countries around 1993–5. Churning, as a percentage of income before taxes and transfers, ranged from 6.5 percent in Australia and 9.0 percent in the United States to 28 percent in Denmark and 34.2 percent in Sweden. Furthermore, the percentage of churning is directly related to the size of public spending. (See Table VII.1.) This indicates the large scope for expenditure and tax reductions.[13] If all churning were eliminated, public spending would not have to be more than about 30 percent of GDP. This does not even take into account possible expenditure reductions from privatization.

The role of government in stabilizing the economy, through the Keynesian manipulation of aggregate demand has been seen by many informed observers in recent years as having been a failure.[14] One basic reason is that cyclical developments have often been used as a pretext to increase permanent public spending. Political, legal, or

12. The costs of expenditure programs should be compared not only to the potential costs of market failures but also to the costs arising from distortionary taxation, rent seeking, financing, and potential macroeconomic destabilization.
13. When the government taxes and subsidizes the same households by the same amount, it may not change the household's disposable income, but it introduces inefficiencies on both the revenue and the expenditure side.
14. The rational expectation literature of the 1970s launched a strong attack on traditional Keynesian thinking. See especially Lucas (1973, 1976, and Prescott, 1986). However, in the policy world, Keynesian thinking still seems to be very influential.

Table VII.1. *Level of Fiscal Churning in Selected Industrial Countries*[a] (Percent)

Country/Year	Churning as a percentage of income taxes and transfers	Government expenditure as a percentage of GDP	Public expenditures without Churning
United States (1995)	9.0	32.9	23.9
Japan (1994)	11.6	34.4	22.8
Germany (1994)	15.7	48.9	33.2
Italy (1993)	22.7	57.4	34.7
Canada (1994)	11.7	47.5	35.8
Australia (1993–4)	6.5	36.8	30.3
Belgium (1995)	23.7	53.8	30.1
Denmark (1994)	28.0	59.3	31.3
Finland (1995)	15.5	57.9	42.4
Netherlands (1994)	21.1	52.8	31.7
Sweden (1994)	34.2	68.3	34.1
Average	**18.2**	**50.0**	**31.8**

Source: Arranged from OECD *Economic Outlook* (June 1998), p. 163.
[a] Fiscal churning measures the extent to which the same households both receive government payments and pay taxes.

administrative constraints make it difficult for many governments to run on and off the faucets of tax revenue and public spending to follow the Keynesian prescriptions. As far as taxes are concerned, parliaments have refused to give the executive the power to change tax rates for short-run purposes and the legislative process of changing taxes has, in many countries, proven to be lengthy and unpredictable in results. As far as public spending is concerned, evidence shows that increasing it is always much easier than reducing it.[15] Thus, the symmetry in fiscal action required by Keynesian economics is often missing.

Again there is no precise road map for reform, but scaling down social programs that make up the welfare state is of prime importance. In the long run, pensions and health systems' reform could yield

15. During the Kennedy administration, an attempt was made to give the executive the power to change tax rates for limited periods of time within specified limits, but the attempt was not successful. In some countries, however, such as Argentina, the executive has the prerogative to change the rates of specific taxes within specified limits. Often, temporary changes have become permanent.

considerable budgetary savings in most countries. One could argue that there is no compelling economic reason for far-reaching state involvement in these areas beyond basic social assistance, e.g., in the form of a basic allowance for the poor or the unemployed, and of insurance against uninsurable catastrophic events including major illnesses or accidents. With proper reforms and intelligent government regulation, most pension, health, and social insurance needs could be satisfied by the private sector, thus reducing the need for public spending. The public sector could regulate private sector activities and could subsidize the buying of basic insurance on the part of the poor. These drastic changes would require a major departure from the present way of doing things. We will discuss some of these changes below.

We will also show that there is considerable scope for the privatization of many government activities. There is no need for the government to be engaged in banking, airlines, telecommunication, or heavy industries. The role of the private sector in the building and operation of roads, prisons, airports, railroads, and municipal services could be extended considerably. The need for free public primary and secondary education is rarely questioned, because of the externalities associated with these activities. However, more and more observers are coming to the conclusion that this need can be satisfied more efficiently and more cheaply through provision of vouchers and not necessarily through provision of public schools. At the level of tertiary or university education, fully or partly privately financed and operated universities could replace often inefficient public university systems.[16]

Access to credit could be made available to help liquidity-constrained individuals. This would in many cases require an efficient regulatory role for the government while reducing its role as a provider of the services.

The question of where to draw the line between government and private sector activities, however, cannot be answered universally. Where the line should be drawn will change with time and, possibly, across countries. The better the market economy is working, the less extended can be the role of the public sector indirectly providing the services. Also, the more efficient and honest is the public admin-

16. Because higher education is supposed to generate few, if any, externalities, there is no reason why it should be publicly provided.

istration and the less important are rent-seeking activities, the greater could be, ceteris paribus, the role assigned to the public sector. Technical considerations and competent analysis should routinely complement the political process in deciding who should perform which function in the economy. Thus, it is important to create institutions (such as the Congressional Budget Office and the Government Accounting Office in the United States) that are capable of carrying out such analyses in an efficient, neutral, and apolitical way.[17]

Reducing public expenditure will free up resources for private use and reduce the demands on the tax system. The overly strong reliance on direct taxes and social security contributions in many industrial countries could be reduced. Marginal tax and contribution rates could, thus, become lower.[18] This would reduce the disincentive effects of taxation and would stimulate growth. The tax base would be broadened if the tax-induced incentives to leave the formal economy and go underground, or to seek tax exemptions, are reduced. Budget surpluses could be generated to retire part of the accumulated public debt and thereby reduce the interest burden for the budget. In summary, public expenditure as a share of GDP could be lowered considerably without necessarily compromising social and economic welfare.

4. THE IMPLEMENTATION OF REFORMS

Important and pertinent questions are raised when a case is made for reducing the role of the state in the economy: How can reforms be implemented politically? And what time frame should be expected? Again, there is no precise road map. Reforms aimed at changing the economic policy regime of countries and reducing public expenditure programs cannot ignore the commonly made argument that a significant cut in public spending might have a negative impact on growth. In the short run, the distributional implications of reform are also very important because some groups will inevitably be hurt by the reforms. The political opposition that this will generate, the debate

17. The Congressional Budget Office with a relatively small staff of about 400 is likely to have saved a multiple of its cost in terms of fiscal resources of the U.S. government.
18. After 1986, the marginal tax rates for personal income taxes fell by an average of about 12 percentage points, while the basic corporate income tax rates fell by an average of about 10 percentage points. However, the revenue loss was frequently compensated by the broadening of the tax bases.

that this will require, and the administrative constraints of government and the political process suggest that the full implementation of the reforms may take decades rather than a few years.

Public Expenditure Reduction and Growth

Many economists and policymakers worry that reduction of public expenditure may be costly in terms of growth, employment, and political support because of the resulting reduction in aggregate demand, which under certain circumstances could reduce output and raise unemployment. A slowing of economic activity would also make the reduction of public debt stocks more difficult. In recent years a growing body of literature has emerged challenging the traditional Keynesian view that fiscal consolidation necessarily leads to recession (Giavazzi and Pagano, 1990; Alesina and Perotti, 1995b, 1996b; McDermott and Wescott, 1996; Perotti, 1998a,b). This literature has argued that Keynesian recessionary effects from fiscal consolidation may be partly or fully offset by positive effects on demand from anticipated higher consumption and investment when declining government expenditure and taxation raises the expected future private disposable income. Lower real interest rates as a result of higher public savings, and positive effects on supply through lower unit labor costs from lower tax burdens could also counterbalance the recessionary effects from reduction of public expenditure.

Giavazzi and Pagano found that successful fiscal adjustment in Ireland and Denmark had not led to recessions because of the expectation effects on consumption and investment. Alesina and Perotti, McDermott and Wescott, and Perotti have looked at a broader sample of countries and a longer adjustment periods in various OECD countries and have distinguished two types of fiscal adjustments:

- those that relied on expenditure reduction, carried out especially through a reduction in the government wage bill and in subsidies and transfers;
- and those that relied mainly on higher revenue without major expenditure reductions.

These studies found that the first type of adjustment was more favorable to growth and debt reduction than the second. McDermott and

Wescott have emphasized the importance of demand side factors, while Alesina and Perotti have stressed the beneficial effects of adjustment on unit labor costs and competitiveness.

All these studies measure successful adjustment in terms of durable reduction in debt and fiscal deficits. However, they tacitly assume that confidence in the durability of the new public policy course can be established instantaneously and that expectations therefore adjust rapidly as well.[19] This may be true if the reforms undertaken change the policy stance of government quickly and credibly. However, it is more likely that fiscal adjustment and reform of government will take a long time to plan and implement and to establish the necessary credibility. While marginal effects on growth may be generated quickly, a move to a higher economic growth path can only be expected after a number of years of persistent reform. The examples of New Zealand, Chile, and, perhaps, Ireland, which we will discuss later, indicate that initially fiscal reform may not be costless in terms of economic growth.[20] Unemployment, which causes some of the severest hardships of reform, may not come down significantly for a long period.[21] However, a reduction of recessionary tendencies in the short run is certainly welcome and may help strengthen support for reform.

Winners and Losers from Reform

The main obstacles to successful fiscal reform lie in their distributional implications. Reforms will inevitably be painful, especially in the short run, for those groups that had gained from public spending. These groups will oppose reforms and will make their introduction and implementation more difficult. These attitudes have been defined as wars of attrition by Alesina and Drazen (1994). Despite the long-term benefits that may derive from less state involvement, the opposition by potential (short-term) losers can easily turn reform efforts into political nightmares. This is particularly true when politically well-organized and vocal groups oppose the reforms, be they government employees, employees of public enterprises, farmers, school

19. The importance of credibility for policy commitments is discussed in Borner, Brunetti, and Weder (1995) and Brunetti et al. (1997b).
20. The experiences of Finland and Canada, where fiscal deficits were reduced sharply, are also of interest.
21. In Canada, an 8 percent reduction in the fiscal deficit has in fact resulted in a decrease of about 1.5 percent in the unemployment rate.

teachers, or social security recipients. Uncertainty about the appropriate solution or about the outcome can further reduce support for the reforms. This is especially true when the objectives of the reforms and the reasons for them have not been well articulated and clearly communicated to the public.

The detrimental short-run effects of reform on some groups need to be addressed by policymakers. Although there is surprisingly little hard evidence on what makes reforms succeed, there are a number of circumstances and complementary policies that raise the likelihood of success. As a basic principle, compensation for large losses and insurance against catastrophic events should be considered in order to gain political support for reforms. Compensation can take the form of privatization vouchers in privatized enterprises. Sunset clauses for certain benefits deter opposition to reform. Retraining programs and retrenchment packages for civil servants or public enterprise workers can compensate for the employment loss from privatization and the downsizing of government. Social safety nets can compensate to some extent for the hardship that individuals might experience as a result of reform. (See Chu and Gupta, editors, 1998.) The reform of social security programs should, therefore, not destroy the basic social safety nets. Compensation may reduce resistance to reform, but not without a cost. Initial budgetary savings will decline and certain reforms – involving, for example, civil service retrenchment – may even lead to net spending increases initially.

If reforms are implemented with a lag after their announcement, this may facilitate the reform although it may also lead some groups to organize to reverse the decisions about the reform. Lagged or gradual implementation may, however, reduce the costs of adjustment to the new economic environment and the number of losers.[22] At the same time, a lag between announcement of the reform and its actual implementation creates new stakeholders in the continuation of reform. Private companies, for example, need time to prepare for the privatization of enterprises, public services, or pensions if they will invest resources in these new opportunities. If opposition forces

---

22. This strategy benefited the implementation of the Common Market in the European Union. The adjustment of all parties involved, including opponents to free trade, was facilitated considerably by the fact that announcing and advertising the reforms planned for end 1992 started already in 1986 after agreement on the Single European Act (Schuknecht, 1992).

threaten to derail reform, these companies will lobby against the disruption of the privatization policy. Stakeholders in reform can also be created in the government itself. Ministries or agencies exclusively designated to undertake certain reforms, such as privatization, become pressure groups for the implementation of reform.

There is some controversy over the importance of consensus building for the success of government reform. Reforms achieved under autocratic leadership in Chile and the apparent success of shock therapy in a few former socialist economies have led some economists to conclude that the population needs to be confronted with a fait accompli before the success of reform will generate the necessary consensus on their usefulness. Numerous failed reforms under autocratic leadership and the success of the consensus approach of New Zealand and some European countries, however, may suggest that economists should have more faith in the rationality of voters. However, the reformers need to do a better job than is normally the case at explaining to the public the reasons and the objectives of the reform. They also need to emphasize the consequences of not carrying out the reform.

There are fundamental differences between the Chilean and the Eastern European "shock therapy," on the one hand, and the reforms suggested here for industrialized countries on the other. In spite of the large government intervention in their economies, industrialized countries are basically still market economies, and all the recommended reforms would take place within the existing market environment. Hence, the outcome of reform is much less revolutionary and uncertain. In addition, voters in industrial countries are generally quite educated and are more inclined to accept the necessity of reforming unsustainable government policies provided that the government clearly explains the unsustainability of the current policies.[23] Problems arise when a government is half-hearted about a reform and when the policymakers are unable to articulate the need and the rationale for the reforms.

Often reforms could not be pushed through the countries' political systems of checks and balances without broad-based political support. Except, possibly, for the United Kingdom, where the execu-

---

23. See, for example, *Frankfurter Allgemeine Zeitung* (September 1996) on widespread political support for expenditure reforms in Germany.

tive is very strong, the countries' political systems are often geared to preventing far-reaching political reform without major political support.[24] These arguments suggest that, in industrial countries, considerable importance should be attached to political consensus building and to the need to explain to the public the reforms.[25]

A number of circumstances can promote reforms. Crisis or near crisis situations can stimulate action. Crises reduce the benefits and point to the consequences of maintaining the status quo and increase the welfare benefits from reform.[26] In addition, in crisis situations, the distinction between winners and losers of reform becomes more blurred and more people become less sure that maintaining the status quo is the best option for them.

5. REFORM AND THE GLOBALIZATION OF ECONOMIES

Up to now, we have ignored the globalization of economies which, in the coming years, will create additional pressure for fiscal reform, especially for smaller countries. The pressure will originate from several angles. To start with, information on international success stories has become much more readily available, thus inspiring or encouraging imitations by the other countries. A later chapter will describe the influence of the experiences of New Zealand and Chile, two much-admired role models, for many other countries. These two countries have initiated major, radical reforms that have encouraged other countries to imitate them.

Second, international mobility of capital and labor puts pressure on governments to reform. In many European countries, the exodus of capital, jobs, and qualified labor has put pressure on governments to reduce taxes and spending. See Tanzi (1995, 1998a). Capital markets are viewed as punishing policy sins mercilessly with higher interest rates and major financial crises. Internet trade and the use of

24. The United States is a case in point, where both the Clinton health plan in 1993–4 and the Republican revolution of 1995–6 failed because of lack of political consensus.
25. Although broad consensus for reform is essential in most countries, governments are more likely to push for reform if their own constituencies do not contain very strong and powerful opponents to reform (World Bank, *Bureaucrats in Business*, 1995). Privatization, for example, is more likely to be undertaken by a conservative or right-wing government than by a labor or union-based government.
26. Financial crises and other difficulties have pushed Korea, Japan, Thailand, and other South East Asian countries toward some structural reforms.

electronic money will erode part of the domestic indirect tax base because trade across borders will be difficult to track and tax. (See Owens, 1997, and King, 1997.) These developments will put pressure on tax rates, thus reducing the governments' ability to finance large levels of public spending. Globalization and capital mobility have also increased the scope of and the benefits from privatizing government activities. The sale of companies in international markets, international competition over service contracts, and the possibility for pension funds to be invested abroad, for example, have provided powerful incentives for governments to disengage from many traditionally public activities.

Third, governments can not easily respond to globalization and its constraining effect on fiscal policies by reintroducing domestic regulations. The control of capital flows has become much more difficult and countries subscribe to international commitments on open trade and financial flows (under the World Trade Organization, or the International Monetary Fund) or on fiscal targets (as part of the European Monetary Union). Therefore, to deal with imbalances, countries can not resort to restrictions instead of reforms as easily as they could in the past.

Finally, in part because of the changing intellectual winds that we described earlier; because of the experience of recent decades; and because of many studies that have analyzed these issues, there is now much more information and realism than in the past about the limitations of many government programs and about their real cost. All these factors will put growing pressure on governments to reduce public spending.

6. THE TIME FRAME FOR REFORM

The debate and the political bargaining over reform, the establishment of credibility for the reforms, the need for grandfathering clauses and for implementation lags, and the existence of other administrative constraints suggest that reform of major expenditure programs will take a long time, possibly decades, to be fully implemented. An increase in public spending of 20 percent of GDP, which required thirty-five years in industrial countries, may require an equal length of time to reverse fully or in part. Current economic policies are to varying degrees slaves of past governments' decisions (Tanzi,

1997). Many policies have long-lasting consequences. Therefore, the role of the state at a given moment has been much influenced by *past* policies (in addition to being influenced by the theories of defunct economists as suggested by Keynes). Policy decisions made by previous governments continue to determine, to a large extent, the economic role of the state and the level of public spending and thus constrain the actions of current governments. Often, past policy decisions have created a role for the state that is different from the one that the current policymakers might prefer. Yet, legal, political, or administrative constraints may significantly limit the current government's power to change economic policies. This is an important reason why ministers often agree with the need for some reform but argue that its implementation is difficult or impossible.

Examples of decisions with long-term consequences are those related to the size of the civil service, to whether enterprises are public or private, to the level of public sector salaries, to pension rights, to tenure in public jobs, to tax incentives and subsidies to particular groups or sectors, and so on. The current difficulties that many industrial countries and some developing countries, such as Brazil, are having in reforming pension laws or in scaling down some social programs are good examples of the long-term effects of such decisions. These past decisions create legal or implicit entitlements or other claims that the current government often finds difficult or impossible to change, especially in the short run. In some countries, the interest on public debt and other hard-to-reduce spending, such as entitlements, accounts for three-fourths of total spending.[27] The reality is that no government has the freedom to start with a clean slate or with a tabula rasa, so to speak, unaffected by past commitments.

Examples of the long time it takes to implement a new policy regime are provided by New Zealand or Chile, where it took over a decade to implement the major reforms. Some countries are likely to need much longer. The United Kingdom's privatization program is still not complete after fifteen years. The interval between the start of discussions and the actual privatization of the German telecom company has lasted more than a decade, and this is just one company

---

27. See especially Steuerle and Kawai, editors (1996, Part Two, Chaps. 5–7: "The Yoke of Prior Commitments").

(albeit a very big and important on). Downsizing of the civil service is bound to be a lengthy process in most countries as lifetime tenure and vocal and highly organized labor representations require a very gradual approach. Important political opposition to reform other than labor also has to be won over. Compensation packages may have to be negotiated. Transition periods will be important, especially in social security reform. The transition period between pension systems in the context of pension reform, for example, may take a whole working life of thirty-five or forty years.

7. CONCLUDING REMARKS

There is considerable scope for reducing the size of the state in industrial countries as measured by public spending. Many changes within countries and internationally have increased the feasibility of major reforms. Reforms that were not possible in the past are now possible. Governments should take advantage of this new environment and should reform their fiscal policy regime and withdraw from much of their role in providing goods, services, and in insuring against some risks. Their new role should lie in setting appropriate rules of the game, both for economic actors and for their own policies. More realism about what government can reasonably do and international pressure for small and efficient states will help to move in this direction. Political implementability, however, is an important constraint that needs to be addressed and strengthened. The next two chapters will provide more specific guideposts for government reform.

VIII Fiscal Rules and Institutions

1. THE IMPORTANCE OF FISCAL RULES AND INSTITUTIONS

The institutional framework of a country is of particular importance for fiscal policy. Fiscal rules and institutions create the environment, the incentives, and the constraints under which policymakers and bureaucrats operate. These rules and institutions can promote smaller and more efficient governments or high and unproductive levels of public spending, high deficits, and the accumulation over time of public debt. For example, fiscal rules and institutions that establish effective budget constraints are more likely to lead to leaner and more efficient governments, while institutional frameworks that result in soft budget constraints and provide little incentive for expenditure prioritization are likely to lead to larger and less efficient governments. Several studies have concluded that small and effective governments with high-quality institutions are conducive to economic growth and development (see, for two recent examples, The World Bank, *World Development Report*, 1997; and Commander, Davoodi, and Lee, 1997).

We will first discuss some key institutional features that have typically contributed to sound fiscal policy and that should therefore feature prominently in the reform efforts of countries. These features are the budget process, fiscal rules, and new trends in expenditure management borrowed from the corporate sector. A transparent budgetary process that sets clear and enforceable spending ceilings

152

that can not be easily undermined by parliament or by the spending agencies will help limit expenditure growth and fiscal deficits. Fiscal rules, and particularly constitutional limits, could be important to enforce the deficit targets envisaged in the budgetary process. Task-oriented agencies, with decentralized decision making, performance-oriented rewards, competitive tendering of public contracts, and strong accountability to the ministry of finance and to other auditing institutions, can help the government prioritize spending requests and increase the efficiency with which essential services are delivered to the public. In strengthening transparency and accountability, and in promoting prioritization and efficiency in the use of public funds, such institutional reforms would also contribute to what is now called "good governance."[1]

The recent emphasis by economists, political scientists, and policy-makers on rules and institutions has been strongly supported by the new institutional economics and by the public choice literature. One of the main contributors to institutional economics, Nobel Laureate Douglas North, has argued that institutions will be stable only if assisted by organizations that have a stake in their own perpetuation (see North, 1994). In other words, what is needed is agencies capable of implementing and enforcing the clear rules of the game.[2] There-fore, the role of some key government agencies and the desirable qualities of their staff will also be discussed below.

The "rules of the game" have to be seen as a coherent body or a system, where changing one element in the right direction may not improve the outcome if escape valves are available. It will be argued that, in particular, quasi-fiscal policies can be an important (and dangerous) substitute for otherwise restricted taxing and spend-ing powers of government. In fact, lack of transparency in fiscal policy often results from the use of quasi-fiscal activities.[3] Finally, we will discuss how poor rules and regulations, in conjunction with inadequately controlled implementation agencies, can breed corruption. Lack of fiscal transparency and corruption undermine

---

1. In the area of budget reform in industrial countries, the work by the Public Manage-ment Service (PUMA), within the OECD, is especially helpful. (See PUMA, 1997a.)
2. Referees and linesmen are good examples for a type of court that watches over the rules in many sports.
3. Quasi-fiscal activities exist when the government attempts to use regulations or extra-budgetary institutions to achieve results that could have been achieved in a far more transparent way through the budget.

the very purpose of rules because they place those who buy favors above the law, destroy the level playing field, and undermine good governance.

2. THE BUDGETARY PROCESS

In most countries, the budgetary process is an integral part of the basic law or constitution.[4] That process links the executive and the legislative branches through a system of checks and balances (Premchand, 1983). The budget is typically prepared and executed by the ministry of finance, but other agencies or institutions influence the budgetary process as well. The power to tax, for example, is typically assigned to parliament, which has a lot of discretion vis-à-vis tax decisions. Parliament also plays an important role vis-à-vis spending policies. In principle, the budget must be approved by parliament, but parliament may have less or more discretion in the details of spending decisions. This establishes the political accountability of the executive to the legislature and allows some ex ante pressure regarding expenditure policies on the executive. In addition, and especially regarding taxation, the checks and balances in this process also protect individuals from arbitrary taxation. In particular circumstances, the converse has happened: tax legislation aimed at helping one or a few individuals has been approved by the legislature of some countries. This may happen either because parliament shows little interest in what it may consider a trivial decision or because the preferential treatment is not apparent from the tax proposals sent to parliament by the executive. It may also happen when de facto the executive controls parliament.

The budget office and the processes that accompany the formulation and execution of the budget are among the most important institutions affecting fiscal policies. Provided that the budget is comprehensive, it sets the framework for aggregate levels of expenditure in the public sector and specifies the composition of spending. The budget also determines how the spending will be financed. The process leading to the "production" of the budget document is there-

---

4. Interestingly, centrally planned economies, where quasi-fiscal activities proliferated, did not have budget laws. The creation of such laws and of a budget office has been one of the important reforms introduced by economies in transition.

fore fundamental in promoting fiscal prudence. The process associated with the execution of the budgetary decisions is equally fundamental to ensure that the budgetary decisions are carried out as intended. In this context, the role of the treasury as the institution that oversees spending is of fundamental importance.

The budgetary process consists of three different stages. First is the stage where the budget is formulated and is submitted to parliament. Second is the stage where it is discussed and eventually approved by parliament in the original or a modified version, thus becoming law.[5] And third is the stage in which the budget is implemented by the executive. That is when public expenditure is actually made. At each of these stages, transparency is fundamental. Without transparency, the final results may diverge significantly in size or in composition from the legislated ones.

Transparency in fiscal policy is an aspect attracting a lot of attention at this time. Citing a recent IMF study:

Transparency in government operation has several dimensions. First, at an aggregate level, transparency requires the provision of reliable information on the government's fiscal policy intentions and forecasts. Second, detailed data and information are required on government operations, including the publication of comprehensive budget documents that contain properly classified accounts for the general government and estimates of quasi-fiscal activities conducted outside the government. The third dimension consists of mainly behavioral aspects, including clearly established conflict-of-interest rules for elected and appointed officials, freedom-of-information requirements, a transparent regulatory framework, open public procurement and employment practices, a code of conduct for tax officials, and published performance audits. (Kopits and Craig, 1998, p. 1)

At the budget formulation stage, centralized procedures guided by a strong minister of finance or prime minister can keep spending pressures coming from other ministries and deficits at bay. In this "top-down" approach the macroeconomic limits for the budget are decided at the top before the various ministries are asked to submit their requests. This approach is in evidence mainly in large countries with two-party systems, such as the United States or the United Kingdom.[6] Some smaller European countries, such as Denmark, have

---

5. In some countries, parliament can only approve or reject the budget proposal presented by the executive. In other countries, parliament can amend the budget and change its composition.
6. However, in the United States, while the minister of finance (i.e., the treasury secretary) is very strong within the executive, parliament (i.e., Congress), has a lot of prerogatives in changing the composition of the budget.

successfully introduced binding numerical budget targets at an early stage of the budget formulation process (Von Hagen and Harden, 1996). In the Netherlands, parties have agreed to multiyear budget targets, with the exception of social security spending. The difference in institutions between country groups may depend on the frequent multiparty coalitions that characterize the governments of some countries. Parties within coalitions may not want to assign strong power to the person in charge of the budget who may come from another party and may thus pursue objectives with which these parties do not fully agree.

Prudent budget formulation can easily be undermined by parliament when parliament is allowed to introduce budget amendments that result in higher spending and deficits. This had been the situation in both Italy and the United States until recent years when a strong finance (treasury) minister in Italy and a conservative opposition with a majority in Congress in the United States have contained the expansion of public spending, or, in the case of Italy, have also increased the tax level. The budgetary process is more effective when amendments in parliament are not allowed to increase spending. It is also more effective when: (a) parliament discusses aggregate budgetary amount ahead of the actual budgetary discussion; (b) when effective and well-informed committees discuss the budget proposal ahead of the discussion by the whole parliament; (c) when the budget document is transparent; and (d) when parliament has a well-informed staff available and reporting to it.

In the absence of strong and effective institutions, such as the Treasury, budget *implementation* can undermine a prudent budget approved by parliament. The Treasury must allocate cash as required and limit the spending by the ministries and of the other spending units to the budgeted amounts. Unpenalized overspending and subsequent requests for additional appropriations have undermined the hardness of budget constraints in many countries. Such practices can be avoided only by binding budget laws that provide little flexibility for upward revisions in expenditure and by strict controls not only on cash payments but also on expenditure commitments. In some cases, as in Italy in earlier years, while the total budgeted limits have been observed, the composition of spending has undergone major changes at the execution stage.

In the European Union, countries with budgetary processes that emphasize centralized control over spending typically have lower fiscal deficits (de Haan, Moessen, and Volkerink, 1997). France and Germany have the most restrictive budget implementation procedures (Von Hagen and Harden, 1994, 1996). Italy, on the other hand, at least until recently, had expenditure management problems that undermined prudent fiscal policies. In that country, amendments to the budget can be easily proposed by parliament.[7] Furthermore, budget laws were not very binding on some expenditures such as health and pensions, and changes in the composition of spending could be carried out by the executive branch through the operation of the Treasury. This had resulted in soft budget constraints especially for some lines of spending and in almost constant bargaining over the budget. However, since 1997, a strong determination to meet the Maastricht fiscal criterion has resulted in much better outcomes.[8] In Latin America, centralized budget processes, which formulate budgets in the context of a realistic macroeconomic framework and limit the ability of parliament to make deficit-increasing amendments, have resulted in lower fiscal deficits (Alesina et al., 1995). Similar constraints have been crucial in many of the better performing countries in Africa, Asia, and Oceania. In Russia, however, unrealistic budgets have often resulted in the building up of large arrears as cash was constrained while commitments to spend were not.

3. FISCAL RULES

The transparency of the budgetary process should be seen as complementary to other constraints that prevent lax fiscal policies. Fiscal rules feature prominently in a number of countries, and in earlier chapters we argued that probably constitutional rules had limited fiscal laxity before the Keynesian revolution.[9] The changed attitude vis-à-vis fiscal policy that accompanied Keynesian economics legitimized fiscal deficits and the accumulation of public debts during peace time. This left governments without a yardstick to measure the

7. In some years, as many as 3,000 amendments have been proposed in parliament after the budget has been submitted for approval.
8. In 1997, Italy cut its fiscal deficit by a remarkable 4 percent in one year.
9. Feld and Kirchgaessner (1997) point to the positive effect of direct democratic controls on fiscal policies via referenda in Switzerland.

desirable level of fiscal deficit (or surplus). In the past two decades, even governments with good budgetary processes experienced chronic deficits and the accumulation of public debt.

These developments have stimulated a vigorous debate over the new yardsticks for fiscal policies which would more efficiently prevent excessive and unproductive public spending. In the 1990s, interest in fiscal rules has increased considerably. (See Kopits and Symansky, 1998.) Many policymakers and some economists have come to sympathize with the old rule that indicated that in normal time budgets should be balanced. This rule has become particularly popular in the United States where it now has broad political support by both parties. Some American economists have argued that constitutional deficit limits are the best way to tie the hands of government to prevent overspending. However, so far attempts to introduce such an amendment in the U.S. Constitution have failed, although in 1998 and 1999 the United States had, for the first time in many years, a surplus in its budget. Apart from various other problematic issues about this rule, there is the problem that the rule says nothing about the level of taxation and public spending, as shares of GDP, at which the budget has to be balanced. Obviously, it makes a big difference for an economy whether the budget is balanced when revenue and expenditure are 30 percent of GDP or 50 percent of GDP.

Various fiscal rules can constrain the government behavior. Most rules target the fiscal deficit, some the public debt. The most popular and, in a way the simplest, fiscal rule is the balanced-budget rule. This rule would prohibit (in normal times) the running of fiscal deficits regardless of cyclical developments. A more relaxed and better alternative to this rule would balance the budget over the business cycle.[10] In a similar vain, a rule could specify a certain maximum budget deficit as, for example, the 3 percent of GDP deficit limit required by European Monetary Union membership or the maximum level of the debt to GDP ratio. Other rules include prohibitions on domestic borrowing as in Indonesia; and prohibitions for the central bank to finance government deficits as in many countries.

All the aforementioned rules address the problem of disequilibrium in the fiscal accounts – that is, the difference between public

---

10. Of course, this assumes that business cycles are well defined and well behaved.

spending and public revenue, not the size of the public sector. Other rules are needed to address the question of the size of the public sector. Such rules may, for example, specify the maximum ratio of public expenditure or tax revenue into GDP. These rules are, of course, more relevant to the issue of the growth of public spending which is the topic of interest in this book.

Fiscal rules have to be introduced in the context of a country's institutional framework. In countries where constitutions are very specific and enforced faithfully, constitutional rules would form the most binding constraints on government policymaking. In other countries, legal statutes, administrative guidelines, or even custom could be the vehicles for introducing or maintaining fiscal restraint. We mentioned earlier that in the nineteenth century, budgets were generally balanced during peacetime largely as the result of custom and tradition. At that time only some countries introduced specific legal provisions.

Monitoring and enforcement are other key elements for the success of fiscal rules. A strong and independent monitoring agency may be considered essential. This could be the ministry of finance, but it could also be a supranational institution. For example, within the European Monetary Union, the EU Commission monitors the member countries' fiscal performance. Enforcement can be strengthened by appropriate checks and balances as discussed in the previous section on budgetary institutions. Public accountability and penalties could also be used as enforcement mechanisms. Reasonable escape clauses are essential to allow fiscal reactions to crisis situations such as wars or deep recessions.

A model fiscal rule would target a well-defined variable (such as the budget deficit), the coverage (that is, what is included in the calculation of the deficit), and the escape clauses (to prevent the possibility that all years become "exceptional" years). To maintain political support for it, the rule must be adequate and simple in the eyes of policymakers and the public. This has been the major feature of the Maastricht rule, which is easily understood by everyone. If the rule is too complex, its credibility and longevity will be jeopardized. For the same reasons, the application of the rule must be consistent with other economic objectives. In this context, time consistency problems must be avoided. For example, a balanced budget rule with limits on tax revenue would conflict with a growing share of pension payments in the GDP. Adequate enforcement provisions and operational transparency are also essential to prevent creative accounting and other attempts at circumventing the spirit of the rule.

Apart from the concerns about the operational feasibility of fiscal rules, some opponents have questioned the very principle of rules because of the loss of fiscal discretion for stabilization policies.[11] However, since the ability of governments' to stabilize the economy effectively through countercyclical fiscal policy has proven limited or even illusory in the past, this loss of discretion may actually be desirable.[12] However, fiscal rules are in fact not easily feasible in many countries, because some of the prerequisites for their success are not met. For example, a country with weak budgetary procedures may not be able to conform to a constitutional balanced budget amendment. On the contrary, the ineffectiveness of the rule may even further undermine the credibility of the constitution. In many countries, however, fiscal rules could assist appropriate budgetary institutions and provide some support to policymakers in their pursuit of a sound fiscal policy.

A number of countries constrain their fiscal deficits, debt levels, or methods of deficit financing at the highest legal or even constitutional level. Simple but "hard" rules, such as balanced budget rules, have thereby proven useful in maintaining fiscal equilibrium under appropriate circumstances.[13] For example, almost two-thirds of the American states have balanced budget rules in their constitutions. There is empirical evidence that these rules have kept the debt of American states very small. Germany's constitution requires that the budget deficit must not exceed the investment component of the budget. Such a rule, of course, raises the question of how investment is to be defined and may lead to the possibility that expenditures are misclassified. The Treaty of Rome does not allow the European Union to accumulate debt. In addition to the rules for EMU entry, the "stability and growth pact," prescribes that budgets be "close to balance or in surplus" in normal times, but more importantly, it can penalize countries with deficits above 3 percent of GDP. Once again,

---

11. The existence of a fiscal rule goes to the heart of the traditional controversy about rules versus discretion.
12. Simulation exercises in Kopits and Symansky's paper (1998) indicate that the loss of discretion does not contribute to economic instability.
13. The shortcomings of rules and the definition of its components may be the unavoidable cost of imposing a simple budget rule.

these rules do nothing to limit the size of the public sector, because they are directed at the difference between revenue and expenditure.[14] Only the Netherlands has so far introduced legally binding expenditure ceilings in its medium-term fiscal plans.

Some countries with weaker constitutional provisions have been less successful at constraining public spending and deficits because the constrains could be easily circumvented. For example, Indonesia has had a balanced budget rule requiring that expenditure must not exceed ordinary revenue plus *foreign* financing. The fact that expenditure could be financed by borrowing externally softened this constraint considerably and led to excessive foreign borrowing. When Indonesia faced a currency crisis at the end of 1997, the large foreign debt was a factor and became a major problem. A still weaker constitutional constraint applies in many countries (including Italy and some Latin American countries) which require that the deficit must be fully financed but does not specify whether the financing has to come from *ordinary* revenue or from any sources including borrowing. A rule of this kind, of course, becomes irrelevant for controlling fiscal deficits and public spending.

Although empirical results on the effect of fiscal rules on fiscal performance are not unambiguous, and are limited mostly to balanced budget rules and to specific situations such as those of American states, several studies have concluded that such rules may be important complements to proper budgetary procedures. De Haan, Moessen, and Volkerink (1997) have found that fiscal discipline is strengthened by binding constraints. Bohn and Inman (1996) have found that balanced budget rules work best when they are constitutionally grounded and when they do refer not just to the budget preparation but also to the actual results at the end of the fiscal year.

4. NEW TRENDS IN PUBLIC EXPENDITURE MANAGEMENT

The 1990s have seen much interest in budgetary institutions and in fiscal rules to prioritize and improve the efficiency of public spend-

---

14. A number of governments have introduced expenditure targets in their political platforms, but the nonbinding nature of such targets has made them relatively ineffective.

ing and to make government live within its means. Many countries, and especially the industrial countries, have introduced important reforms that have been helping to make fiscal policy more sound. Furthermore, the adoption of market mechanisms and managerial practices borrowed from the corporate sector have started to influence the thinking and the practice of public expenditure management in many countries. These practices that started in New Zealand, Australia, and the United Kingdom are slowly spreading to other countries. They should progressively allow governments to focus their public spending on essential tasks and to provide basic services in more cost-effective ways.[15] Unlike the rules discussed in the previous section, these approaches are in fact aimed at reducing the size of public spending and in time may be instrumental in achieving that objective. They may bring a quiet revolution in the way governments operate.

The key element of this new managerial approach to expenditure management is the buyer–provider link that dominates expenditure relations. With approval from the legislature (which is supposed to be the principal representing the public), the government buys various goods and provides services with the overall budget. Departments or agencies provide these services or outputs while the government appropriates the needed funds. The broad policy objectives and the overall budget are decided at the top; however, the details on how the objectives are achieved and how the money is actually spent is decided by the providers. The assumption, and it is a very strong one, is that most government outputs can be defined and can be costed. Thus, a monetary cost can be linked to a given output even if this is nothing else but a meeting of civil servants.[16] In the new approach, buyers and providers are linked to performance agreements that specify the objectives, the quality of the outputs, the money allocated to buy the inputs, and, at times, the time needed to achieve the objective.[17] There can be a chain of buyers and providers down from the government to divisions within ministries or to the private sector to which government agencies can subcontract. This approach decentralizes

15. See Premchand (1996) and PUMA, OECD (1997a, b) for a detailed discussion of this topic.
16. In this case, the value of the meeting is compared to the cost (in terms of salaries, etc.) of those who participated in it.
17. For example, an agreement with a passport office will specify the number of expected passports prepared or renewed and the time it should take to get a passport.

expenditure decisions, ultimately to the last provider in the chain, but it does not sacrifice accountability, because all the buyers and the providers are linked by the aforementioned performance contracts that hold each provider accountable to the next higher buyer. In this approach, it becomes more difficult to diffuse responsibility among many offices so that no one is held accountable for failure. Each one must live within the conditions of the contract.

The full efficiency gain can materialize only if the potential providers compete with each other and bid for contracts. This idea is not new for public procurement and for outsourcing to the private sector.[18] However, this concept is rather revolutionary within the public sector when departments, divisions, or individual staff have to compete for the performance of a certain task. In the extreme version of this approach, rewards (salaries) become performance oriented and contracts are limited in time. Personnel relations within the civil service become less career oriented as well. In fact, the traditional concept of civil service of employees with tenure in their jobs disappears and employees can be hired and fired without constraints. Thus, government jobs no longer guarantee a lifetime income unrelated to performance as has been the case for most civil services until recently. In the extreme version of this approach, during the period of their contracts, managers have the discretion of hiring or firing, or of replacing individuals by capital equipment as long as they stay within the budget.

Capacities for strategic policy formulation and expenditure prioritization need to be strengthened. Otherwise the administration may become more efficient in executing existing programs but not in prioritizing among programs. An important aim of these reforms is the need to get a way from incremental budgeting that rarely challenged established priorities. In this context, line ministries need to develop management capacities. The ministry of finance needs to strengthen its institutional capacities as overseer; and, sophisticated information systems must allow regular monitoring and analysis of developments. Without monitoring, the "task-oriented" agencies are not accountable and can behave as if they were little governments. However, performance contracts can lead to abuses, especially if the outputs are

---

18. See PUMA, OECD (1997c), *Contracting Out Government Services: Best Practices Guidelines and Case Studies*, Occasional Papers, No. 20.

difficult to define or monitor, or if tendering is not transparent. Therefore, corporate principles are only applicable within limits, and these limits depend on the quality of the existing institutions, on the existing legal constraints – some imposed by labor unions and labor laws – and on the quality of civil services. The application of these principles clearly requires a cultural revolution that may not be possible in many countries.[19]

In expenditure management more than in many other areas, the evolution and reform of institutions need to be adequately rooted in the local institutional situations if they are to represent genuine improvement. After reviewing the adequacy of existing systems, a strategy for changing the incentive structure should be formulated and the limits of task-oriented agencies should be defined. Mechanisms for consultation and negotiation between the various parties involved, be they political or administrative, should also be designed. The final objective must be to develop a culture that makes the achievement of efficiency an important objective for all involved.

Despite the need for prudence to establish the limits and implementation problems, the new trends in expenditure management can change the way the government operates quite dramatically.[20] Governments become the financier, arranger, and overseer rather than necessarily the direct provider of services (Premchand, 1996).[21] This change can have a powerful impact on public spending. In the previous chapter we argued that governments should set the rules of the game, rather than provide many government services themselves, in order to reduce the scope for public sector involvement. We now see that even within a more limited role for government, there is considerable scope for the useful application of market principles. The application of these principles may both reduce public spending and increase its value to a country's citizens.

---

19. However, after reviewing the "management revolution" in Australia, France, New Zealand, Sweden, and the United Kingdom, the PUMA (1997b) *Survey of Modern Budgeting* concludes that "there is professed consensus within government that the centralized model no longer suits the needs and conditions of public management" (p. 7).
20. For a warning that these developments may not be acceptable by all cultures, see Schick (1998).
21. The ministry of finance as the overseer of the overall budget envelope typically has a strong role in this process, in particular, in the initial definition of objectives, outputs, and budget allocations, and in the monitoring of performance, although such a monitoring should also be done by other institutions, some attached to parliament.

5. IMPLEMENTATION AGENCIES

In addition to a "good" overall, institutional framework, governments need a number of *core agencies* with well-defined roles, well-qualified staff, and adequate means. As mentioned previously, prudent fiscal policies typically require a relatively strong ministry of finance that can impose and enforce budget constraints on other ministries and that can monitor the latter's performance. Without a strong ministry of finance, each ministry or spending unit will attempt to shift the cost of public sector retrenchment to somebody else. The ministry of finance should include an efficient budget formulation (budget office) and an efficient budget implementation (treasury office). Public expenditure by each spending unit must be accounted for and must be closely monitored by a well-functioning treasury that keeps track of budgetary developments, economizes on the use of cash, and ensures that actual spending reflects closely the decisions in the budget law. The treasury must also ensure that the budgeted money is spent wisely and efficiently. Tax collection requires a well-equipped and competent tax administration, and the same holds for the customs administration. Audit departments – both internal (for each spending unit) and external – should ensure both quality control and accountability. Unfortunately, in many countries the auditing agencies have worried more about whether the money received by the various ministries and other spending units was used according to the guidelines of bureaucratic rules and less about whether the money spent was achieving the maximum possible results. Value for money has not been a concern for many auditing agencies.

In addition to these core fiscal agencies, a number of other agencies should indirectly support prudent fiscal policies and efficient spending. We argued above that governments should not be able to switch from policies that require actual taxing and spending authorized through the budget to quasi-fiscal activities when they want to reduce public spending without actually reducing government involvement. Thus, some agency must have the responsibility of overseeing this important area. This agency must keep track of the number of economic regulations and develop a kind of regulatory budget so that regulations are kept under observation and eliminated when they are no longer necessary. An antitrust agency is also important to prevent monopolization and cartelization. Such an agency must ensure that privatization does not change public into private monopolies.

These agencies are all part of the executive. A well-functioning legislature and judiciary are also key to an efficient public sector. An independent judiciary has been given great importance since the time of the great Greek state philosophers. The courts monitor administrative decisions and thereby protect public officials from political intervention and private agents from arbitrary decisions. They protect property rights and enforce contracts. A well-functioning judiciary also publicizes and penalizes inappropriate government behavior and thereby keeps corruption at bay, an issue to which we will return in the next section.[22] The weakness of the judiciary and at times its corruption have had great, negative, effects on many areas of policy and have reduced the ability of the government to promote some of its core functions.

Conditions for an Efficient Civil Service

Public agencies cannot be better than their staff. Transparency and clarity of the rules, and clear incentives for employees should reduce uncertainty over the desired performance of officials. Private sector management rules such as performance contracts that reward target achievement, if enforced objectively and efficiently, can improve public sector output, reduce public spending, and strengthen the motivation of staff. A certain independence from political interference in operations also boosts staff morale. In too many countries, accountability for good performance is weak while, at the same time, officials are constantly subject to pressure and interference from the political level. In addition, it is important that officials be well trained, well equipped, and adequately paid for their jobs so that they do not have to recourse to moonlighting or other questionable income sources. In many administrations, the correlation between the skills needed to perform a job well and those needed to get the job has

22. Frederick the Great of eighteenth-century Prussia saw the role of courts as "protecting people's property, and thereby make them happy, as much as human nature permits." To him "an unjust judge [was] worse than a thief." We predict that in the next decade, there will be major reforms of the judiciary. As in several other areas, Chile has been on the forefront with major reform plans in 1997 to bring "a new justice for Chile." However, many countries are now facing the need to reform the judiciary. At the time of this writing no fewer than fourteen Latin American countries were contemplating reforms of their judiciary systems.

been very low. An efficient public sector would require changes also in this area.

There are considerable differences in the perception of the quality of the public service which also, most likely, affect the quality of its output: In Japan, for example, employment in the government has traditionally been considered an honor; therefore, the government has been able to choose from the top universities the best candidates for public office.[23] To a large extent the same has been true in France, where a very prestigious school (ENA) prepares graduates who generally assume the top positions in the government and in society. In the United States, however, government employees came to be viewed with some contempt during the early 1980s and top students often avoided government jobs.[24] Such an attitude cannot be conducive to an efficient public administration, and it is quite remarkable that the United States' administration has remained as good as it is. A negative attitude toward the civil service may even promote a vicious circle of poor performance, declining public support, declining appropriations for the functioning of the government, and lower efficiency. When such attitudes prevail, the smartest people do not go into government jobs. Or when they go, they do so to benefit privately from the power that these jobs give them.

6. CORRUPTION AND THE RULE OF LAW

In our discussion of fiscal policies and the role of government so far, we have assumed that personal relations play no role in policy decisions and in the interaction between government officials and private agents. Arm's length relations have been assumed to prevail and nobody can buy favors from civil servants.[25] Political philosophers widely agree that the rule of law is one of the great achievements of modern society and one of the most important prerequisites of a well-functioning and well-governed market economy in which policies and

23. Unfortunately, recently Japanese bureaucrats have come under strong attack because of some corruption scandals and their inability to deal with some serious economic problems.
24. In the early 1980s a top official of the U.S. Civil Service Administration stated publicly that public salaries should be low because bright people should go into private sector jobs, where they can be productive.
25. For a detailed discussion of issues related to corruption, see Tanzi (1998a).

policy implementation are not "for sale" (see, for example, Hayek, 1960).

However, history is full of corrupt rulers and government officials, starting with the Bible's tax collectors. But it is interesting to note that over the centuries the rule of law has been establishing its predominance. "Since the 12th century in all countries of the West, even under absolute monarchies, it has been widely said . . . that law transcends politics. The monarch may make law but until he has remade it, he is bound by it" (Berman, 1983). An interesting little anecdote about Frederick the Great of Prussia shows that the rule of law may have been well established in Prussia even before the Industrial Revolution. Frederick the Great wanted to extend the gardens of his chateau Sans Souci. He summoned a miller who owned a mill on the planned extension and asked him to sell it to him. The miller, who wanted to keep the mill for his children, declined. The king replied that he would be able to take it from him without any compensation. "Yes majesty," replied the miller, "if our courts did not exist." The mill still rises above the chateau and thereby symbolizes the submission of the ruler to the law.

Nonetheless, newspapers report on the prevalence of corruption in many countries and even seemingly virtuous governments are plagued by occasional scandals. Corruption of course undermines the supremacy of the law and destroys the level playing field in society and thereby the functioning of market economies. Corruption makes policymakers and officials pursue personal gain, which drains resources from the achievement of economic or social welfare.

There are two levels at which corruption occurs: at the political and at the bureaucratic level. Under *political corruption*, policymakers sell policies to those who are willing to pay the most. The sale of certain production or trading monopolies would fall under this category. The direct or at least the explicit sale of policies is not often an issue in the industrialized countries. In these countries, only the indirect effect of party contributions on policymaking is very important. Some, of course, may argue that the results are the same, namely distorted policies and probably more public spending.

The other form of corruption, which refers to the relation between government officials and private agents, where people pay for a favorable interpretation or circumvention of existing laws and regulations, is *administrative corruption*. To some extent, the presence of corruption has its roots in the cultural background of many societies, where cultural, religious, or family networks are very important, so that it becomes difficult to resist pressures for favorable treatment from related individuals or from others. Especially in these societies corruption may be difficult to eliminate. The issue of administrative corruption is closely related to the issue of government institutions and economic incentives. When the rules of the games for bureaucrats are not clearly defined, and when they have discretion in awarding economically valuable licenses or government contracts, or making recruitment decisions, officials may be tempted to accept bribes. The greater their discretion and the more opaque the rules, the greater the potential for corruption.

In a country where corruption is rampant, the corrective role of government is likely to suffer and the cost of government intervention to rise. The allocative function of the state suffers as decisions get distorted by corruption. The redistributive role suffers because program benefits or subsidies do not go to the most needy but to the best connected. The stabilization role of government is adversely affected by the higher costs of running the government and by the loss of revenue, which raises the fiscal deficit. In addition, there is a learning curve on the part of civil servants, and the private "buyers" of services learn how to bend the rules. This can have a corrosive effect on the whole machinery of government. What corruption can do to an economy is illustrated by the example of the Soviet Union.[26]

What is the role of the state in a country suffering from corruption, and how should the state be reformed? Most importantly, opportunities to engage in corruption need to be scaled down by reducing the government role in the economy. The very growth of government creates rents that tempt bureaucrats and policymakers to favor their "friends." In addition, rules and regulations carefully drafted to provide incentives that promote arm's-length relations make corruption less attractive. Increased penalties, audits, transparency of rules, laws, and regulations, and reasonable wages also reduce the incentive to accept favors. (See Tanzi, 1998a.)

---

26. In his Pulitzer Prize–winning account of the last days of the Soviet Empire *Lenin's Tomb* (1994), David Remnick writes: "The Communist Party apparatus was the most gigantic mafia the world has ever known" (p. 183) and "It was as if the entire Soviet Union were ruled by a gigantic mob family; virtually all relations were in some form mafia relations" (p. 185).

7. CONCLUDING REMARKS

Fiscal rules and institutions are very important in order for government to be small and efficient. The budget process, fiscal rules and institutions, and managerial practices can induce governments to prioritize spending on its main objectives, to spend in an efficient manner, and to live within its means. However, public spending must not be replaced by (market-unfriendly) quasi-fiscal regulations, and government agencies must operate in ways that are conducive to "good government."

IX Blueprint for Public Expenditure Reduction

1. THE IMPORTANCE OF REFORMING EXPENDITURE POLICIES

In the first two parts of this study we argued that in recent decades, governments have been doing too many things and often they have not done them in the most efficient manner to achieve the stated social and economic objectives. Thus, they end up spending much more than necessary. Governments, therefore, need to reform themselves while disengaging from many current activities that are not directly connected with well-defined social goals. This will allow them to focus more effectively on their main economic and social objectives, thus making it possible for public spending to come down *without sacrificing much in terms of economic and social well-being.* In fact, the key message of this book is not that the government should become indifferent to the welfare of the population, but rather that it should consider alternative ways of pursuing its objectives. The book argues that these alternative ways are often available and feasible.

We have argued in the previous chapter that fiscal rules and institutions are important prerequisites for achieving these objectives. Good institutions improve government efficiency and can reduce, over time, the growth of government spending. However, good institutions will not necessarily generate the reforms of expenditure programs that will reduce the role and, with it, the size of the state. The needed reforms require difficult policy choices. This

171

chapter aims at providing some broad guidelines on what the options are and on the direction the reforms could take. There is now a broad menu of options available to governments intent on reducing their role in the economy and the share of GDP represented by public spending.

A considerable body of literature and policy experience has emerged in recent years that suggests that government does not need to play an extensive, direct role in the *production* of goods and services, in investment, or even in social security. There is no essential social objective that is necessarily satisfied by such direct government involvement. The allocative role of government, à la Musgrave, could and should be much smaller than it has been in most countries. Most public enterprises and the provision of many (traditionally public) services and even many infrastructures can in principle be privatized.

There is also considerable skepticism about the redistributive role of government beyond the pursuit of basic social objectives such as poverty alleviation. Widespread criticism of inefficient, unsustainable, and poorly targeted welfare systems is a case in point. If the objective of the government is to insure citizens against the risks associated with old age and illness, the private sector could satisfy that objective for much of the population. Much of income maintenance for the aged and health services, the main objectives of social security in industrial countries, could be satisfied privately. Budgetary resources should be used only to secure minimum standards and basic social services for those without the means to buy private insurance. Much of the population is not in this category. Thus, if the citizens were taxed more lightly by reducing the extent of fiscal churning, they could use their extra income to buy their own insurance.

Table IX.1 provides some broad ideas on the reform options for major expenditure programs. These ideas have been borrowed mainly from World Bank reports. We do not necessarily endorse all of them, but we believe that they provide a rich enough set of options so that almost any government could benefit from considering them.

It needs to be emphasized that privatization of government functions does not eliminate the role of government in many of these areas. It just changes the nature of that role. Effective and efficient regulations will be necessary to prevent mismanagement of privately

Table IX.1. *Blueprint for Government Reform of Various Expenditure Programs*

Public Expenditure	Reform Options
	Goods and services
Subsidies to state-owned enterprises	Privatization usually better than management or performance contracts or direct government operation
	Regulate/subsidize to avoid monopolies, quality problems, externalities, distributional/community conflicts
Other goods and services	Widespread privatization possible, very few areas producing genuine "public goods"
	Regulate/subsidize to avoid monopolies, quality problems, externalities, distributional/community conflicts
	Social security and social services
Education	Dual public and private secondary and tertiary education providers with consumer choice via vouchers
	Privatize tertiary education with extended scholarship system for equity reasons and with access to credit to finance education.
	Strengthen competitiveness/lower costs of public system through out-contracting, private and public funding
Health	Mandatory (public or private) for catastrophic illness insurance and for basic health packages
	No model clearly best for cost and quality control; strengthen incentives for quality and cost control
Pensions	Reform pay-as-you-go schemes with higher retirement age and streamlined benefits and eligibility
	Introduce multipillar system; public equity-oriented minimum coverage; funded mandatory occupational and private plans for additional coverage, funded voluntary pillar
Unemployment	Mandatory public insurance with minimum coverage
	Out-contracting of job search and training support
	Labor market liberalization with more flexible wage and/or employment regulation

Sources: Compiled by Tanzi and Schuknecht based on Gómez-Ibáñez and Meyer (1993); World Bank, *Averting the Old Age Crisis* (1994a); World Bank, *Bureaucrats in Business: The Economics and Politics of Government Ownership* (1955).

held funds, the abuse of monopoly powers, or the generation of negative externalities such as environmental damage. Antitrust and environmental regulations, the supervision of banks and investment funds, and the supervision of services providers will be very important.[1] Private provision does not necessarily lead to better and more efficient services and, depending on the country and the sector, government provision of services may at times be preferable. The decision requires careful weighing of the options: the productive and regulatory capacity differs across governments, and the choice of government production or the regulation of private providers depends very much on the particular circumstance of each country. Nevertheless, bold decisions on the part of governments to reform important public expenditure programs are necessary and possible in most countries. As a result, government could operate with much smaller budgets and still create an environment in which essential goods and services and social insurance are provided and the basic social and economic objectives are achieved.

2. PRIVATIZING PUBLIC ENTERPRISES, SERVICES, AND INVESTMENT

All industrial countries' governments are involved, to some extent, in the production of goods and services. However, there is no convincing economic argument which suggests that governments should own and run banks, airlines, steel companies, railroads, military industries, or postal and telephone companies.[2] The experience with state airlines and banks in many countries, including France, Italy, Spain, and Sweden, which required massive government subsidies confirms the perception that governments are typically unable or unwilling to run public enterprises on commercial terms. In Portugal, for example, public enterprise losses at one point brought the government budget into serious difficulties; in 1982, public enterprise losses exceeded

1. Of course, there are new pitfalls in assigning government this role, as has been demonstrated by the literature on regulatory capture and corruption. Nevertheless, we will argue later that the role of government in setting and enforcing the rules of the game will increase and shift to many new areas in the future.
2. The World Bank Study, *Bureaucrats in Business*, assesses government involvement in production and discusses in detail the scope and prerequisites for reform.

10 percent of GDP. See Cardoso (1985). Inefficiencies in the provision of government services from garbage collection to gardening are also frequently lamented.[3] Given that industrial countries now spend almost 20 percent of GDP on average on goods and services, the privatization of the activities that provide these goods and services needs to be one of the major ways to reduce the role of the state and public expenditure.[4]

Similarly, the provision, financing, and operation of investment projects ranging from infrastructure, utilities, public schools, public hospitals to swimming pools are not necessarily tasks of the state. The traditional public investment budgets of 3–5 percent of GDP could, therefore, come down as well, without much adverse effect on the welfare of society.

Assessing the Scope for Privatization

A considerable body of literature about privatization and experience with privatization shows that hardly any area is fully unsuitable for private sector involvement. Privatization can be particularly useful from a budgetary perspective when public enterprises operate at a loss or when user fees do not cover the costs of providing government services. Privatization can also reduce operating inefficiencies resulting from overstaffing or poor management. Privatization isolates the decisions of the enterprises (as to hiring, pricing, and so on) from political pressures.

In some areas, there is hardly any reasonable justification for giving government a role beyond that of regulator and overseer. Banks, steel companies, or the gardening in public parks and the operation of swimming pools are essentially private goods or activities that should be undertaken by the private sector. If necessary, budgetary subsidies and transfers could be used to achieve social policy objectives.[5] One

---

3. For example, before it went broke a few years ago, the city of Naples had 1,600 gardeners and very few gardens.
4. Over time, considerable savings could come from reversing the trend of growing public sector employment (see Table II.2 in Chapter II). Public sector employees, however, are very vocal and typically have lifetime tenure. Their numbers can only be reduced slowly, and sometimes at high initial costs of severance pay or other compensation packages. As discussed earlier, this is an important reason why reforms are likely to take a long time to have a significant positive budgetary impact.
5. Social objectives have in fact often been mentioned as the main reasons for government involvement.

could envisage, for example, that instead of running the swimming pool, government could subsidize the use of swimming pools for swimming lessons or swimming pools in poor areas of the city. Also, instead of having public employees to clean and take care of public parks, private enterprises could be hired to do the job.[6]

In the broader area of infrastructure, the division between public and private goods is not clear-cut, and the government will continue to play an important role in many areas. Nevertheless, there are areas where privatization can replace direct government involvement. There are a number of criteria which can be used to assess the prospects and prerequisites for successful privatization in infrastructure, and which the World Bank's 1994 *World Development Report* discussed in some detail.[7] First, privatization tends to be more desirable when there is potential for competition in a sector. Regulatory requirements would not be too strong, so that the public will be less weary of the abuse of monopoly power by the private sector. In passenger transportation, for example, private bus transport is more desirable when several bus companies can compete for customers. The privatization of road operation in rural areas, however, may not be desirable from this perspective.

Second, enterprises that produce private goods and services are (by definition) easier to privatize than those that generate public goods. However, many public goods of the past have become private goods because of technological changes. Telephone services, which used to be largely in the public domain, for example, are now provided by private sector enterprises. Third, the cost-recovery potential from user charges must be high. Again, telecommunication is a good example where the full price for the service can easily be charged. Cost recovery from a toll on the use of rural roads may not be feasible, however. Fourth, the absence of social policy objectives facilitates

6. For many examples of contracting out government services, from the operations of international airports and highway developments and operations to cleaning services and catering for hospitals or the military, see PUMA, OECD (1997c). In Buenos Aires, the government has allowed private corporations to "adopt" private parks. The corporations take care of the parks in exchange for public signs in the parks that announce their responsibility. The parks are now kept in good shape at no cost to the government.

7. The World Bank study, *Bureaucrats in Business*, discusses in detail the scope and implementation issues for privatization in developing and newly industrialized countries, but much of the discussion is also relevant for industrialized countries. See also Heald (1997), Irwin et al. (1998), and Engel, Fischer, and Galetovic (1998) for issues that arise with respect to infrastructure privatization.

privatization. Provision of telephone services has much less of a "social policy" function than provision of rural roads and is therefore easier to privatize. Finally, environmental externalities may require government intervention in the provision of certain goods and services, such as sanitation.

Based on these criteria, the World Bank has ranked the potential for privatization of certain services and industries and produced a marketability index ranging from "3" for goods and services that are most marketable to "1" for those that are least suitable for privatization (Table IX.2). The indices show that there is no reason to publicly provide long-distance telephone services. Airlines, intercity buses, rail services, or electricity generation are similarly suitable for privatization. Gas production and distribution or waste collection also have a high marketability index. Toll financing is a suitable method for financing road construction and maintenance in many cases; the exception may be rural and intracity roads.[8]

The scope for privatization also depends on the regulatory capacity of government. Strict regulatory standards may be necessary if the scope for competition is small, or if social and environmental considerations are important. Antitrust regulation and oversight can mitigate the problems associated with monopoly power. Government regulation can reduce adverse environmental effects of privatization. As mentioned, budgetary support to groups that are negatively affected by privatization can help achieve the desired social policy objectives.

The scope for privatization should not be assessed in a static sense. The regulatory capacity of government can be significantly improved with institutional reforms and, at times, with foreign assistance. New contractual arrangements and better monitoring possibilities have given rise to more effective buyer–provider relations between the public and the private sector. This has created more scope for the privatization of activities formerly considered in the government domain. Technological developments have also changed the scope for privatization considerably. Individual billing on telephone calls has turned phone services into more of a private good. The possibility of

8. See OECD (1987). The role of the private sector in airport infrastructure is discussed in detail by Kapur (1995). A problem with the privatization of infrastructure is that the government often guarantees to the private investors a certain rate of return. This may create large contingent liabilities for the government.

Table IX.2. *Assessing Benefits of Private versus Public Provision of Goods and Services in Infrastructure*

	Potential for competition	Characteristics of goods and services	Potential cost recovery from user charges	Public service obligations (equity concerns)	Environmental externalities	Marketability index[a]
Telecommunications						
Local services	Medium	Private	High	Medium	Low	2.6
Long distance and value-added	High	Private	High	Few	Low	3.0
Power/gas						
Thermal generation	High	Private	High	Few	High	2.6
Transmission	Low	Club	High	Few	Low	2.4
Distribution	Medium	Private	High	Many	Low	2.4
Gas production/transmission	High	Private	High	Few	Low	3.0
Transport						
Railbed and stations	Low	Club	High	Medium	Medium	2.0
Rail freight and passenger services	High	Private	High	Medium	Medium	2.6
Urban bus	High	Private	High	Many	Medium	2.4
Urban rail	High	Private	Medium	Medium	Medium	2.4
Rural roads	Low	Public	Low	Many	High	1.0
Primary and secondary roads	Medium	Club	Medium	Few	Low	2.4
Urban roads	Low	Common property	Medium	Few	High	1.8
Port and airport facilities	Low	Club	High	Few	High	2.0
Port and airport services	High	Private	High	Few	High	2.6

Water						
Urban piped network	Medium	Private	High	Many	High	2.0
Nonpiped system	High	Private	High	Medium	High	2.4
Sanitation						
Piped sewage treatment	Low	Club	Medium	Few	High	1.8
Condominial sewage	Medium	Club	High	Medium	High	2.0
On-site disposal	High	Private	High	Medium	High	2.4
Waste						
Collection	High	Private	Medium	Few	Low	2.8
Sanitary disposal	Medium	Common property	Medium	Few	High	2.0
Irrigation						
Primary and secondary networks	Low	Club	Low	Medium	High	2.4
Tertiary (on farm)	Medium	Private	High	Medium	Medium	1.4

Source: World Bank, *World Development Report: An Infrastructure for Development* (1994).
[a] Average for five indicators with indicators quantified as in World Bank, *World Development Report*, 1994.

excluding viewers from certain television programs has also increased the scope for private television channels. Future developments, such as electronic measurement of road utilization, will increase the marketability of sectors that traditionally were considered public goods because potential consumers could not be excluded from their use and could not be charged in relation to their use.

Political economy considerations are very important for the success of reform, as majorities have to be won and opposition, including that by the public employees who had been providing the service, must be appeased in the process (Gómez-Ibáñez and Meyer, 1993). Activities that are more labor intensive and thus have more public employees, such as health and education, would encounter more resistance. Privatization has better chances of succeeding when it promises high efficiency gains. These gains increase the chance that many people will be better off, raising the political support for privatization. This has often happened with the privatization of services such as telephone.

Experiences with Privatization

Many industrialized and developing countries have privatized public enterprises and the provision of many services. Privatization has been prominent in telecommunications, utilities, transportation, and infrastructure provision.[9] In the United Kingdom, for example, the share of state-owned enterprises in the economy has declined from over 6 percent of GDP to 2 percent of GDP. Data are sketchy for other industrialized countries, but public enterprises have also become less important in Germany, Italy, Japan, Spain, or the United States.[10] In Portugal, the combined deficit of nonfinancial public enterprises declined from 10 percent of GDP in the early 1980s to 1–1.5 percent of GDP in the early 1990s after important privatization.

Short of privatization, contracting out by the public sector can reduce the budgetary burden of public services. (See PUMA, OECD, 1997c.) Governments sometimes introduce performance contracts for the management of these enterprises. However, insufficient

9. Gómez-Ibáñez and Meyer (1993) discuss numerous case studies of transport privatization from toll roads in France to airports in Britain. The World Bank study "Bureaucrats in Business" also discusses experiences with privatization mainly in developing and newly industrialized countries.
10. In some developing countries such as Argentina, Brazil, and Mexico, and in some transition economies such as Hungary, and Poland, privatization has gone a long way.

autonomy over operations and incentives to generate profits have frequently undermined these contracts. Management contracts assign management companies the task of running a public enterprise. Again, contractual problems have often undermined the performance of management companies.[11] Management contracts have been used also for the running of customs organizations in some developing countries.

Contracting out is already quite common in some areas of government services such as cleaning or garbage collection, but it also extends to health and educational services and even to jails in some states. Numerous studies have shown that private provision of services has often proven cheaper than public provision of services. Only a few studies, some dealing with hospitals or railroads, have not shown much of a differences in the costs of public and private provision. Table 9.3 shows that even in areas that have almost always been under the public domain, such as intracity transportation or road construction and operation, private sector participation is possible and often more efficient. (See also PUMA, OECD, 1997c.) Expenditure savings have been significant and private providers have at times been up to 60 percent cheaper than public providers.

The privatization of assets can bring considerable revenue to the treasury. If the government captures part of the potential efficiency gains from privatization in the sales price or through higher tax revenue, it can yield considerable net receipts. In England and in several Latin American countries and transition economies such as Hungary, net privatization proceeds have been very significant in the past decade. However, privatization can also be a costly exercise if other, noneconomic objectives are imposed on the privatization process. The German mass privatization of East German industry, for example, resulted in a net loss of over 2 percent of GDP over the first three years of privatization (1990–2) for the "Treuhand," the German privatization agency, because it often had to pay for the restructuring and rehabilitation of companies and for job guarantees (Schwartz and Lopes, 1993). These costs may be high when the enterprises have caused serious environmental damage that needs to be corrected before the privatization process is complete. Also, to get a higher price from the sale of public assets, the government may agree to leave some monopoly power to the purchaser. This

---

11. It is difficult to write contracts that are precise enough to cover all the eventualities. (See World Bank, 1995.)

Table IX.3. *Private versus Public Provision of Goods and Services*

Activity	Case; country	Private performance compared to public sector	Efficiency lead of private sector
Airlines	Private vs. public domestic airline; Australia	+	Private efficiency index 12–100% higher
Banks	Private vs. public bank; Australia	+	...
Bus service	Private vs. public buses; Germany, United Kingdom, United States	+	Private providers have 20–60% lower costs/km
Cleaning services	Public vs. private contracting; Germany	+	Private providers 30–40% cheaper
Debt collection	Public vs. private contracting; United States	+	Private two-thirds less expensive per dollar collected
Electric utilities	Electricity production; United States	+, −	Private provision ranges from "slightly more expensive" to 30–40% cheaper
Fire protection	Public vs. private contracting; United States	+	Private provisions 30–40% cheaper per capita
Forestry	Public vs. private forests; Germany	+	Private labor productivity twice as high as public
Hospitals	Public or non-profit vs. private hospitals; United States	+, −	Mixed results on efficiency
Housing	Public vs. private construction; Germany, United States	+	Private providers about 20% cheaper

Insurance	Public vs. private life insurance; Germany	0	No cost differences, private service quality better
Ocean tanker repair	Navy vs. commercial servicing; United States	+	Private provider less than half the price of U.S. Navy
Railroads	Public vs. private railroad; Canada	0	No productivity differences
Refuse collection	Public vs. various private modes; various countries	+, 0	Private provision 0–30% cheaper
Savings and loans	Public vs. private institutions; United States	+	Private operating costs 10–35% lower
Slaughterhouses	Public vs. private firms; Germany	+	…
Toll road construction	Public vs. private construction; France	+	Private builder 20% cheaper
Water utilities	Public vs. private suppliers; United States	+	Private operation 15–60% cheaper
Weather forecasting	Public vs. private service; United States	+	Private service 33% cheaper

Sources: Compiled by Tanzi and Schuknecht based on Ibáñez-Gómez and Meyer (1993) and Mueller (1989).

[a] + = private provision cheaper and/or better; 0 = no significant difference in performance between public and private sector; − = public provision cheaper and/or better.

would, of course, reduce the efficiency of the economy and reduce competition.

3. EDUCATION

From an economic perspective, a good educational system strengthens equality of opportunities, human capital endowment, and income distribution. (See Tanzi, 1998b.) Furthermore, education may be an important prerequisite for the functioning of democracies. (See Friedman, 1955, or West, 1970.) Hence the provision of basic education is both an individual and a social investment. The responsibility of the state in its provision is justified by the belief that education, and especially basic education, generates high, positive externalities. The social importance of universal primary and secondary education is therefore almost unquestioned in industrial countries, and to secure a high level of education has so far been considered one of the core activities of government. As it was shown in earlier chapters, spending in this area increased significantly in recent decades. Public expenditure on education is one of the most important expenditure categories in governments' budgets. It averages about 6 percent of GDP in industrial countries.

In some countries, effective government provision provides a strong case for continued government involvement, especially in primary and secondary schooling. However, countries that face problems with the quality of education or with its cost could probably improve its quality or reduce its cost with more private sector participation (and competition). In such a case, the government would finance the activity, say through vouchers, while the private sector would provide the services. In general, however, budgetary savings from more private sector involvement in primary and secondary education are likely to be small. Therefore, any privatization of this activity should be justified in terms of its impact on quality and other objectives of education.[12]

In tertiary education, the situation is somewhat different. Tertiary

---

12. However, there seem to be wide differences in student/teacher ratios among countries. For example, these ratios are much higher in Japan than in Italy. The differences are in part explained by the political power of the teachers. In Italy, the fall in the number of children in the past two decades was not accompanied by a fall in the number of teachers.

or university education provides mostly marketable, and thus privately usable, skills. It also generates less obvious externalities because individuals can internalize most of the benefits that they receive from it through higher incomes. User fees and improved cost effectiveness via private universities could yield budgetary savings and relieve costly and overburdened public systems in many countries. This has happened to a significant degree in several Latin American countries, including Argentina and Chile, where in recent years private and financially successful universities have been created. Such a development would not represent a withdrawal of the state from a basic, core function such as education. Given the importance of good education for economic and social reasons, some limited budgetary support, in the form of scholarships or loans, could help secure equality of opportunity for poorer students. Also, the state could continue to subsidize activities by universities that have strong externalities, such as basic research.

Primary and Secondary Education: Scope for Expenditure Reduction

On average, industrial countries spent 5 percent of GDP on primary and secondary education. This spending has not gone down in recent years when, in many countries, because of demographic developments, the number of school age children fell significantly. Countries have a multitude of different educational systems with a widely differing mix of public and private schools. Depending on the particularities of the school systems, in some countries public schools provide a superior education while in others private schools are perceived to be better. Quantitatively, however, public schools are much more important. Three-quarters of all children in the EU attend public primary or secondary schools, and only in Belgium, Ireland, and the Netherlands do a majority of children attend private schools. (See Psacharopoulos, 1992.)

Rising costs and a deteriorating quality of public education, however, have reopened the discussion, especially in the Anglo-Saxon countries, on the appropriate role for government and for the private sector in providing educational services. In some parts of the United States, for example, the public education system is characterized by a bloated administration, outdated curricula, and especially a lack of discipline and motivation. Teachers' salaries and their social status have deteriorated. The deterioration of family life and violence have overburdened many public schools with nonacademic functions. At the same time, increasing mobility has allowed wealthy (and vocal) parents to opt out of the public school system into private schools, or to aggregate themselves in rich areas that can afford better public schools. The poor then are stuck with inferior public schools that at times are not much more than parking lots for children. As a consequence, the children receive an inferior education and fewer economic opportunities in life and the perception of social and economic injustice follows suit.

Few people doubt that primary and secondary education should be largely publicly *financed*. However, there are increasing doubts on whether that education should necessarily be publicly *provided*. The way the system is financed and who provides the education are issues that have been discussed vigorously in recent years. Many proposals have been made to increase competition, quality, cost control, and choice in school systems mainly by "contracting out the management of instructional services and combining them with adequate planning."[13] A number of school districts in the United States, for example, have given private companies management contracts for formerly public schools with the objective of strengthening performance and reducing costs. Although this experiment is still ongoing, and the effects depend very much on the specific contractual arrangements, this might be a useful option for schools and school districts that are perceived as being of particularly bad quality.

Voucher systems of various kinds have also been experimented with in several countries. In Chile, since the early 1980s, vouchers in the form of grants to primary and secondary schools on a per student basis have given parents the choice of schools, and schools an incentive to provide a quality education within the budget constraints of

---

13. See Brown (1995) for a summary of the debate on privatizing public education; and West (1997) on voucher systems. See also Walford (1989) for an assessment of the diversity in educational structures in ten industrial countries; James (1984) on experiences with public funding of private universities in the Netherlands; and James (1987) or Gradstein and Justman (1996) for a model on the division of responsibility for education between the public and the private sector.

fixed grants. In 1997, three-quarters of the educational budget was allocated through vouchers. When students move, they take their vouchers with them. Chile is also considering vouchers for preschool children. Favorable experience has also been reported for a number of other countries and U.S. states. Voucher systems have often improved the quality of education and also the opportunities for the poor. They have also put pressure on public schools to improve their services (West, 1997).[14]

The experience with educational vouchers has, of course, not been all positive. Some countries, for example Finland, experimented with vouchers but encountered difficulties. Other countries, such as Australia, rejected higher education vouchers because they considered them just another form of subsidy. In still other countries, such as the United Kingdom, teachers in public schools threatened strikes. Furthermore, administrative costs tend to be high, and there is a tendency for the best students to concentrate in the best schools. In Chile, this problem led the government to intervene directly to assist the poorer schools, leading to greater progress for the latter than for other schools.

Vouchers work best when there is competitive potential. They do not work in cases of no actual or potential competition. Thus, conceptually they require the government to recognize the need for choice. Of course, choice is based on information so that the use of vouchers gives some responsibility for the government to provide the needed information. In addition to education, vouchers have been used or can be used in other areas such as health and public housing.

Management contracts and voucher systems may help improve the quality of education in countries where public education is deficient. However, appropriate teachers' pay and regulation have secured high-quality schooling in countries such as Germany, Switzerland, and Japan and may serve as useful examples for reinvigorating the public education system.

14. Of course, these reforms do not guarantee better education for everybody and will still require adequate government financing and regulation. Competition over students, for example, could result in a deterioration of standards and the teaching of more fads at school. A voucher system with a limited subsidy per student could induce the middle class to opt into private schools and leave the poor to the remaining public schools as they may still not be able to afford private education.

Tertiary Education: A Case for More private Sector Involvement

Although tertiary education on average absorbs only about 1 percent of GDP, or one-sixth of the industrial countries' education budget, public spending on higher education is much more controversial than on primary or secondary education. Higher education is considered at least in part a private economic investment. Public financing of higher education often constitutes a subsidy to the future higher income groups and is, therefore, regressive. This suggests that budgetary costs of higher education could be reduced through user charges in the form of tuition. The adverse impact on the poor could be cushioned by means-tested grants or earmarked loans. Tuition payments would increase the incentive to study more efficiently and to demand better quality services. It would also create a higher incentive for the establishment of more private universities and more competition. It should be recalled that some of the top universities in the world are private.

Private financing via tuition or through private institutions seems to matter for the quality of public education. Tuition covers 15–35 percent of the costs for higher education in the United Kingdom, the United States, Spain, and Japan. This is more than in the other industrial countries for which data are available (Table IX.4). Universities in Japan, the United Kingdom, and the United States receive also the highest share of other incomes, such as industry or alumni funding. These countries have more than their share of the most prestigious universities.

Not only the financing but also the provision of tertiary education is controversial. Public provision does not automatically mean poor quality, as there are many outstanding public universities. Capital market imperfections and the demand for educated labor are often mentioned as arguments for public provision of tertiary education. However, these arguments concern the financing of tertiary education and would support extensive subsidization of private education as an alternative to the public provision. Proponents of private education insist that public provision of tertiary education generates no externality that could not be emulated by private provisions cum targeted public support. Therefore, the private sector should be able to provide this service efficiently (Blomqvist and Jimenez, 1989).

Table IX.4. *Sources of Income of Higher Education Institutions,*
Mid-1980s

	General public funds[a] (In percent)	Fees	Other income
Australia	88.0	2.1	9.9
France	89.5	4.7	5.8
Germany	68.5	. . .	31.5
Japan	42.0	35.8	22.2
Netherlands	80.0	12.0	8.0
Norway	90.0	. . .	10.0
Spain	80.0	20.0	. . .
United Kingdom			
Universities	55.0	13.7	31.3
Polytechnics (England)	72.4	16.2	11.4
United States[b]	44.8	22.4	32.8

Source: Compiled by Tanzi and Schuknecht based on OECD, *Financing Higher Education, Current Patterns* (1990).
[a] Expenditure of National Ministry of Education for Australia, France, Germany, and the Netherlands.
[b] Figures include all government expenditure at all levels. Loans and grants to students amounted to about 80 percent of fees in 1969–70 and 95 percent in 1984–5.

Empirical evidence on the performance of public versus private universities is quite mixed. Publicly provided higher education in continental Europe often suffers from overcrowding and poor quality of teaching and research. The University of Rome is reported to have 150,000 students. German and Italian universities, for example, induce people to study "forever" since subsidized insurance and other services, the absence of tuition, and the option of postponing examinations until late in programs does not give students strong incentives to finish quickly. A very bureaucratic lifetime employment system for professors with limited incentives to do well and to keep up with their fields, as well as underfunding and overcrowding are also lamented for limited research opportunities. A hundred years ago, however, Germany's public universities were considered among the best in the world. In Switzerland public universities are the predominant form of tertiary education, with very high standards, and in Japan the universities with the best reputation are also public. Even countries that boost a strong private sector participation in tertiary education, such as the United States or England, have important public institutions as well.

Despite these caveats, the case for private provision *and financing* of tertiary education is much stronger than for primary and secondary education. Private provision and funding and better cost recovery through tuition could improve the cost effectiveness and the quality of higher education, especially when public systems have deteriorated. Looking ahead, the growing demand for higher education and budgetary pressures suggest that we are likely to see much stronger private sector involvement in this area in the future with potential savings for the budget. (See Psacharopoulos, 1992.)

4. PENSION REFORM

All industrialized countries will have to face the fiscal consequences of a rapidly aging population over the next decades. The share of people over the age of sixty will rise from less than 20 percent in 1990 to almost 30 percent of the population by the year 2020 in OECD countries. However, pension expenditures already average about 10 percent of GDP in industrialized countries with peaks of 15 percent of GDP in Austria and Italy (see Table II.10). In past decades, the extension of benefits and eligibility, for example through a reduction in the effective retirement age, rather than the aging of the population, was the main factor contributing to the rise in pension expenditure.[15] In the future, population aging is likely to become the more important factor because financial pressure will not allow further extensions of benefits or eligibility. Nevertheless, budgetary costs could become unsustainable if, on the basis of current systems, pension expenditure rose significantly in the next decades. Pensions are therefore one of the most important expenditure areas requiring reform in industrial countries.

In recent years there has been an intellectual movement suggesting that governments progressively withdraw from the provision of old-age insurance except for a publicly secured basic or minimum pension. Several countries have demonstrated how privatizing the pension system (that is, moving to a private, fully funded and defined-

---

15. See Holzmann (1988) for the factors explaining growing pension spending between 1960 and 1985 and Scherer (1996) for the effects of early retirement and declining labor market participation on social expenditure in OECD countries in the 1980s.

contribution system with government regulation) could significantly reduce the long-term budgetary costs. This change could have positive effects on growth and on the social climate because it would reduce the burden of social security taxes on labor and would largely depoliticize pension decisions, thus rebuilding confidence in the productive role of the state. However, the shift to a privately managed and fully funded system requires some conditions and has some important implications, which need to be carefully assessed.

Current Pension Systems in OECD Countries

Current pension systems are broadly and typically pay-as-you-go and defined-benefit public systems where benefits to the pensioners are largely paid from current contributions by the workers. These systems can be very costly in budgetary terms and can have adverse effects on growth by discouraging private saving, encouraging early retirement, and stimulating underground economic activities. They can have major fiscal consequences. In many countries, high payroll taxes lead to tax evasion and push many small enterprises underground. Early retirement provisions inflate pension costs because benefits are generally based on recent earnings and not on lifetime contributions. In most countries, pension benefits redistribute income from the relatively young to the first generation of retirees. These systems imply large implicit financial liabilities for governments.[16]

Economists have calculated the governments' implicit pension liabilities that will arise in future years on the basis of demographic trends, current contribution, and benefit levels, and some assumptions about interest rates and productivity growth. Net pension liabilities are highest in Germany, France, Italy, and Japan (see earlier Table 3.6) and point to the likely challenges lying ahead. These liabilities tend to be much higher than the current levels of public debt. Among the larger industrial countries, only the United Kingdom, the United States, and Sweden have relatively low uncovered pension liabilities. Given these projections, it is not surprising that experts in the industrialized world have been discussing the soundness of the pension systems and questioning the governments' ability to honor the

16. For an overview of current public and private pension schemes, see various OECD studies on this topic. See also Group of Ten (1998). Generational accounting has emerged as a way of assessing fiscal policies and financial liabilities of a country arising particularly from its future pension obligations (see, for example, Hagemann and John, 1995, for generational accounting in Sweden).

present commitments. Pension reform has become a major topic for debate in several countries.

Guidelines for Pension Reform: The Option of a Multipillar System

In response to the challenge of pension reform, few years ago the World Bank staff provided a blueprint for reform in a study titled *Averting the Old Age Crisis* (World Bank, 1994a).[17] In this study, the staff of the World Bank presented its own vision of a pension system based on full funding and defined contributions rather than on defined benefits. It gives a strong role to the private sector although the government continues to play an important regulatory role. The World Bank study was largely inspired by the pension reform pioneered by Chile in the early 1980s. The latter has influenced several countries to reform their systems and to introduce some of the features introduced by Chile.

A problem with the existing pension systems with macroeconomic consequences is that their implicit future liabilities, arising from too generous benefit levels and eligibility, need to be reduced. See Chand and Jaeger (1997). Most of the future increases in contribution rates could be avoided if the effective retirement age were raised, if the replacement rate were lowered, and if pensions were indexed only to inflation instead of net (or even gross) earnings (see Table IX.5). These changes could largely take care of the macroeconomic imbalances that now exist in many pension systems. However, they would not represent genuine structural reform and would not reduce public spending for pensions over the long run.

Systemic reform is necessary to transform at least parts of the prevailing pay-as-you-go pension systems into a fully funded and defined-contribution system. This is where the World Bank study and the Chilean reform come into the picture. The new system should maintain a safety net against poverty in old age and should minimize adverse effects on growth. The World Bank study suggested the introduction of a three-pillar system similar to the one introduced in Chile. The first pillar should be a mandatory, publicly managed

17. For a proposal for pension reform in the United States along similar lines, see Kotlikoff (1995). Siebert (1998) discusses pension systems and their reform in a number of industrialized and newly industrialized countries.

Table IX.5. *Contribution Gaps of Pension Systems and the Effects of Reform in Selected Industrial Countries*
(Percent of GDP)

	Contribution gap under current policies			Effects of reforms on contribution gap by		
	Projected average contribution rate 1995–2050 (1)	Sustainable contribution rate 1995–2050[a] (2)	Contribution gap (3) = (1) – (2)	Reduce replacement ratio by 5 percentage points for new pensioners	Limit increase to 100% CPI indexation	Increase retirement age to 67 years from 1995
Canada	3.8	5.8	−2.0	−1.0	…	−0.7
France	12.1	15.4	−3.3	−0.9	−0.8	−3.7
Germany	10.3	13.7	−3.4	−1.2	−1.9	−1.2
Italy	16.0	18.5	−2.5	−0.7	…	−5.7
Japan	3.9	7.2	−3.3	−0.5	−1.4	−1.6
Sweden	7.1	8.0	−0.9	−1.0	…	−1.0
United Kingdom	4.2	4.3	−0.1	−0.7	…	−1.1
United States	4.7	5.5	−0.8	−0.7	…	−0.3

Source: Chand and Jaeger (1997).

[a]The sustainable contribution rate is defined as the constant rate over 1995–2050 that equalizes the net asset position in 2050 with the initial net asset position in 1995.

pillar, financed by tax revenue, which would provide a flat or a means-tested minimum pension to provide an essential safety net.[18] The second pillar should be a mandatory, privately managed, defined-contribution system with individual accounts that would reflect the accumulated contributions made by the participants. These accounts would grow in line with the accumulated contributions made and the rate of return earned on the balances. The contributions would be equal to a given, legally defined share of the incomes of the partici-pants. These contributions would be placed in the hands of private managers who would invest them. At retirement, an annuity option would be available, based on the accumulated assets in the accounts, to guarantee an income over the remaining period of life. The third pillar would be voluntary contributions to savings accounts to allow for individual insurance preferences. Those who would prefer higher assets at retirement could thus make larger voluntary contributions during their active life.

In this system, the role of the government would change dramatically, but it would remain very important. First of all, it would continue to provide minimum pensions that would serve as a safety net. Second, it would decide on the percentage of wages and salaries that must be set aside for the retirement accounts. Third, it would regulate those who manage the funds to insure accountability and to limit risk taking. Fourth, it would decide on what kind of limitations to impose on the managers as to the assets on which the funds can be invested. These assets, of course, could be limited to domestic assets or could be extended to foreign assets. The wider the range, the lower the volatility of the rate of return but the more difficult the controls.

A number of factors could increase the economic benefits from moving from the current pension systems to such a multipillar system. To have a positive effect on the sustainability of pension systems, on savings, and on growth, the funded pillars should not be too small compared to the unfunded and government-financed pillar.[19] The managers of the funds should be free to pursue the highest rates of

18. Country-specific social assistance programs that are already in place can sometimes substitute for the first pillar. Social assistance in Germany, for example, already complements pension benefits to reach a minimum threshold.
19. Obviously in this system there will continue to be pressures on the government to increase the levels of the guaranteed, minimum, and government-financed pensions.

return within given risk limits. Basic financial markets with sufficient regulatory capacity would be required as a prerequisite for moving toward funded systems. However, some experts have argued that the existence of such a system would itself be an incentive for the development of domestic capital markets.

Countries that have started making systemic changes in their pension systems include the Netherlands and the United Kingdom with a flat minimum public pension and Australia with a means- and asset-tested public pillar and an occupation-based second pillar. Other countries such as Argentina, Mexico, Hungary, and Poland, have moved or are moving toward a Chilean-type pension system.

Economic Benefits from Moving to a Funded System

The movement from a pay-as-you-go to a fully funded, defined-contribution pension system once completed would increase fiscal transparency by making explicit the implicit pension liabilities. It would also guarantee that savings are accumulated by current workers to cover future dissavings when they retire. Contributors would tend to see their contributions as savings rather than taxes. Such reforms can also have considerable positive effects on the economic performance of countries. Pension funds would help develop financial markets, which in turn stimulate savings and capital accumulation. This aspect could be particularly interesting for some of the less-developed capital markets in Europe and elsewhere. Capital market development also stimulates technical progress and labor productivity. Payroll taxes in a defined-contribution system would be more modest than they are now in some countries or, if the minimum pensions are paid out of general revenue, they could even disappear. As a result, employment in the official economy would grow because individuals and firms have less of an incentive to go underground. Such change would have a beneficial effect on tax revenue, thus allowing the countries to reduce tax rates.

A funded system based on a defined-contribution plan with individualized savings accounts enhances labor mobility because people do not lose their pension rights when they change jobs. This argument will become particularly important within the European Union, where growing labor mobility should raise the ability to deal with regional shocks and asymmetric developments. The introduction of the European Monetary Union has reduced the individual countries' ability to deal with these shocks (Holzmann, 1996a).

The current defined-benefit systems suffer from the fact that they are subject to political pressures from pensioners to raise benefits. Also, some governments have tended to use the pension systems to pursue redistributive policies. In such systems, reforms can always be introduced which raise or reduce benefits or contribution rates. Taking the politics out of the pension system by introducing a fully funded and contribution-based system raises the credibility of the reform and its positive long-term effects on the economy. Trust in the pension system would increase particularly in countries where governments have not met their commitments in the past. Savings can also arise from the reduction in rent-seeking opportunities when pension policies cannot be lobbied any more. However, in a contribution-based system administered by the private sector, *the regulatory activity of the government becomes particularly important.* The government must regulate the managers to ensure that they do not take excessive risks, but it must not impose stifling conditions on how to invest the funds.

Transition Problems

One of the main problem with moving to a funded and defined-contribution pension system lies in the financing of the transition period.[20] Typically, there is a cutoff point where people enter the new system (young workers plus new entrants); middle-aged people have a choice between the funded system and the old scheme; and people near retirement continue under the old scheme. Thus, for a while the government continues to pay pensions while it receives less contributions. Chile has given its active workers "recognition bonds" for benefits accumulated under the old system, which can be redeemed upon retirement. This way, active workers can easily enter the new funded system if they opt to do so.

There are several ways in which the amount and the timing of transition costs can be influenced. If the unfunded system is downsized

---

20. See Holzmann (1997a) for more details on this important issue.

before moving to a funded system so that the implicit liabilities decline, the subsequent financing gap is smaller. In fact, this is the practice of many countries whether they move to a funded system or not. Fiscal costs can be front-loaded if all active workers enter the funded system immediately. Then the government would have to pay for existing pensioners without receiving any contributions. Fiscal costs can be back-loaded if only new labor market entrants become part of the funded system. As existing workers retire and young workers contribute into funds, less financing is available under the pay-as-you-go scheme to pay for the retired. The deficit grows over time. Independent of whether the costs are front- or back-loaded, they need to be financed. Depending on the particularities of the transition and the level of implicit pension liabilities, additional costs can reach several percent of GDP for many years. The sale of public assets might be used to cover transition costs (but of course this is no net gain because the proceeds could also be used to pay for other government liabilities). But it should not be neglected that a considerably tightened fiscal stance may be necessary to generate the savings to finance the transition period.

Lastly, we should emphasize that the success of pension reform depends very much on public support. This is a reform area that affects everybody at a vulnerable stage in life, and the public debate has shown how nervous people are over pension reform. The information and education of the public is therefore very important. However, while pension reform would be costly, the postponement of reform would lead to even larger adjustment problems in the future.

Reform of Existing Pay-as-You-Go, Defined-Benefit Schemes

In some countries, the notion of pay-as-you-go schemes as a "compact between generations" has been very important in the past. Therefore it seems worthwhile discussing reform of such systems in more detail as well. Although the notion of a compact between generations has probably been much abused to award unsustainable benefits for political purposes, a careful reform of these schemes may yield significant benefits, if the preservation of the compact between generations is considered an overriding social benefit (see Chand and Jaeger, 1996, for a detailed discussion).

As a first step, as mentioned above, indexation arrangements should be changed, and the retirement age should be raised and early retirement should be penalized. It can be argued that the period of retirement should be a constant fraction of life expectancy so that the normal retirement age rises in steps with life expectancy. Furthermore, the benefits should be indexed to net wages or even to price changes. Second, the contribution rate should be raised such that it can be kept relatively stable over time. In demographically favorable periods, the system would thereby accumulate reserves that would be used up in less favorable periods.[21] The key benefit from these reforms would be the elimination of intergenerational transfers because the contribution rate and the relative value of pensions compared to wages would stay constant. Measures aimed at raising labor force participation and reducing unemployment could also help reduce pressure on pension systems, through raising the contribution base, in a number of industrialized countries (see Foot, 1989 for a discussion of the Canadian situation).

In many countries, the increase in the contribution rate would have to be quite significant unless eligibility and benefits are restricted considerably. This, of course, can aggravate tax evasion and stimulate even more the growth of the underground economy. Transition costs would be lower, but the effects on savings might not be as favorable. Furthermore, the credibility of the system would always suffer from the very fact that politics is not kept out of the pension system, and strong institutional safeguards would be necessary to prevent opportunistic future policy changes. More fundamentally, *these reforms are not likely to reduce the public spending's share of GDP.*

5. REFORM OF THE HEALTH SECTOR

Health care policies are another important area with a considerable potential for government reform that could reduce public expenditure. As with education, access to affordable high-quality health care affects the equality of opportunity of people. In the public debate on this issue, social justice and equity issues are therefore often seen

---

21. See Sadka and Tanzi (1998) for a discussion of these issues.

as more important than economics. However, as a share of GDP, public expenditure on health has almost tripled since 1960 and now absorbs resources of the same order of magnitude as public education. Progress in medical technology and, increasingly, population aging will put further upward pressure on public spending for health. (See Roseveare et al., 1996.)

Reform of the health sector started in the early 1980s in many countries and has focused mainly on the cost effectiveness of health systems. Government regulation to strengthen incentives has proven useful in many countries to control costs and to improve quality. However, important further reforms seem possible in the health sector. Budgetary support should largely be limited to areas with important externalities and to insurance against catastrophic illness; other services can normally be provided and financed privately.

Existing Health Care Systems

There is an enormous variation in health care systems among OECD countries with respect to the provision and the financing of health care, ranging from tax-financed and publicly provided systems in many European countries to significantly privately financed and provided services in the United States.[22]

In the past, the debate of health care systems has focused on who should provide and finance health care. As for education, there is no simple answer. Private, unregulated systems have considerable drawbacks because insurance markets make it difficult for high-risk patients to get insurance. Asymmetric information between patients and providers drives up the costs of services. These arguments are supported by empirical evidence: systems with a large share of private financing have been much less successful, on average, at controlling aggregate costs of health care. Austria, Canada, France, Switzerland, and in particular the United States have the highest health care costs in the world (Table IX.6). Despite the high costs, the U.S. system leaves a large percentage of the population uninsured. The public provision of health services is also seen very critically and countries

---

22. For a detailed discussion of health systems and reforms efforts in OECD countries see, OECD Health Policy Studies No. 2 (1992) and 5 (1995).

Table IX.6. *Cost Control and Public versus Private Health Expenditure, 1992*

	Health expenditure as percent of GDP	Health expenditure as percent of total	
		Private	Public
Australia	7.9	14.4	85.6
Austria	8.8	34.8	65.2
Belgium	7.9	11.1	88.9
Canada	10.8	27.3	72.7
France	9.4	25.2	74.8
Germany	8.7	28.5	71.5
Ireland	7.1	23.9	76.1
Italy	8.5	24.8	75.2
Japan	7.0	28.8	71.2
Netherlands[a]	8.6	23.4	76.6
New Zealand	7.7	21.0	79.0
Norway	8.0	5.2	94.8
Spain	7.5	19.5	80.5
Sweden	7.9	14.4	85.6
Switzerland	9.3	32.1	67.9
United Kingdom	7.1	15.6	84.4
United States	14.0	54.3	45.7
Average	**8.6**	**23.8**	**76.2**

Source: Oxley and MacFarlan (1995).
[a] 1991.

that relied heavily on public sector provision in the past (such as the United Kingdom and Italy) have faced problems with the quality of services. In some of these countries individuals may have to wait for long periods before they can get particular medical attention such as major surgery.

A first wave of reforms in the 1980s focused on spending caps or other macro instruments to slow the growth of spending. This has only been partly successful as the underlying incentive structures were not taken into account and the quality of services suffered. In fact, the regulatory framework and the incentives facing health care providers have been identified as a driving force behind spending increases equally important as aging of the population and growth in income (Oxley and MacFarlan, 1995).

Strengthening Incentives

Reforms in the health sector since the 1980s have moved away from the public provision of services. Instead the more recent reforms focus on the most efficient public regulation and on the incentives of private providers, insurers, and patients to control costs and to choose the most economic form of treatment. Patients, for example, are encouraged to economize on recourse to health services. They often have to contribute an increasing share to the costs of drugs, doctors' visits, or hospital charges. In some countries, patients have a choice among different insurance companies, which gives the latter an incentive to control the costs of providers such as doctors or hospitals. Doctors are encouraged to prescribe generic drugs, and price curbs are negotiated with pharmaceutical firms. The United Kingdom and New Zealand have introduced elements of buyer–provider relations in health care. The government buys health care, and health-service providers (hospitals etc.) compete for such contracts. In the United States, health maintenance organizations (HMOs) cover about one-third of patients and combine insurance and provider functions to reduce unnecessary tests and treatments and to keep costs under control. Performance contracts for doctors with fixed salaries who receive premiums when costs are kept down have also been applied.[23] In the past, government regulation often prevented cost saving by the private sector, and significant further savings can be conceived with the help of appropriate regulation and better incentive-oriented private contractual arrangements. There is some evidence that these reforms have slowed down the rise in the cost of health care in the most recent years.

Reducing the Role of Government in Health

In addition to strengthening cost and quality control in the health sector, there is a strong case for reducing the role of the government budget in providing health services beyond a minimum. Governments should secure universal coverage for basic preventive care and against catastrophic illnesses. For these it may have to support espe-

---

23. See Oxley and MacFarlan (1995) for a detailed discussion of the main principles of health care reform, or the *Financial Times* comment by Mark Suzman (September 9, 1996) on health care reform.

cially the most vulnerable groups, possibly by providing them with vouchers that would allow them to buy insurance. The government ought also to play a major role in providing vaccination against infectious diseases. Beyond this, people may either want to purchase private insurance or finance the residual risk themselves. If health reform is guided by these principles, the role of government can be scaled back and health services can be more efficient and more easily financeable in the future. However, the regulatory role of the government becomes more important.

6. SCALING DOWN OTHER INCOME TRANSFER PROGRAMS

The previous sections discussed some of the main public expenditure components and provided some general principles for reform. In addition, in the early 1990s, industrialized countries spent, on average, almost 3 percent of GDP on labor market programs and unemployment compensation and another 5 percent of GDP on other income transfer programs, including disability, sickness, maternity, occupational injury and disease, early retirement, housing, family, and other benefits (see Tables II.11 and II.12). The costs of unemployment are probably underestimated significantly because many countries "eliminated" some of their unemployed via early retirement.

Reform of the unemployment insurance system should yield some budgetary savings from curtailing benefits and privatizing some of the related services. More importantly however, labor market reform is necessary in many countries to reduce unemployment.[24] In addition, very high costs of disability and sickness benefits, for example in the Netherlands or Norway suggest the need for reform in other areas as well. In the Netherlands and Norway, the "other income transfer programs" add up to about 10 percent of GDP and many countries spend over 5 percent of GDP. Without going into detail, considerable budgetary savings may therefore be possible by better targeting of benefits in these various programs.

---

24. See, for example, Coe and Snower (1996) for reform proposals for the EU.

7. QUASI-FISCAL POLICIES

In earlier chapters we assumed that governments aim to achieve their objectives through taxing and spending, and economists generally agree that in most cases these are the best instruments with which to implement fiscal policy objectives. However, if governments face political or administrative limits to their taxing and spending powers, and if the rules of the game do not clearly specify the policy instruments by which to pursue the desired objectives, policymakers may pursue these objectives through reliance on inefficient instruments. Regulatory control could become a (less efficient) substitute for spending whereby governments cut their fiscal role but not their overall role in the economy.

Certain types of regulations, can become alternatives to taxing and spending. For example, governments have often introduced rent controls when they were unable to give subsidies to allow families to reduce their rental costs. Such a control is equivalent to a tax on the owners of the houses with controlled rents and a subsidy to those who rent the houses. Therefore, these controls can substitute for budgetary action but are generally economically more costly. For example, an overvalued exchange rate implicitly "taxes" exports and "subsidizes" imports, thus allowing some imported goods to be sold more cheaply. However similar effects can be achieved more efficiently via taxes and subsidies providing that this is a feasible alternative. (On these quasi-fiscal policies, see Tanzi 1998c.)

Regulations that have the clear though unstated objective of replacing taxing and spending (quasi-fiscal regulations) are most prevalent in developing and transition economies, where the potential for tax revenue is limited, but they also occur in industrial countries. For example, regulations on the financial system were used by Italy until the 1980s to service its public debt more cheaply, through repressed interest rates and requirements on the banks to invest some of their deposits in public debt instruments. See Bruni, Penati, and Porta (1989). The implicit revenue from these regulations of the financial system can be very large. For example, Giovannini and De Melo (1993) found that financial market controls in Zimbabwe and Mexico in the early 1980s had allowed these two governments to finance themselves at artificially low interest rates, thus reducing the interest cost on servicing their public debt by more than 5 percent of GDP. The governments of Greece, Portugal, and Turkey each "saved" over 2 percent of GDP by adopting similar measures.[25]

The widespread use of quasi-fiscal instruments implies that governments should not only be constrained in their fiscal policies but also in their scope to engage in quasi-fiscal (and market-unfriendly) policies. Concretely, this may require that central banks not be allowed to lend at subsidized rates or with exchange rate guarantees, that exchange-rate systems are unified, and that the government pays a market-based interest rate on its debt (Mackenzie and Stella, 1996). But there are numerous other regulations, such as rent controls, unpaid military service, and so on that may have high economic costs and that can significantly undermine the functioning of markets and distort the role of government. Thus, the objective of government reform should not only be to reduce explicit public spending but to change the culture so that quasi-fiscal activities disappear. It is important to keep in mind that quasi-fiscal regulations can often be imposed without accountability and that unlike budgetary expenditures, there is no limit as to how many regulations can be imposed. A limitation for the latter can only come from a change in the rules and the culture as to what role the government should play.[26] The same rules and culture that lead to high spending in some circumstances lead to a proliferation of quasi-fiscal regulations.

8. ACCOUNTING FOR RESOURCE USE

The governments of all countries own a lot of valuable assets such as public enterprises, land, buildings, gold and cash, foreign exchange, natural resources, patents, shops, planes and other means of transportation, and many others. These assets are often under the control of ministries and other spending units. For example, education

25. Mackenzie and Stella (1996) discuss quasi-fiscal operations of public financial institutions in detail and provide case studies on Ghana, Jamaica, Poland, Romania, and Uruguay.
26. To the best of the authors' knowledge, no country has made a complete inventory of all the quasi-fiscal regulations in existence and no country has created an institution charged with the objective of getting rid of most of these quasi-fiscal regulations.

ministries control school buildings, health ministries control public hospitals, public museums control works of art, interior ministries control public lands, and so on. Of course, subnational governments, such as provinces, counties, or municipalities, control other assets.

For most countries two statements could be made that fairly accurately reflect the current situation with respect to these assets. First, most governments to do not have a full, updated inventory of the assets that they own, and especially of the potential market value of what they own. It is thus impossible for them to determine, for example, the net worth of the public sector or the opportunity cost of the rental value of, say, using a given building for a particular use, such as a school or a hospital. Second, these assets are not used in ways that maximize the social rate of return.

In fact, normal budgetary procedures do not account for the use of these resources. For example, the cost of running a school often does not include the fair rental value of the building.

As a consequence of these facts, one finds in the public sector some of the most glaring examples of unproductive use of valuable assets. Examples could be schools located in the most expensive areas of a city, works of art that are never seen because they remain in museums' basements, buildings that are left empty for long periods of time, cash that is left in low-yielding accounts for too long, and so on. These examples imply that the real cost of the government is often much higher than the budgetary cost.

While the private sector must take into account the opportunity cost of using assets that it owns, the public sector, in most cases, is not in the habit of doing so. In recent years, some attempts have started to be made in Australia, New Zealand, the United Kingdom, and a few other countries to address this problem The objective is to take better account of the resources used by the public sector so that a fuller view of the real costs of various public sector activities is available. The control of public expenditure will be much helped by a more rational approach to resource accounting in the preparation of public budgets.[27]

27. David Heald, in the Department of Accountancy at the University of Aberdeen, and the Aberdeen research team have been doing particularly valuable work in this area. For a few countries, attempts have been made in recent years to determine the net worth of the public sector. However, the objective of this exercise is different from that of improving the quality of the budget.

9. CONCLUDING REMARKS

Governments will need to make difficult choices if they want to bring about a reduction in public expenditure to more reasonable levels. Privatization of the provision and financing of many goods and services, including the provision of infrastructures, and the reform of education, pension, and health systems, and of numerous other social programs, toward greater private sector participation should enable the governments of industrial countries to reduce public spending and taxes significantly. This chapter has discussed in a broad and somewhat informal way the various possibilities now available. Not all of these will be possible to all governments, but some of them should be feasible for all. The next chapter will discuss some of the recent experiences with government reform in a number of industrialized and newly industrialized countries.

PART FOUR

Recent Experiences of Countries in Reforming the Government

In previous chapters of this study, it was shown that the rapid growth in public spending in recent decades did not generate clearly identifiable achievements in social and economic objectives. Declining returns to government growth or, in some cases, even negative returns (in terms of socioeconomic objectives) suggest that a smaller economic role for the state would be desirable in the future. With major reforms, and once the full effects of these reforms are felt, government spending could come down significantly. To achieve this radical change, governments would need to focus on setting the rules of the game and on pursuing their core objectives in an efficient manner. They would have to shed many of the responsibilities they assumed in recent decades. In Part Three we provided some guidelines for reforming fiscal rules and institutions and for streamlining public expenditure programs. Although we do not claim that these guidelines provide precise instructions on how to solve the problems that have justified big government in the past, we hope that they can provide a useful brief for a debate on what could be done to achieve more efficient governments with much lower levels of public spending.

The following chapters illustrate how much public policies and public opinion have changed since the 1970s. Government reform is not just a mind game for eccentric academics, but it is a process that is already well advanced or gaining momentum in some countries. New Zealand and Chile, for example, have pioneered far-reaching reforms that have addressed the whole spectrum of fiscal institutions and expenditure programs. In a less radical way other countries have also introduced major reforms. As a result, public spending has declined significantly in these countries without any evidence that socioeconomic objectives have been damaged. Furthermore, the public debate as presented in the media illustrates that the need for government reform is now widely accepted. Finally, we will speculate on the future role of governments in a more global environment.

X   Recent Reform Experience

A number of industrial and newly industrialized countries have already gone a long way in reducing the role of the state. Dramatic reforms in the way government is organized and in the scope of government involvement in producing goods and services and providing social security have in some cases resulted in reductions of public spending of 10 or even 20 percent of GDP. Two examples, in particular, show that a change in the policy regime is most important to reinvigorate the economy and raise economic growth while maintaining adequate standards of social welfare. In New Zealand and Chile, but to a lesser extent also in some other countries, governments have changed from using economic policies largely to redistribute rents to providing needed services and a regulatory framework appropriate to allow market forces to raise growth rates and social welfare. In this process, some of the reforms outlined in earlier chapters have in fact been successfully implemented. Thus, they do not represent pipedreams of armchair economists.

In the following pages we report on some of the reform experiences in OECD and newly industrialized countries. In the choice of case studies we had to be selective, and only a limited sample of countries and reform experiences are represented. As time goes by, new countries are likely to engage in significant reforms while a few others may experience policy standstill or even reversal. The implementation of concrete reforms has been conducted in often differing circumstances, and reforms that succeeded in one country may not always work in exactly the same way elsewhere. Nevertheless, many of the broader issues and experiences reported here are likely to be relevant and informative for other countries interested in fiscal reform for many years to come.

1. CHANGING THE POLICY REGIME IN NEW ZEALAND

In the early 1980s, New Zealand was one of the most protectionist and interventionist countries. Its economic growth and living standards had fallen behind most other Western economies. At that time, the government role in the economy was very large. After 1984, New Zealand undertook the most radical economic reform program of any OECD member country (Massey, 1995). Its reform program can provide a useful guide for reform elsewhere. The policy regime was intentionally and fundamentally shifted toward a smaller, more efficient, and rule-governed state and a significantly increased role for the private sector.

In New Zealand, the reform process started in 1984, and fiscal reform was a very important element of the program. (See IMF, 1996b; Massey, 1995; Cangiano, 1996; Evans, Grimes, and Wilkinson with Teece, 1996 and Scott, 1996, for surveys.) In a first step, the government disengaged from much of the production of goods and services. Most state enterprises were commercialized and then privatized, including the steel industry, the banks, the telecommunication sector, and the national airline. Price support and subsidies for agriculture were abolished. Implicit subsidies through low government charges or prices were reduced, user fees were introduced, and ministries were given targets for cost recovery. The tax system was greatly simplified, marginal tax rates were sharply reduced, and the tax bases were widely broadened. In 1990–1, social policy reform restructured the health, education, welfare, housing, pension, and accident insurance system. It raised the retirement age from sixty to sixty-five years and replaced universal entitlements by a modest safety net with means testing. In education, school autonomy was increased and fees on university education were introduced.

The public administration was also restructured with a view to enhancing expenditure prioritization and service delivery.[1] The new system of task-oriented expenditure management included buyer–provider relations with a clear definition of policy goals, competition over service delivery, and performance contracts. This has raised efficiency and transparency in many areas of the public administration. The restructuring also involved significant decentralization of decision making. Chief executives, such as heads of departments, are given five-year contracts with performance-based compensation and considerable autonomy on how to manage their affairs. They have great discretion on how to use their budget. Accountability through monitoring of managers and their outputs was also strengthened, and information systems to inform senior managers as well as the legislature and the public on the performance of the various agencies or offices were created or improved. The prioritization of public expenditure was strengthened through capacity building in strategic policy formulation and management.[1]

In 1994, the Fiscal Responsibility Act established the rules and objectives for fiscal policies. This rule based fiscal policy is also influencing other countries. The government is required to run fiscal surpluses under normal circumstances until a prudent debt level is reached. A balanced fiscal position will be required thereafter. Tax rates are to be stable and predictable. The Act enshrines budgetary accounting principles and disclosure requirements so that the processes and the outcome of fiscal policy become transparent. Fiscal discipline is backed from the monetary side: the main objective of the independent central bank is to stay within the agreed inflation target range and the governor's pay is related to inflation performance. Inflation targeting has been influencing monetary policy in other countries.

The reform efforts did not result in immediate fiscal savings or faster growth. In fact, public expenditure initially increased and peaked in 1988 at over 45 percent of GDP (Table X.1), indicating that, in the short run, major reform may require higher spending.[2] However, by 1994, spending had declined by a remarkable 10 percent

---

1. See Scott (1996) for a detailed account of New Zealand's experience in this area. See also New Zealand State Services Commission (1998).
2. The table compares expenditure policies during the year when total expenditure was at a historic maximum with the most recent year available.

Table X.1. *Public Expenditure Development and Government Reform: Chile and New Zealand* (Percent of GDP)

	Chile		New Zealand[b]	
	1982	1995	1988	1994
Public expenditure				
Total expenditure	34.1	19.9	45.6	35.7
Government consumption	10.8	8.8	11.5	15.4
Interest[b]	0.5	0.7	7.2	5.7
Transfers and subsidies[b]	20.6	10.0	24.8	13.2
Capital expenditure	2.2	3.2	2.1	1.3
Overall deficit (+/surplus)	−2.3	3.9	−1.6	3.3
Health[b]	1.8	2.5	3.0	5.6
Education[b]	4.0	2.8	5.7	5.6
Economic and social indicators				
Real GDP growth[c]	0.3	8.2	1.4	3.3
Gross fixed capital formation[c]	16.2	23.0	21.5	18.0
Inflation[c]	21.8	16.6	11.6	1.9
Unemployment rate[c]	13.8	5.3	4.9	6.2[d]

Source: Tanzi and Schuknecht (1997b).
[a] 1995 is preliminary data.
[b] Central government data. For New Zealand, includes all state-owned enterprises (SOEs) and Crown entities, as well as the Reserve Bank of New Zealand.
[c] Three-year average up to observation year.
[d] 1995–6 average, after a peak of 10.3 percent in 1991 and 1992.

of GDP. This reduction was achieved almost exclusively in the area of transfers and subsidies, which were reduced from almost 25 percent of GDP in 1988 to 13.2 percent of GDP in 1994. The bulk of this spending had constituted support to industry, which declined from 14 percent of GDP in 1984 to only 3 percent in 1992. Social welfare spending declined by 2 percent of GDP between 1991 and 1994 and (more importantly) the system's targeting and future financeability were improved. Interest expenditure also came down by over 2 percent of GDP, while spending on health and education was protected from cuts. In fact, government consumption, as distinguished from government spending, even increased over the period shown in the table.

As mentioned, liberalization in New Zealand altered in a fundamental way how things were done. Rent-seeking opportunities were sharply reduced through privatization, transfer, subsidy reduction, and through institutional reforms in the public administration. However, it should also be noted that the reforms introduced took five years before they started translating into measurable falls in public sector spending and even longer before real economic growth started to accelerate. Thus, a lot of patience is required on the part of policymakers and the public. It helped that both the main political parties supported the reform program. This support secured continuity even when the ruling party changed. Vested interests in the new policy regime were strengthened, e.g., through the introduction of a privatization ministry.

Reform in New Zealand was also facilitated by the Westminster-style political system, which features a strong executive. However, reforms in such a system can more easily be reversed. In anticipation of this possibility, and to strengthen the credibility and durability of the new economic policies, New Zealand changed its electoral system to a German-type system, mixing elements of direct and proportional representation. This is intended to strengthen stability-oriented policymaking in the future.

The New Zealand experience should be studied closely by all those with serious intentions to reduce public spending and to reform government. Although it undoubtedly has special features that are not easily duplicated in countries with different cultures, it provides significant lessons for other countries. The New Zealand experiment has of course not been without critics. (For a strong criticism, see Kelsey, 1997.) More recently the earlier, almost missionary zeal of the policymakers has mellowed somewhat, but the policies have not been changed.

2. CHANGING THE POLICY REGIME IN CHILE

The second country that reformed its economy and economic policy regime most radically is Chile. Although it is not yet classified as an industrial country, it is getting to the point where, if the economic performance of recent years is maintained, it soon will be. In the early 1970s Chile had undergone a socialist experiment that resulted in high inflation and high fiscal deficits. Over the following fifteen years, a mixture of constitutional and quasi-constitutional reforms fundamentally altered the character of the Chilean economy and of its economic policy making processes.[3] Unfortunately, the military regime's economic success over that period is tarnished by its human rights record.

The new 1980 constitution guarantees property rights and limits the role of government as a discretionary regulator. Budgetary procedures were reformed and government procedures were subjected to stricter rules and accountability. The government disengaged itself from most public enterprises, privatized much of the pension and health insurance system, and decentralized health and education. All these reforms reduced the scope for lobbying by special interests for preferential tax treatment, social benefits, and favorable regulation and rendered government services more efficient. It replaced a "clientelistic state with a more autonomous state" where "the costs of government transfers and interventions are (at least partially) internalized, and therefore sound fiscal policy becomes achievable" (See Velasco in Bosworth, Dornbusch, and Laban 1994.[4])

The main phase of privatization in Chile started in 1984. Most core state enterprises were privatized, including, for example, the utilities and transportation sector. Although some shortcomings remain, the privatization process also took into account regulatory requirements such as creating a competitive market structure and a sound financing and ownership structure for the privatized enterprises.

In social insurance, the government introduced a fully funded, mandatory pension system with defined contributions and individual savings accounts. Pension funds are privately managed. Members can choose the managers and change managers if they wish. They can also choose between phased withdrawal of benefits and a real annuity when they reach retirement age. A guaranteed minimum pension (together with a number of other well-targeted programs) provides a social safety net for everyone. The reform of the social security system in Chile has attracted attention from around the world, and its main features are being imitated by many countries.

3. The road to reform was quite rocky initially. A first period of reforms after 1975 followed the socialist period under Allende and focused on privatization and fiscal stabilization. The economic and banking crises of 1981–2, however, revealed considerable problems with these reforms and resulted in the renationalization of enterprises and another period of fiscal destabilization.
4. See also the studies by Marcel and Solimano, Diamond and Valdés-Prieto, and Bitran and Saez in the same volume for a detailed discussion of the Chilean reforms.

In the social services, private sector participation was also encouraged and management was decentralized. Funding of public schools was changed to a standard grant per student (voucher) scheme, which also encourages private provision. Only 14 percent of education spending currently goes to higher education. Several first rate private universities have come into existence and have been attracting even foreign students. Public health is only provided for low-income groups. Consequently, social benefits are relatively well targeted, with two-thirds of public health benefits and half of the benefits of public education spending going to the poorest 40 percent of households. Overall spending on these sectors was 30 percent higher in real terms in 1992 than in 1970. However, facilities have frequently been underfunded and staff underpaid (as employment and real wages came down in the 1980s). The new democratic government therefore has been attempting to reorient spending toward the social sectors (without increasing the overall level of public spending) to equalize access to education and social services and to improve the quality of services further. (See Aninat, 1999.)

The reforms in the role of the state have resulted in an impressive reduction in public expenditure. Overall expenditure declined from 34 percent of GDP in 1982 to less than 20 percent of GDP in 1995. While government consumption declined from 10.8 to 8.8 percent, the biggest decline, from over 20 to 10 percent of GDP, was in subsidies and transfers. This generated considerable primary surpluses, which helped to finance the transition to a fully funded and defined contribution pension system. High public savings and the pension reform contributed to a deepening of financial markets, growing factor productivity and an increase in investment from less than 15 percent to over 25 percent of GDP over this period (Holzmann, 1997a). Economic growth has been high and unemployment low.

3. FISCAL REFORM IN OECD COUNTRIES

A number of OECD countries besides New Zealand have also reformed their fiscal institutions and expenditure programs (for a summary of fiscal data, see Table X.2).[5] The reform of the institutional framework has strengthened the policymakers' incentives for prudent fiscal policies.[6] Privatization of public enterprises has made considerable progress, and private provision of goods and services or traditionally public investment projects is on the increase. Social security reform is a high priority in a number of countries. In this context, efforts made by EU governments to meet the Maastricht criteria illustrate the incentive coming from global competition and international agreements for government reform.

Despite some progress, the number of countries that have introduced far-reaching reforms such as large-scale privatization of public enterprises or the privatization of social security is still limited. Welfare reforms have started reducing the costs of existing systems, but the next step – fundamental systemic reform – has largely yet to be taken.

Australia

Australia introduced bold institutional reforms to improve the efficiency of public spending and the strategic policymaking ability of the government. In the budget formulation process, provisions for existing programs and policies that are not changed are locked in for a three-year forecast period while policymakers can focus on priority areas where changes are envisaged. Ministries have considerable autonomy and flexibility in identifying spending and savings options to stay beneath their budget ceilings. Annual efficiency increases of 1 percent of "running costs" are expected as a payoff from the additional flexibility. Program management and budgeting with ex-post evaluations has strengthened accountability and has created a "performance-oriented culture" (Campos and Pradhan, 1996).[7] Aggregate

5. Selected literature will be referenced when discussing individual country experience. In addition, a discussion of fiscal reforms is provided in Recent Economic Development Reports by the International Monetary Fund for Argentina, Australia, Finland, Ireland, and Portugal. OECD Economic Surveys for Belgium, Finland, Sweden, Ireland, Portugal, and the United Kingdom are also useful.
6. For a study of budgetary institutions in EU countries see Von Hagen (1992); and for Latin America, see Alesina et al. (1996); Burki and Perry (1997); and Inter-American Development Bank (1997). For a more general discussion, see Alesina and Perotti (1996b).
7. Although both the Australian and New Zealand reforms were very successful, they had somewhat different focuses. The Australian reforms focused on policy prioritization, while the New Zealand reforms gave more weight to aggregate fiscal discipline and efficiency.

Table X.2. *Public Expenditure Development and Government Reform: Selected Industrial Countries*
(Percent of GDP)

	Australia		Belgium		Finland		Ireland		Portugal		Sweden		United Kingdom		
	1991–2	1995–6	1983	1996	1993	1995	1983	1994	1984	1994	1993	1995	1983	1989	1995–6
Public expenditure[a]															
Total expenditure	37.5	34.5	60.5	51.1	62.0	58.1	53.2	43.8	46.0	45.4	72.8	68.2	44.7	37.5	42.8
Government consumption	...	...	14.8	11.5	23.4	20.9	19.3	15.8	14.3	17.6	25.8	...	21.7	19.4	21.2
Interest[b]	...	...	9.4	8.7	4.6	5.2	9.1	7.5	9.2	5.8	7.1	...	3.9	3.3	3.6
Transfers and subsidies[a,b,c]	...	...	33.0	28.6	31.1	29.6	30.9	23.4	16.6	16.4	24.3	...	21.9	17.3	22.0
Capital expenditure[b]	...	...	4.5	2.3	2.9	2.4	3.8	2.6	4.5	6.6	3.0	...	2.0	2.1	2.3
Overall fiscal balance	-4.6	0.5	-2.2	-3.4	-7.8	-4.7	-15.6	-2.3	-9.6	-5.9	-12.7	-8.1	-3.4	-1.2	-4.7
Main fiscal reform areas:	Budgetary institutions; privatization; civil service reduction		Investment; goods and services		Local government; subsidies; health insurance		Social security; subsidies; civil service; tax system		Privatization; budgetary institutions; debt management		Budgetary institutions; social security		Privatization; social security		

Sources: Tanzi and Schuknecht (1997); IMF, *Belgium: Selected Issues* (1997); IMF, *United Kingdom: Recent Economic Developments* (1996).
[a] The table typically compares the year of maximum public expenditure with the most recent available data, or closest year available.
[b] Central government data, except Belgium, Finland, Portugal, and Sweden (1993).
[c] Includes transfers to other levels of government. Therefore, some double counting may occur in the government consumption and transfers and subsidies categories.

fiscal targets are publicly announced and implicitly enforced by media and by financial markets, thus raising the pressure on the government to perform.

Australia introduced a kind of cost/benefit analysis for government regulations, called a Regulation Impact Statement. These statements aim at making the objectives of regulations and their costs and benefits more transparent, so that pressure to choose the economically best alternative increases (Australia Office of Regulation Review, 1995). A new planning and performance accountability mechanism, and a Code of Ministerial Conduct that clearly defines obligations and responsibilities also aim at "improving the consistency, quality, transparency, and public accountability of government activities" (Australian Minister for Industrial Relations and Minister Assisting the Prime Minister for the Public Service, 1996).

Since 1990, Australia has also improved controls over state expenditure. Reforms in expenditure programs reduced state spending on goods and services. The state of Victoria, for example, cut government employment by 20 percent over 3 years. Other fiscal savings came from public enterprise reform.

Reform of fiscal institutions and expenditure programs helped Australia to shave another 3 percent off already low levels of public spending between 1991–2 and 1995–6. Public spending of about one-third of GDP is one of the lowest spending levels among OECD countries, and the budget is nearly in balance.

Belgium

Belgium achieved a considerable adjustment in public expenditure between 1983 and the mid-1990s. The outside constraints of the Common Market, the Maastricht Treaty setting strict fiscal eligibility criteria for entering European Monetary Union, and a heavy debt burden appear to have driven the adjustment of public expenditure. Total expenditure declined from over 60 to 51 percent of GDP. However, the reform package consisted of a number of marginal policy adjustments rather than bold changes in the country's policy regime. After 1996 there was little further progress in reducing public expenditure.

Finland

In the aftermath of a severe recession in the early 1990s, the development of public finances in Finland has been characterized by strict expenditure restraint. As a result, the general government expenditure-to-GDP ratio declined from its peak of 60 percent in 1993 to an estimated 51 percent in 1998. This outcome was achieved by modest annual increases in expenditure, averaging about 2 percent, in real terms, over the period 1994–8, while real GDP increased by almost 5 percent on average over the same period. Consequently, the cumulative increase in real expenditure of about 11 percent since 1993 was more than offset by real GDP growth of about 27 percent.

The authorities estimated that in the absence of savings decisions by the government, central government expenditure in 1999 would have been higher by about 3.5 percent of 1999 GDP. Almost one-third of this is attributed to a reduction in central government transfers to local governments, which resulted in considerable expenditure cuts by the latter, albeit to a lesser extent than the reduction in transfers. The additional cuts were achieved largely in income transfers to households and in subsidies to firms.

Ireland

One of the most impressive reductions in public expenditure among OECD countries was achieved by Ireland between 1983 and 1994. A staggering public debt of 130 percent of GDP, high unemployment, and low growth and the emerging common market project gave rise to a public consensus in the mid-1980s that fiscal consolidation was urgently needed. Later, the Maastricht Treaty and its convergence criteria provided an additional strong external incentive for Ireland to get its fiscal house in order by scaling back the role of the state and reducing public spending. Thus, to some extent, Ireland followed the experience of New Zealand and Chile, where major economic and fiscal reform became politically feasible. After 1994, however, the fiscal position only improved slowly despite almost double-digit growth, and some concerns about more lax expenditure policies have emerged.

Irish total expenditure declined from 53 percent of GDP in 1983 to 43.8 percent in 1994. As in New Zealand, reductions in subsidies and transfers contributed the lion's share by declining from over 30 percent of GDP to 23.4 percent of GDP. Eligibility for social security benefits was tightened, and targeting was improved, while the real value of benefits was frozen. Significant reforms in the provision of government services also featured prominently. Reforms included, for example, a reduction in the size of the civil service by 8 percent, a significant cut in housing and producer subsidies, and an increase in user fees for universities and hospital care. Capital spending was linked to the availability of funds from the EU. Fiscal retrenchment also resulted in a decline in interest payments by 3 percent of GDP.

Higher growth and small fiscal deficits made possible a reduction in public debt to less than 70 percent of GDP in 1997, thereby approaching the Maastricht limit of 60 percent of GDP. Tax cuts also became possible. The top marginal income tax rate was reduced from over 60 to 48 percent and the standard value-added tax (VAT) rate came down by 3 percent to 21 percent. Most investment in manufacturing has been subject to a profit tax of only 10 percent.

The Irish experience shows that reduction in public spending does not have damaging consequences for social welfare or macroeconomic stability. After the reform program started, strong economic growth resumed. This experience is consistent with that of some other countries that experienced consumption and investment booms rather than recession after substantial fiscal consolidation (see Perotti, 1998; and Alesina and Perotti, 1996b).

The Netherlands

In the Netherlands, fiscal policy changes coupled with labor market and other structural reforms were similarly successful in bringing down public spending. Public spending fell by a remarkable 10 percent of GDP from its peak of almost 60 percent of GDP in 1982 to less than 50 percent of GDP in 1996. At the same time, the budget deficit declined from over 6 percent to about 2 percent of GDP. Economic growth revived and unemployment came down markedly. Some observers, especially in continental Europe, have started looking at the Netherlands as a model of government reform, talking of the "Dutch miracle."

Institutional reform started in 1983 with a time path for deficit reduction coupled with revenue ceilings. This forced the government to achieve the envisaged declines in the deficit through expenditure reductions. In 1994, a medium-term expenditure plan was introduced putting ceilings on central government, social security, and health care spending. Higher-than-expected revenue, which allowed higher expenditure in the pre-1994 period, has to translate into lower taxes and lower deficits while the expenditure ceiling remains unchanged.

Reforms of expenditure programs included public sector wage restraint and a small cut in the size of the civil service. Reductions in official lending and capital transfers to enterprises contributed to reorienting public expenditure policies and to bringing down public spending. The Netherlands also introduced important reforms in the social sectors. The replacement rate on unemployment and disability was reduced from 80 percent to 70 percent and eligibility for disability benefits was tightened. This helped to cut the link between the growth of benefits and of average wages. In health care, contractual arrangements were changed and specialists whose expenses are difficult to control increasingly became employed by hospitals and were thus paid well-defined salaries. The use of generic drugs and discounted drugs as negotiated between insurers and industries was encouraged.

The Dutch pension system could also provide some guidance to policymakers in other industrialized countries. For a long time, it has relied on a strong occupational and fully funded pillar that complements the moderate benefits from the government's pay-as-you-go scheme.

Portugal

Portugal introduced important fiscal and economic reforms in the 1980s. For some of these reforms Portugal could probably serve as a model for European transition economies.[8] In the early 1980s, support for public enterprises and high interest payments burdened the budget. This gave rise to destabilizing fiscal deficits of almost 10 percent of GDP. Since then, Portugal has moved from a quasi-

---

8. See *Frankfurter Allgemeine Zeitung*, March 9, 1996.

socialist economy, with large fiscal deficits and large public ownership to a market economy with sound public finances. These reforms considerably reduced the role of the state. However, they did not translate into major expenditure reductions because social spending was increased.[9]

Fiscal reforms included both institutional and policy reforms. Nominal ceilings on primary expenditure, strengthened authorization procedures, and ex-post control laid the institutional foundations for fiscal consolidation. In addition, the quality of debt management was improved considerably. Government involvement in industry, utilities, and transport declined notably through an extensive privatization program. By the mid-1990s, privatization proceeds had reached 9 percent of GDP, third, as shares of GDP, after the United Kingdom and New Zealand among OECD countries.

Sweden

In the early 1990s, Sweden faced problems similar to those encountered by Ireland in the early 1980s. High fiscal deficits and rising public debt coincided with slow growth and growing unemployment. Although not as dramatically as in Ireland, Sweden cut public spending from 70 percent to 63 percent of GDP through important fiscal reforms.

Weak expenditure control and the absence of strict budget ceilings had exacerbated the dramatic deterioration of the fiscal position in Sweden in the early 1990s. In response, nominal overall expenditure ceilings on a three-year rolling basis were introduced. Overspending in one area then required compensatory savings somewhere else. This system was refined in 1997 when separate ceilings were introduced on state, local government, and pension budgets. Monthly monitoring of spending and semiannual reporting to parliament further strengthened fiscal discipline.

Sweden also started to tackle its much extended welfare state. However, it focused on cost-cutting measures rather than on systemic reform. The government reduced the replacement ratio for unem-

---

9. See the *Financial Times* survey from February 22, 1994, and the *Euromoney* survey from March 1994 for a review Portugal's modernization efforts, including public finances and privatization.

ployment benefits, sick pay, and parental leave, changed the indexation of pensions, and cut child allowances and family support.

United Kingdom

In the United Kingdom, significant fiscal and structural reforms were introduced by the Thatcher government in the 1980s. Among them, the United Kingdom's privatization program has been probably one of the most far-reaching privatization programs in history. It did not stop at traditional public enterprises such as steel, telecommunications, or railway operation. Many former public services were privatized.[10] The Private Finance Initiative, in which private companies finance, provide, and operate investment projects, became the main instrument for implementing capital projects identified by government. This initiative is also a good example of how changes in fiscal institutions and management spill over into expenditure policies and help making government policies more prioritized and efficient. Very large privatization proceeds helped reduce public debt. Furthermore, tax revenue from privatized enterprises started contributing positively to the budget.

Reform of the welfare system also featured prominently. Social security reform tackled the problem of implicit pension liabilities and addressed some of the shortcomings of the National Health Service. The reformed pension system provides very modest tax-financed public benefits. These can be complemented by private pension insurance. The private component is typically fully funded and is based on occupational savings plans. Individual retirement accounts (in a system similar to the one in the United States) can also complement the public pension. Private health insurance was allowed to provide some competition to the national health service, which still provides publicly financed services for everybody. In addition, cost control was strengthened through performance and output-based contracts between the National Health Service and health care providers.

10. See Bishop, Kay, and Mayer (1994, 1995) for a thorough discussion of the United Kingdom's privatization program, the regulatory challenge, shortcomings and strengths of the programs, and economic effects. See also Gómez-Ibáñez and Meyer (1993) for some case studies on British privatization in infrastructure. This study also looks at some of the pioneering private sector involvement in road financing, construction, and operation in France and Spain.

Fiscal reforms initially reduced public spending quite dramatically, from 45 percent of GDP in 1983 to 37.5 percent in 1989. This allowed a considerable reduction in marginal income tax rates and still reduced the public debt and fiscal deficits. However, public expenditure crept up again rapidly in the early 1990s. In 1996, total public expenditure was only 2 percent below its previous peak in 1983, and subsidies and transfers were just as high as they had been before the Thatcher reforms. Clearly, the reforms of the 1980s were not fundamental enough, which may in part be due to the characteristics of the English political system.[11]

United States

Fiscal rules and constitutional deficit limits experienced a renaissance in the 1990s. In the United States, a number of balanced-budget amendments were brought before Congress, but they were rejected. However, most U.S. states have to balance their respective budgets annually.

European Union

The European Union itself is not allowed to incur debt, and member countries have ratified formal deficit limits for members of the European Monetary Union under the Stability and Growth Pact. The European Union is watched particularly carefully because of the poor fiscal record of some of its member countries and the fear that lax fiscal policies by individual governments could result in difficulties for the Union.

The EU Stability and Growth Pact shows the importance of institutional underpinnings for the credibility of fiscal rules. Not only does it foresee numerical targets, but it also defines very clear procedural rules to strengthen its credibility. The pact obliges member governments to aim at balanced budgets, or even at surpluses, as medium-term objectives. Cyclical output variations should not result in a breach of the Maastricht deficit limit of 3 percent of GDP. The EU Commission monitors fiscal performance of member governments and makes proposals on penalties if the 3 percent limit is exceeded.

---

11. Mullard (1993) describes the British reforms and their shortcomings from a political economy perspective.

Waivers for penalties have to be approved by the EU Council of Ministers, the main forum of EU member governments. Countries in trouble will have to submit "stability programs" to the European Union months before they go to parliament. After a ten-month warning period, "delinquent governments" will have to make large non–interest-bearing deposits to the European Union, which would turn into fines after two years. The deposits would be between 0.2 percent of GDP (when the deficit exceeds 3 percent of GDP) up to a maximum of 0.5 percent of GDP (for a deficit of 6 percent or more). "Temporary and exceptional circumstances" would allow a deviation from the deficit limit without penalty. Countries are exempted from paying penalties on excessive fiscal deficits only when output declines by more than 2 percent of GDP in the previous 12 months. If output declines between 0.75 and 2 percent, governments can plead a special case to the EU Council of Ministers.[12]

Another deterrent to lax fiscal behavior has also been agreed on. The European Commission will alert member countries publicly when they become liable for penalties. The reputational costs from such public announcements are expected to prevent "bad" policies in the first place or at least to increase pressure for sounder policies and fiscal reform.

4. FISCAL REFORM IN SELECTED NEWLY INDUSTRIALIZED COUNTRIES

Newly industrialized countries have been much more successful than OECD countries in reducing the scope of government or in keeping government small from the outset. In the case of Chile we saw how well-conceived government reforms can contribute to promoting economic growth and social welfare while sharply reducing public spending. A few other countries have achieved major reforms in the past decade as well, and we only want to mention four in this place: Argentina, Mauritius, Malaysia, and Singapore.[13]

12. A detailed discussion of the implications of the Maastricht Treaty and the Stability and Growth Pact for assessing sustainability and credibility of the public finances can be found in Perotti, Strauch, and Von Hagen (1998).
13. The financial crisis in Southeast Asia in 1997–8 has temporarily cast a different light on some of these countries. In this discussion we focus on longer trends.

Table X.3. *Public Expenditure Development and Government Reform: Selected Newly Industrialized Countries* (Percent of GDP)[a]

	Argentina		Malaysia		Mauritius	
	1985	1994	1982	1995	1980–1	1995–6
Public expenditure						
Total expenditure	26.3	22.5	44.7	22.6	36.4	25.4
Government consumption	10.3[b]	13.0[b]	. . .	9.6	12.7	10.4
Interest[c]	5.9	1.2	. . .	3.0	5.0	3.2
Transfers and subsidies[c]	6.8[d]	5.4[d]	. . .	5.1	9.1	7.5
Capital expenditure[c]	3.3	2.9	18.7	5.0	9.7	4.9
Overall fiscal balance	−5.1	−1.2	−16.9	1.2	−14.0	−2.9
Main fiscal reform areas:	Privatization; civil service; social security		Privatization, incl. infrastructure investment; government employment		Consumer and producer subsidies; civil service	

Sources: Tanzi and Schuknecht (1997); and IMF, *Mauritius: Background Papers and Statistical Annex* (1996); IMF, *Thailand, Statistical Appendix* (1996).
[a] The table typically compares the year of maximum public expenditure with the most recent available data or closest year available.
[b] Includes transfers to provinces.
[c] Central government data, except Argentina and Malaysia.
[d] Mainly pensions.

Argentina

For a long time, Argentina was perceived as one of the great tragedies in world economic development. It had slipped from being one of the richest countries in the world to one of the most regulated and stagnant economies, with a large public enterprise sector, high public debt, and public finances often out of control. The reforms of the early 1990s significantly changed this picture through stabilization and liberalization. Public expenditure declined from 26.3 percent of GDP in 1985 to 22.5 percent in 1994, reaching a level close to that of Chile or of the East-Asian newly industrialized countries (Table 10.3).

Argentina introduced far-reaching expenditure policy reforms. Important public enterprises including utilities, transportation, telecommunications, and petroleum were privatized. Public employment at the national level was sharply reduced, partly through the elimination of functions. Health and education were decentralized, and provincial finances (which had run up significant debt and deficits before) were being controlled more tightly than in the past. The privatization of formerly public services generally brought major improvements in their quality.[14] Pension reform was partly based on the Chilean model. It reduced the fiscal pressure from an aging population by raising the retirement age to sixty-five years and by introducing a new fully funded privately managed pillar.

Mauritius

Mauritius is probably one of the least known countries that experienced rapid economic growth after major government reform in the past decade. Until the late 1970s, Mauritius suffered from repeated downturns in the sugar sector, high fiscal deficits, and high unemployment. However, a political and social consensus was gradually built for the need of radical changes in economic and fiscal policies. At the outset of reform, in 1980–1, public expenditure exceeded 36 percent of GDP and the fiscal deficit was 14 percent of GDP. As a result of major reforms, within a few years public expenditure had come down by 10 percent of GDP, while growth and employment creation accelerated. Reforms included conservative wage and employment policies and lower producer and generalized consumer subsidies. In addition, the government liberalized the economy and restructured a number of public enterprises.[15]

Malaysia

Malaysia experienced a similar degree of destabilization as Mauritius in the early 1980s. In 1982, public expenditure stood at almost 45 percent of GDP and the fiscal deficit was almost 17 percent of GDP

14. Reforms of expenditure policies in Latin America are discussed in Burki and Perry (1997) and Inter-American Development Bank (1997).
15. Literature on the Mauritian reforms is very scarce. A brief description is provided in Gulhati and Nallari (1990). See *Financial Times* Surveys from September 14, 1992 and September 27, 1994, which include a useful description of the overall economic situation of the country after successful reform. *Financial Times* from February 12, 1997 mentions the potential for further reform of the civil service and the welfare system.

while public investment absorbed a staggering 18.7 percent of GDP. Malaysia managed to turn around its policies, and by 1995 spending had fallen to half the level of the early 1980s. Public spending reached 22.6 percent of GDP, similar to the levels prevailing in other newly industrialized countries, and the budget was in surplus. In addition to reform, rapid growth helped achieve such impressive expenditure reductions. Most importantly, the government brought significant deregulation to the economy and reduced its direct engagement in many activities. Public investment spending came down significantly, and Malaysia pioneered privately financed capital projects in areas traditionally reserved for the public sector, such as roads or water supplies. The government was also successful in improving public enterprise performance. A number of public enterprises were privatized and the remaining ones were commercialized with considerable private sector equity participation. Conservative wage and employment policies also kept public spending at bay.[16]

Unfortunately, in 1997 Malaysia was affected by the financial crisis that hit Southeast Asia. It also started engaging in more controversial economic policies, including strong interventions in financial policies and capital controls. It remains to be seen whether Malaysia can regain its good record in economic policy in the years to come.

Singapore

Singapore may be a good example of how to avoid fiscal problems in the first place. Singapore has kept its government small and efficient since its existence and its economy has been considered one of the most competitive and free to operate in. This country has also been remarkably successful at reducing corruption. In 1992, public employment constituted only 4 percent of Singapore's labor force, a sign of a very lean administration. At the same time, its well-paid civil servants have a very good reputation for honesty and efficiency. Budgetary subsidies to public enterprises were avoided because they had to largely finance themselves. Singapore was among the first

16. See *Financial Times* surveys from September 19, 1995 and June 19, 1996 and Parker (1994) for a useful discussion of public expenditure policies and privatization in Malaysia. See also *Asiamoney* (1994) for private sector involvement in construction and infrastructure projects.

countries to charge user fees for the use of (formerly congested) inner-city roads. This reduced the need for costly road building.

The most interesting feature of Singapore's economy is the Central Provident Fund, which was put in place in 1955. The Central Provident Fund is a compulsory savings scheme with individual accounts to which employees and employers contribute. Originally, the objective was to finance a basic retirement income, but it has grown into a saving vehicle to finance housing, health, or investment outlays as well. This fully funded scheme has relieved the budget of much of the social security expenditure pressure that industrialized economies are experiencing (Bercuson, 1995). However, the account has lost much of its transparency because of the confidentiality with which the funds are invested.

5. CONCLUDING REMARKS

Our short survey indicates that the role of the state declined in several countries since the early 1980s. Our review of public expenditure in many countries has convinced us that 30 percent of GDP may be a reasonable target for public spending in industrial countries. This is, of course, only an indicative target that can be used as a general reference for industrial countries. One would expect that some countries would aim at a higher and some at a lower figure. Newly industrialized countries may be well advised to maintain the public spending level at about 20 percent of GDP. Models for radical reforms aimed at reducing public spending are now available from a variety of countries. These models can show hesitant policymakers and special interest groups that reforms can work and can provide considerable benefits when seriously and consistently adopted. The common experience seems to be that the citizens of countries that have reformed their governments do not want to go back to the old ways. (See Rodrik, 1996.) In fact, the remarkable thing is the way the public now backs the new programs in the countries that undertook them.

XI Fiscal Reform in the Public Debate

1. THE PROMINENCE OF FISCAL REFORM IN THE PUBLIC DEBATE

The public debate in industrial countries shows a keen awareness of the fiscal problems and recognizes the need for substantial changes in government programs. All major international financial and economic newspapers provide almost daily coverage of fiscal issues and of reform proposals. It is also rare now to find politicians running for election on a platform to increase the level of public spending. Of course, some groups or individuals would still like to have their own pet spending increased, but at the cost of someone else's reduction rather than through an increase in the total. Even relatively left-leaning governments, such as the French, Italian, and British governments of 1998, were advocating reductions in, or at least better control of, public spending.

Fiscal deficits, high public debt, and high public spending are seen at times as reasons why growth is sluggish, real interest rates and unemployment are high, and some social problems are getting worse. There are no Galbraiths at this time arguing that total public spending should increase. The climate has really changed from recent decades. To give a feel for the prevalent current mood, we shall cite from some influential newspapers. This is, of course, far from a scientific approach. Still, newspapers, better than anything else, reflect the current thinking. Obviously we can only cite selectively.

In the *Independent* of October 1, 1996, McRae pointed out that fewer than 10 countries in the world (out of almost 200 countries) had a fiscal surplus in 1995 and argued that this was an indication of "system failure for the world." He went on to write that: "Something is very wrong with the way that tax and spending policies are determined throughout the developed world." Along the same lines, in a January 6, 1996 editorial, the *Financial Times* (*FT*) suggested that "everybody has got a fiscal problem, the US has one, Europe has one, and now even Japan has one." Policymakers around the world have also acknowledged the need for tackling high public spending levels and fiscal deficits. President Bill Clinton, for example, made balancing the federal budget the first priority of his second term as president;[1] and French President Jacques Chirac criticized the unfortunate fiscal habits of EU countries and demanded that the "perverse system" of chronic deficits be "broken" (Agence France Press, November 19, 1996).

In its commentaries, the international press has also been lamenting the excessive role of the government in the economy and stressing the need for significant reform: "High spending, taxes and deficits, and excessive regulation undermine individual liberty and self reliance, and discourage private sector initiative" (*Frankfurter Allgemeine Zeitung*, March 8, 1997). "Public spending has reached levels which governments are unable or unwilling to cover by taxation, and public debt has sky-rocketed. Policymakers know that they have to tighten their belts as they will not be allowed to inflate or tax out of these problems without punishment" (*FT*, January 6, 1996). International organizations, such as the IMF, "urge an assault on public borrowing" (*FT*, April 18, 1996), and central banks urge cutting budget deficits (*FT*, August 14, 1996). "Reinventing government," a popular buzzword in America, has crossed the Atlantic as well (see *FT,* July 26, 1996). While in the United States some government critics object to almost any government activity, more moderate forces typically demand a "leaner but not meaner" state.

The media agrees that there is ample scope for reforming and downsizing the government.[2] Even left-leaning publications, such as

---

1. An exceptionally strong U.S. economy and some policy changes gave him a balanced budget much earlier than anticipated. In contrast, the fiscal situation in Japan has deteriorated considerably in recent years.
2. See, for example, the survey on "The Future of the State," in *The Economist* of September 20, 1997.

the influential German weekly, *Der Spiegel*, have argued that government is doing too much too inefficiently. *Der Spiegel* (May 13, 1996) reported that Arthur D. Little, a management consulting firm, analyzed the German government like a company in crisis and identified savings of 8 percent of GDP that could be realized within four years. *These savings could be achieved without cutting social services*, through government reorganization according to modern management principles and through the elimination of redundant personnel.

"[It is] time to change the rules of the fiscal game" as "fiscal responsibility is the mood of the hour," McRae argues in the same *Independent* commentary mentioned above. After monetary policy reform in the 1980s, when monetary targets and greater central bank independence took away monetary discretion from politicians and brought back low rates of inflation, the 1990s have seen the beginning of a similar process in the fiscal area which is likely to continue well into the next millennium. Strict rules or even independent bodies may be created to oversee the budgetary process, and social security funds may be separated from the budget and freed from political interference. Downsizing of public expenditure programs and institutional reform are both seen as essential as governments try to "sail" between the Scylla of unforgiving capital markets and the Charybdis of resisting special interests when promoting their reform programs. International trade and globalization may induce in particular the European countries to reduce the size of their governments.[3] If the debate of the past years is a good indicator of what is actually going to be the future role of the state, we are likely to see more reform in future years than is now taking place, and forceful attempts at reducing public spending.

The debate on government reform, however, still reflects an international imbalance. While the Anglo-Saxon world strongly and generally favors smaller governments and a market economy, continental Europe seems to have more apprehension about globalization and less faith in the virtues of the market. Especially in France, resistance to reform remains deep. For example, the influential French sociologist, Pierre Bourdieu (1993), has rejected the "false internationalism of the markets" and the notion that policies must be reformed to gain

3. See Harold James, *The Times* (January 25, 1997) and *The Economist*, September 20, 1997, p. 34. However, *The Economist* believes that big government may survive in a globalized world.

the trust of international investors. Instead, he demands a European welfare state *which prevents such competition*. In a book that became an international bestseller, Viviane Forrester (1996), a French professional writer, decried the "Economic Horror" of recent economic developments that give supremacy to the market-oriented current liberal view. In her not very convincing essay, she states repeatedly but without much analysis that globalization and the market will rob workers of their jobs and dignity. Jobs will simply disappear, and labor will cease to have economic value and workers will come to feel useless. She does not ask the question of who will buy the products produced if the workers do not have an income.

The 1997 elections in France brought a socialist government back to power on the promise of old-style regulation and interventionism to deal with fiscal problems and with the growing international competition. However, the new government seems to be unwilling to repeat the mistakes of the past as far as fiscal issues are concerned. For example, in an interview in *Le Monde* of April 21, 1998 (pp. 6–7), the French Prime Minister, Lionel Jospin stated that:

To create fiscal deficits is not a characteristic of leftist policies. From 1993 to 1997 public debt increased from less than 40 percent of GDP to about 60 percent of GDP. To feed the debt is to damage the future. . . . To service the increasing interest payments is to service rents. . . . The 1999 budget must allow us a well-controlled progression of public expenditure, a reduction in the fiscal deficit, and a favorable action vis-à-vis employment. (our translation)

In the same interview, Jospin also states the need to control expenditures for pensions and health. These statements from the leader of a leftist government would have been unthinkable a decade ago.

With all its rhetoric, the debate in France has clearly identified the need for public sector reform (Bismut and Jacquet, 1997), but fears of the excesses of globalization (*Figaro*, March 19, 1997) seem more prevalent in France than in other countries. In Germany and Italy, much debate is focusing on the challenges of fiscal reform, and some important genuine changes are taking place. However, in all of these countries, some outdated recipes from the past continue to attract some following or even trigger some reform proposals: The former German Finance Minister, Oskar Lafontaine, for example, argued that supply-side policies have failed and "we cannot allow globalization to undermine the German social security system" (*Business Week*, February 24, 1997). One of the first measures of the new social democratic government in fall 1998 was to reverse the modest welfare and labor market reforms introduced by its predecessor. However, Mr. Lafontaine resigned because his views were not shared by the rest of the government. And Sandro Bertinotti, the Secretary of the Italian Communist Party still sees the solution to the unemployment problem through a reduction to thirty-five hours in the work week and the creation of publicly financed jobs. He also opposes privatization of large public enterprises.

2. THE DEBATE ON DEFICIT AND SPENDING LIMITS

Much of the debate on fiscal reform focuses on global spending or on deficit limits, and many governments have announced ambitious objectives for reform, typically suggesting near-balanced budgets or considerable spending reductions or both.

United States

In the United States, the president and Congress agreed to balance the federal budget by 2002, but a strong economy and a booming stock market gave them such an outcome much earlier. In that country, the demands for reform, even by some major political figures, are probably the most extreme of any industrial country – despite the fact that in the United States, public spending is relatively low by international standards. In 1995–6, a major effort to balance the budget and to reduce the size of government was launched by the Republican Party. The "Contract with America," as presented by then majority leader Newt Gingrich, claimed: "we sincerely believe we can reduce spending and at the same time make Government better" (*New York Times*, April 8, 1995).

The U.S. tax system has also been subjected to strong attacks even though the tax burden has changed little in several decades and the ratio of tax revenue to GDP is the lowest among industrial countries. Over recent years, there have been proposals to abolish the Internal Revenue Service, to abolish the income taxes, or to replace existing taxes with a flat rate tax, and there have been continuous calls for tax reductions. Vice President Gore, with the objective of "re-inventing the government," introduced several changes in the way the government operates. These changes have been made by many small steps rather than by major systemic reform. Nevertheless, the number of people working of the U.S. federal government has been reduced by a significant amount. Also, the number of people on welfare has fallen as the result of welfare reform.

In the United States, the debate over balancing the budget and introducing a balanced-budget rule was particularly heated in the winter of 1995–6. In principle, all parties seemed to agree on the objective of a balanced budget, but they disagreed on how to achieve it. One side wanted more revenue; the other wanted less spending and a tax reduction on top of that. The Republican-dominated Congress demanded that the budget be balanced in seven years (by the year 2002) and President Clinton consented (*New York Times*, November 25, 1995), but no *firm* plan for a balanced budget was put in place. Many of the spending cuts were left for the future to specify. A balanced budget amendment to the U.S. Constitution was voted down by a small margin in Congress. New rounds of negotiations and attempts to introduce such a constitutional rule can be expected, although at the moment the surplus in the fiscal accounts may have removed the urgency for such a rule.

EMU Countries

In 1995–8, the debate in Europe was dominated by the run-up to the European Monetary Union (EMU). Many of the EU countries oriented their budgetary policies toward the goal of passing the EMU entry hurdles.[4] We mentioned in the previous chapter that the European Union has introduced standards for future fiscal stability and has requested that a balanced budget be a "normal" deficit target. It remains to be seen what effect EMU membership will have on the level of public spending.

The debate on how to achieve lower deficits and spending limits in industrialized countries is surprisingly vivid and focused. It largely focuses on the "rules of the game" required to achieve these objectives. It has come a long way from the broad acceptance of deficit

---

4. The most important criteria were a fiscal deficit limit of 3 percent of GDP for the general government and a total debt ceiling of 60 percent of GDP. Convergence on interest rates and on inflation were also required.

spending in the 1970s and the 1980s. The erosion of constraints on fiscal policies facilitated the emergence of big governments and high deficits in past decades. Now, people are becoming more aware of the need for binding rules that would limit deficits and spending. In addition to the size of government, the quality of government services is targeted to improve. In Italy, for example, the quality of government services has been attracting serious debate for the first time in decades.

The need for institutional underpinnings that firmly and credibly will force governments to promote fiscal policy objectives is hotly debated as well. The stability pact in the European Union or the Fiscal Responsibility Act in New Zealand reflect attempts to introduce institutions that reduce politicians' discretion in fiscal policy and create a new fiscal order. Although the public debate is well focused on the main rules and objectives for fiscal policymaking, institutional details (for instance on the budgetary process and new management practices) receive relatively less attention.[5] This is due to the complexity of the issues, which are difficult to understand and to discuss, especially in the short space of newspaper articles. It is also due to the fact that expertise in these areas of public administration is very scarce. The fiscal institutions underlying the EU stability pact, however, have attracted a lot of attention.

EU Stability and Growth Pact

In the European Union, the debate on how to guarantee fiscal stability in the EMU is less colorful but equally intense.[6] In December 1996, EU member governments agreed on a "Stability and Growth Pact" to strengthen fiscal discipline and to prevent imbalances arising from large deficits in some member countries. The EU Stability and Growth Pact shows the importance of institutional underpinnings for the credibility of fiscal rules. Not only does it foresee numerical targets, it also defines very clear procedural rules to strengthen its credibility. (See also the previous chapter.)

---

5. Still, they are receiving much more attention than earlier especially in scholarly works. See, for example, Alesina and Perotti (1996a) and Banca d'Italia (1994). Also, the work of the OECD in this area has been noticeable.
6. See Lionel Barber in the *Financial Times*, October 17, 1996 on the European Commission's debate about post-EMU budgetary discipline. The final terms of the Stability and Growth Pact were decided on at the EU summit in Dublin in December 1996.

Most EU countries had to struggle to achieve the Maastricht criterion of a 3 percent deficit, and, for a while, it seemed that only few countries would be able to comply. Since the introduction of the euro on January 1, 1999 it appears that the European Union will grasp this unique opportunity to impose quasi-constitutional constraints, on fiscal policies, that strengthen fiscal discipline. The stability pact, therefore, should promote confidence in fiscal stability in the European Union over the medium and long run.[7] This will set an important precedent for other countries struggling with similar problems.

Institutional reform to strengthen fiscal discipline is not limited to industrial countries. In fact, balanced budgets or even fiscal surpluses have become more common in the past couple of years. In Latin America, institutional constraints against government profligacy have been introduced or are being debated. And, as mentioned earlier, there have been calls by a number of influential economists for an independent fiscal council for Latin America.[8]

3. EXPENDITURE POLICIES IN THE PUBLIC DEBATE

In the current discussion of public spending programs, social security has dominated the political debate. "Government is not a cow which is fed in heaven and milked on earth," German Chancellor Kohl argued; he demanded "real and fundamental reforms" of the German welfare state (*Der Spiegel*, 20/96). Other expenditure issues such as the size of the civil service, the extent of industrial subsidies, the role of the private sector in traditionally public investment, or the control of local and regional expenditure have taken the back bench as the welfare state has come under attack in many countries. However, it should be noted that privatization was at the center of attention during much of the 1980s, and it continues to be so in countries such as France and Italy. The fact that in other countries privatization receives less attention now than in the 1980s is a sign that the debate

7. Efforts to water down the Stability and Growth Pact have resurfaced in some quarters. Of course, only time will tell whether the rules will not be changed again, or whether they will ultimately be enforced.
8. See Eichengreen, Hausmann, and Von Hagen (1996) and the *Financial Times*, March 25, 1996

in this area has been largely settled in favor of a smaller role in production for government.

Social Spending Reform

Reforming social spending is a much more controversial issue than reducing fiscal deficits and public debts. High payroll taxes, high health care costs, and high unemployment costs have created a broad (but still often diffuse) awareness that fundamental change is necessary.[9] The possibility that these elements may promote an underground economy and higher official unemployment has also attracted growing attention. Welfare reform plans have often made front page news, sometimes with dramatic headlines. Headlines read: France is launching private complementary pension insurance and overhauls its health system (*FT*, September 16 and September 25, 1996); public pension debate rages in Spain (*FT*, February 24, 1995); war on welfare saves millions (in the United Kingdom) (*FT*, April 13, 96); budget cuts hit frontline of Sweden's welfare system (*FT*, January 24, 1995), Finland [is] united around a [ ] package of spending cuts, (and) unemployment, sickness and child benefits will be among the main casualties (*FT*, April 11, 1995). The United States has grappled with pressures for welfare reform and with continuing social problems including the fact that a large share of the population is without health insurance while health costs have been rising dramatically and are the highest among countries. The aim of the welfare reform program in the United States has been to reduce aid dependency while maintaining basic safety nets.

Even though, so far, reforms have mostly been limited to relatively marginal changes in benefits and eligibility, rather than to systemic changes in the way social security is provided, the debate is heated and involves all groups of society. However, an increasing number of voices is demanding more fundamental reform, more private sector involvement, and a return to basic social safety nets instead of cradle-to-grave security. These demands are made largely on the grounds of strengthening self-reliance, long-term sustainability of social security

---

9. See for example the *FT* commentary from December 29, 1995, which argues that Germans like their social security system, which has brought peace and prosperity since its implementation during Bismarck's time, but which they know is becoming unaffordable.

systems, and economic growth. Also, the increasing sophistication of the market and globalization will allow individuals to protect themselves against some risk through the private sector. For example, globalization may allow individuals to buy abroad insurance against some risks.

Privatization

The privatization of public enterprises and a growing private sector participation in government-planned investment and public services seems widely accepted. In the United Kingdom, a political consensus emerged that the country's Private Finance Initiative will be the main vehicle for the funding of new capital projects with private companies building, financing and operating the projects (*FT Survey*, October 18, 1996). In Germany, privatization of state enterprises is also proceeding, and the public discussion focuses on the expected returns for private investors rather than on the social, political, or economic repercussions associated with it.

In France, much of the nationalizations of the socialist government in the early 1980s was reversed as awareness grew that government is not well able to manage public enterprises in many sectors. The shift in public opinion on this issue is quite remarkable, as reflected, for instance, in an article in *Le Monde*, one of the public opinion leaders. On October 8, 1996, *Le Monde* wrote that "the solutions of public powers to deal with public enterprises in crisis are too late, badly prepared, and mostly inappropriate." Especially in the banking sector, the Treasury "lacks the tools for evaluating modern banks." The left-leaning government that came into power in 1997, however, has taken a more neutral or more guarded stand vis-à-vis privatization.

Wage and Employment Policies

Government wage and employment policies, raise surprisingly little public debate, given the increase in the size of the civil service in recent decades and the budgetary pressures everywhere. For a long time public employment was used as a way to reduce unemployment, and most countries are still reluctant to reduce public employment for fear that the unemployment rate would go up. Except, perhaps, for Australia, where the civil service has shrunken considerably and further cuts are planned in the near future, basically no OECD government has tried to tackle high spending and deficits with major reductions in public employment. However, as already mentioned, there has been a significant fall in public employment in the United States. Even shrinking the civil service through attrition is not popular. The French government, for example, faced stiff union opposition on the modest plan to reduce the civil service by 6,000 staff, or 0.3 percent, through natural attrition in its 1997 budget. The Italian government has faced strong resistance in its attempt to streamline the railroad and the airline companies. Spain's attempts to reduce spending by freezing civil service wages in its 1997 budget were strongly opposed by the civil service unions. The Finnish government's plan to reduce the number of provincial government authorities ran into considerable political resistance despite its small effects on employment and costs. Given the timid and slow efforts to shrink the public sector work force in OECD countries, and the political resistance against such modest action, it is remarkable that some Latin American and African governments have managed to reduce the size of public sector employment very rapidly. Countries such as Argentina and, of course, Australia might provide future guidance on how this objective is achieved.

Subsidies

Another issue that raises occasional public debate or even upheaval is public subsidies to enterprises and farmers. Typically it is the workforce of subsidized enterprises that protests against the reduction in subsidies to the enterprises, and it is the competition that protests against the continuation of these subsidies. Subsidies for the French, Spanish, and Italian state airlines, for the coal industry in West Germany, and for all the industry in East Germany, or for agriculture throughout the European Union, have periodically come under political and public scrutiny. The European Union has tried to reduce the financial costs and the political repercussions from government subsidies. All state subsidies need to be approved by the EU Commission, following strict criteria. However, the power of the European Union is limited in this context. Thus, subsidies continue to be given as member governments find it politically opportune to pressure the

European Union for "exemptions" for their ailing industries and agriculture, often on grounds that the removal of subsidies would lead to higher unemployment at a time when the unemployment rate is very high.

Implications for Tax Reform

When President Reagan promised to finance large tax cuts with equivalent spending cuts, some experts expected that record fiscal deficits would follow for the United States. Similar fears can arise when European political forces promise major tax cuts to be matched by yet largely unrealized or even identified expenditure cuts. In the United States tax cuts have remained common campaign promises. The 1996 presidential campaign, for example, saw the Republicans promise significant tax cuts. One quarter of these were to be financed from higher economic growth (*New York Times*, August 6, 1996, or *FT* August 6, 1996). In 1999 there is again pressure for cutting taxes. Income tax reductions have been popular promises in France, Italy, and, to some extent, in Germany.

In spite of the rhetoric, the situation in the late 1990s is nevertheless much different from that in the early 1980s. Privatization and welfare reform have started in many countries, generating some scope for public expenditure reduction and for tax cuts in coming years. In addition, international tax competition will force some declines in tax rates and will impose some international constraints (such as those imposed by the EU Stability and Growth Pact or even by IMF surveillance) which will make it difficult for countries to lower revenue without matching spending cuts. In light of this, pressure to cut taxes may actually increase the pressure on governments to cut spending. Thus, plans to overhaul tax systems and to reduce marginal rates may be realized in tandem with expenditure cuts.

4. IMPLEMENTATION OF REFORMS: BETWEEN GLOBALIZATION AND VESTED INTERESTS

Globalization

We mentioned the favorable role international commitments can play to strengthen fiscal discipline. We have also mentioned the political trade-off for governments between sending "good" signals to international financial markets and giving in to the special interests when considering policy reform. Financial markets react positively to good reforms, and reward governments with low interest rates and stable exchange rates. The announcement of the 1997 budget in Australia, for example, was well received by financial markets and the yield on ten-year bonds declined by 16 basis points. The sharp reduction in the fiscal deficit in Italy in 1997 brought a significant decline in real interest rates. Similar effects on long-term bond yields have been registered in many European countries as the chances for realizing EMU and post-EMU fiscal stability increased. Thus, financial markets are a good barometer and, more importantly, they have become a "pressure group" in favor of fiscal discipline and appropriate government reform.

In the future the influence of financial markets is likely to become stronger especially amongst the EMU countries, when countries can have different credit ratings and different interest rates on their public debt. The single European currency will make the perception of national government policies by financial markets much more transparent. This will introduce a new element of beneficial competition among national governments within EMU. Citizens and companies will be able to choose more easily among the countries on the basis of their policy regimes.

A positive verdict from the international financial markets can also have important indirect effects on government popularity. Lower interest rates, or a favorable investment climate, can raise employment and real wages. Lower inflation can enhance the popularity of governments. However, many of these beneficial effects are mainly realized in the long run, once the credibility of the reforms has been established and the reaction by economic agents has translated into more favorable outcomes. The public debate has also taken notice of these effects, as the media report the beneficial effect of government reform in reforming countries and debate the applicability and effect of these reforms for other countries.

Resistance from Special Interests

"Everybody knows that what we need is to cut benefits and start shifting some of the costs of welfare from the state to a private system. It is a crisis of political management," Mark Suzman quoted a German economist in an article entitled "Welfare System Sinks under Its Weight" (*FT*, April 14, 1996). But, despite this presumed general knowledge, resistance against reform is still widespread, and not only in the area of pensions. Pension reform is particularly risky before elections because of the political power of retirees and, often, the opposition of labor unions. Employment or subsidy reductions often provoke immediate and sometimes violent resistance by well-organized special interests which can threaten the authority of governments.

When farmers spill milk in front of national parliaments or the EU Commission, public sector workers paralyze countries' infrastructure, as in the winter of 1995 in France, or rioters demonstrate with sledge-hammers against austerity budgets, after the Australian 1997 budget was announced, or metal workers unions threaten with strike after relatively small reductions in sick pay, as in Germany in the fall of 1996, one can understand the pressure on governments to reverse or even not to start reform programs. In Germany, the government reform proposal to limit sick pay, to tighten pension eligibility, and to reduce employee protection created fierce opposition by unions and by the opposition social democratic party. Australian public servants struck after they heard of cuts in the Australian civil service and, similarly, French civil servants partly went on strike in October 1996, when the government announced a 0.2 percent cut in the size of the civil service. As a result of these strong actions, at times, by relatively small but well-organized groups, some of these reforms were shelved or postponed as politically infeasible.

Consensus Building

Although strong political will by the government is required, major investment in consensus building and careful packaging of reforms seem to have worked better than a purely confrontational approach. Fairly broad public consensus over far-reaching reforms in New Zealand, Ireland, and Chile, has allowed major fiscal reforms to take place, reforms that constrain public spending and deficits and reduce the role of the state in many areas. This suggests that consensus building and broad-based public support are requirements essential for successful fiscal reform and reduction of long-term spending and deficits in democracies. Many governments have made considerable efforts to build such a consensus on austerity packages with opposition parties, trade unions, and employer associations. An agreed perception of the "fair" distribution of reform costs and benefits and the protection or compensation of vulnerable groups has often helped to achieve such consensus. As mentioned, New Zealand and Chile maintained minimum pensions and social safety nets during reform and improved the targeting of social expenditure.

A broad-based political debate and consensus building also raises the ex ante credibility of reform and the expected economic (and noneconomic) pay-off. This was one of the major strengths of the EU's single market project implemented between 1986 and 1992. The same strategy of political marketing and consensus building strengthened the prospects for EMU and made possible the subsequent Stability and Growth Pact as well.

The United States' experience with fiscal reform from the winter of 1995–6 is a good example of how things can go wrong when political diplomacy and consensus building are neglected. Everything seemed to be on the right course when the Republicans agreed with President Clinton on the need to balance the budget within seven years. However, it was less the fundamental differences on the future size and role of the federal government than the lack of willingness to compromise on particular points that ultimately resulted in the failure to reach an agreement. Perhaps dogmatism and lack of political sensitivity by one side, including a very unpopular three-week government shutdown, made it easy for the other side to stop the proposed "revolution." Entitlement reform was key to the Republican agenda to reduce spending and the deficit. But the costs of adjustment were perceived by the public to be distributed unevenly, and the government benefited from presenting the opposition as callous, pro-rich, and determined to cut spending on popular programs such as education, training, the environment, and poor children. The irony in this case was that a fiscal surplus was achieved in 1998 because of a booming economy and stock market. However, the surplus was made possible by a significant increase in tax revenue rather than by large falls in public spending.

Sometimes, however, political stamina and determined action seem necessary to overcome the resistance of special interests. Government persistence in the early Thatcher years certainly helped to establish and maintain a certain momentum of reform. In Germany, the failure to agree on major tax reform in 1997 and the policy reversal of 1998 shows the limits of consensus-based decision making despite widespread acceptance of the broad objectives of lower taxes, less spending, and deregulation. For too long, parties were used to painless changes that did not go very far, and the system became unable to deal with crisis or near-crisis situations. Regarding growing unemployment, high labor costs, excessive labor regulations, and the inability of the involved parties to agree on significant reforms, newspaper headlines commented: "German workplace consensus has failed" or "German work consensus turns to conflict" (*FT*, May 25, 1996).

Policy Regime

Last, but not least, we should reiterate the importance attached to changing the overall policy regime. In the countries that introduced far-reaching reform in their overall policy regimes, the benefits from reform were high, outweighing or at least reducing the costs from redistribution for many special interests. If reforms constitute a broad package with considerable long-term benefits, special interests may eventually come to agree to them. The vision of EMU with broader benefits and widespread fiscal stability enforced first by the Maastricht entry criteria, and then by the Stability and Growth Pact, is also probably one of the main reasons why resistance by national special interests to it has not been stronger. Perhaps a broader vision in reform programs in many continental European countries (instead of marginal reforms to meet the Maastricht targets) would also strengthen public support. This could help them to catch up with some of the Anglo-Saxon and emerging market countries that seem to be well ahead in reforming government and in reducing public spending.

5. CONCLUDING REMARKS

The public debate on government reform in industrialized countries has been and continues to be lively. By and large, and with some important exceptions, the need for government reform and for reducing the role of the state seems to be widely accepted. Reform of fiscal rules and of social spending features most prominently in the public debate, but many other issues from the creation of institutions to privatization and to public employment are also discussed. If ideas indeed matter more than special interests, as Keynes claimed, we should see the public debate on government reform followed by considerable action in the future. For sure, the voices that argued for increased public spending at some key historical moments, such as Keynes in 1927 and Galbraith in 1958, have fallen silent. On the other hand, the most strident voices today are those of individuals who would like the government to get out of the economy. We have argued that the governments should not give up on their fundamental objectives but should limit their activity to achieving these objectives and should attempt to do so more economically.

XII The Future of Public Spending

Part One of this study provided evidence on the growth of public spending in the industrialized countries for the period between 1870 and the present. The data indicated that the growth of public spending over the past 125 years was not smooth. Far from it. For example, there was almost no growth for the first forty years, so that, on average, public spending as a share of GDP was almost the same in 1913 as it had been in 1870 even though the economies of these countries had grown enormously over these four decades. After 1913 public spending started to increase, prompted first by World War I, then by the Great Depression, and again by World War II. More importantly, over these decades attitudes vis-à-vis the role of the government in the economy started changing. Yet, between 1913 and 1960, the growth of public spending could still be considered as moderate.

By the end of the decade of the 1950s, however, the general attitude vis-à-vis the role that the state could play in solving many economic and social problems, and, more broadly, in reducing various risks for the citizens, had changed dramatically. By this time, many had come to believe that the government and not the individuals themselves should provide protection against the risks of getting old, getting sick, becoming disabled or unemployed, remaining illiterate, and so on. And many believed that this role could be played best through higher public spending. At the end of the 1950s, we entered a period of great optimism about the government's ability to make life better for the citizens mainly through higher public spending. In this period, various technical innovations, in budgeting, in project evaluation, and in other aspects of public administration were introduced. These innovations were expected to allow the government to sort out good from bad policies and to make public spending more efficient.

In the 1960–80 period, in most industrial countries public spending as a share of GDP registered the fastest rate of growth even though in that period there were no world wars, no great depressions, and no major disasters that could have contributed to that growth. Part One identified the areas in which spending grew the most. It showed that transfer expenditure, often in cash, was the most dynamic broad category. In many cases citizens paid money with one hand and got it back with the other hand. Furthermore, this growth was widespread, affecting most countries, but especially the European countries. In this period public spending grew faster than public revenue, thus leading to sustained fiscal deficits (a new experience in peacetime) and to rising public debts. For much of this period, these trends did not give rise to major concerns on the part of the public or the policymakers, partly because real interest rates were very low. For example, the growth of public debts as shares of GDP started attracting some attention only around the middle of the 1980s (see Larosière, 1984) and fiscal deficits were often dismissed as being irrelevant on grounds that private saving would increase to neutralize their effects. Ricardian equivalence became an academic and, in the United States, even a political credo.

In Part Two of the study we attempted to establish, in a simple way, whether a relationship existed between higher public spending and higher social welfare. Did the higher spending lead to higher welfare? Because public welfare cannot be measured directly, we showed the changes in a whole range of socioeconomic indicators that had accompanied the increase in public spending. We assumed that these indicators largely determine social welfare. For this purpose, we divided the countries into three groups on the basis of their share of public spending into GDP. We thus had groups of countries with "small," "medium," and "big" government. Our simple empirical test led us to the conclusion that countries with small governments have performed as well, or even better, on the basis of various socioeconomic indicators, as countries with large governments.

Because higher levels of public spending impose obvious costs on the taxpayers and on the economy, costs that do not seem to be compensated by a better performance in terms of socioeconomic indicators, we suggested that the countries should aim at reducing their public spending to, perhaps, around 30 percent of GDP. This is, of course, an indicative figure, and we do not argue that, even if our argumentation is accepted, countries should aim precisely at that figure. Different countries' circumstances and different attitudes toward the role of the government and toward social programs may, of course, justify somewhat different levels. For example, European countries may be more disposed to finance publicly cultural events than, say, the United States. Still, we believe that much of what governments want to achieve through public spending could be achieved by levels of spending ranging from, say, 25 percent to 35 percent of GDP. This range is wide enough to include differences in cultures and in attitudes. It implies that most industrialized countries should reduce their public spending and their taxes by a substantial amount. Reducing fiscal churning would go a long way toward achieving this objective.

In Part Three, we discussed, in very broad terms, reforms that could help reduce public spending while still promoting the social goals that the governments want to pursue. In fact, we argued that direct public spending and the direct public provision of goods and services are not the only way of promoting certain social objectives. Those objectives can often be promoted more clearly and more efficiently in other ways. And lower spending and lower taxes mean that most households would have a higher disposable income that could be used to buy certain services or certain insurances against particular risks from the private sector. Thus, the fact that the public sector reduces its involvement in certain activities does not necessarily imply that most people would benefit less from particular services or would have less protection against particular risks. It only implies that the people would buy the services or the protection directly rather than buying them indirectly through the payment of taxes and through the government provision of the services.

Obviously, some safety nets will be needed for the unfortunate few who, because of conditions beyond their control, end up with incomes so low, or with needs so high, that the government must target them for special assistance. However, these groups needing special protection are not likely to represent a large proportion of the population, especially if present incentives that make it attractive for some groups to be in special, favored categories, are removed. Furthermore, in particular cases, the assistance to these groups may come in ways other than public spending. Additionally, the public sector would still be responsible for genuine public goods.

A concrete example may help clarify the preceding point. Most countries have handicapped or invalid individuals, although the definition of handicapped or invalid is clearly a flexible one that varies from country to country, from time to time, or even from place to place within a country. Culture may play a role in defining a handicapped person. In Italy, for example, in past years the definition of invalid was much influenced by the unemployment rate of a region. In regions with high unemployment, especially in the south, individuals who had the capacity to remain economically active were classified as invalid so as to qualify for disability pensions. In regions with low unemployment, these individuals would not have qualified as invalids. This policy led to a large increase in the number of "invalids" in some regions (see Putnam, 1993). In parts of Sicily there were six times more pensions for invalidity than for normal old age.

Assume now that the invalids are considered part of the unfortunate few deserving the targeted attention of government. This attention can be shown in different ways. One is by providing disability pensions to them. In this way, those officially classified as disabled drop out of the labor force and join the group of retirees; thus many try to be classified as invalids. This has been done by various European countries. The problems with this approach are two: first, public spending goes up; second, there are increasing pressures to broaden the definition of invalid. As the definition becomes more elastic, more individuals will claim to be invalids, and the public spending to satisfy the objective of protecting this group will go up to possibly high levels. In the Netherlands, for example, this type of spending reached almost 5 percent of GDP in the early 1990s. Corrupt doctors may lend themselves to providing certifications of invalidity to individuals who are not invalids. And the disabled may reenter the economically active labor force by joining the unofficial economy.[1]

A second approach would be to provide some special allowance, but not a pension, for those ascertained to be invalid. This allowance,

1. There have been reports of individuals drawing an invalidity pension for being legally blind who were driving taxis or other handicapped who were playing soccer.

which could involve special training, could be seen as providing some compensation for the extra costs of being invalid. This would also lead to higher public spending, but the incentive to "soften" the eligibility criteria to make unemployment statistics look better would be avoided.

A third approach is similar to the one followed by the 1990 Disability Act of the United States. This law requires employers to make provisions such as building modifications that facilitate access by the handicapped; it also requires that employers not discriminate against the handicapped in hiring for jobs they can perform. Claims have been made that in the United States this Act has increased the supply of labor and has decreased public spending. Some costs have of course been borne by the private sector. The point is that, to a large extent, the objectives of providing protection to the disabled has been achieved at low cost in *public* spending and at some cost in private spending.[2] We have not studied this law to determine whether on balance it was a good or bad one, but it does provide a concrete example of possibilities that exist for reducing public spending.[3]

Possibilities for reducing public spending now exist in many areas from the provision of pensions (protecting against the risk of getting old) to the provision of educational and health services and infrastructures in general. There is no scarcity of ideas or even of examples. The "adoption" of public parks by private enterprises in Buenos Aires is an interesting one. They exist in the provision of infrastructures, in the running by the private sector of (previously public) utilities, and so on. Even zoos and museums can be contracted out, thus reducing public spending and even receiving an income. Many of these examples prove that the traditional objectives that justify public sector intervention can still be satisfied while spending less than in the past and giving a bigger role to the private sector. But, of course, some of these changes are costly politically and must overcome the opposition of groups (such as school teachers, railroad workers, health workers) or of the direct beneficiaries of public spending programs (pensioners, students, those with illnesses, etc.) who consider themselves on the losing end.

---

2. See article in *The Economist*, April 18, 1998, pp. 25–6.
3. Similarly, Germany features a system whereby employers have to provide a certain share of jobs for handicapped people or pay a fee to buy themselves out of the obligation.

The discussion in Part Four indicated that many countries have already carried out, or are carrying out, changes that would reform the fiscal role of the state and would reduce the share of public spending in gross domestic product. In recent years, there has been a lot of experimentation, with good and, occasionally, with bad results. In general the more developed is the government's ability to provide a useful or needed regulatory function the more scaling down of public spending can be achieved. Thus, countries set on reducing public spending can choose from these experiments and experiences.[4] As already mentioned, often the main obstacles are special interests, but "the vested interests of the mind," using a Galbraithian expression, and lack of imagination also often impede change.

In most of the reforms discussed in Part Three of this study, the role of the state played through public spending would be reduced. However, if the state does not just want to disengage from its role but wants to promote its fundamental objectives in other ways, it must reinforce its regulatory power. In many cases, good regulations can reduce public spending without losing sight of the social and economic goals of the state. There is now a large literature on regulations. Some of this literature has shown the extent to which regulations can be captured by the regulated and distorted in their objectives. This is clearly a danger. However, as countries become more sophisticated and markets improve, policymakers should be better able to pursue this regulatory role. They can learn from the successes and mistakes of other countries, and can also rely on the expertise of foreign advisers. For example, Chilean experts in pension reform have played a considerable role in advising the policymakers of other countries in making reforms in this area. The same has happened to experts in privatization and in other sectors. And international organizations, such as the OECD and the World Bank, have been providing useful studies that can help the policymakers in making better decisions.[5]

It is also important to realize that globalization itself will put some downward pressure on public spending. It will do so in two ways. First, through its effect on tax revenue. Because of tax competition, it will become progressively more difficult for countries to tax some tax

---

4. Many of the industrial countries have or can develop the needed regulatory ability.
5. See, for example, OECD, *The OECD Report on Regulatory Reform*, Volume I: *Sectoral Studies*, and Volume II: *Thematic Studies* (Paris: OECD, 1997).

bases and, for sure, globalization will limit a country's ability to impose higher tax rates than other countries, especially on mobile factors such as capital and highly skilled labor. (See Tanzi, 1995, 1997.) Second, because the limitation of a domestic market will no longer be a valid justification for the government to take over a given activity. It will become possible for individuals of a given country to buy insurance or even services from other countries capable of providing better quality. This is already happening in education, in health and in insurance against particular risks (such as life insurance).

All these arguments give us reason to believe that governments will become more efficient and public spending (and taxation) will decline in the future in spite of demographic trends that will tend, under existing policies, to increase public spending. Spending will not decline to the levels seen 100 or 70 years ago, but it can be rolled back to levels closer to those experienced around 1960. With this, we are not advocating a return to the "Hobbesian jungle" as some critics may claim. We suggest, rather, a more modest and more focused role for the state and for public spending with which countries are likely to experience much invigorated economies and a growth in social well-being. This will allow the citizens of these countries to lead more balanced lives, enjoying the choice and invigorating effects of markets, the benefits from public goods, and security of social safety nets.

Bibliography

Alesina, Alberto, and Allan Drazen, 1994, "Why Are Stabilizations Delayed?" in Torsten Persson and Guido Tabellini, eds. *Monetary and Fiscal Policy*, Vol. 2 (Cambridge, Mass.: MIT Press), pp. 387–414.

Alesina, Alberto, and Roberto Perotti, 1995a, "Political Economy of Budget Deficits," *IMF Staff Papers*, Vol. 42, No. 1 (March): 1–31.

—— 1995b, "Fiscal Expansions and Fiscal Adjustments in OECD Countries," *Economic Policy*, 21: 205–8.

—— 1996a, "Budget Deficits and Budget Institutions," IMF Working Paper 96/52, International Monetary Fund, Washington.

—— 1996b, "Fiscal Adjustments in OECD Countries: Composition and Macroeconomic Effects," IMF Working Paper 96/70, International Monetary Fund, Washington.

Alesina, Alberto, Ricardo Hausmann, Rudolf Hommes, and Ernesto Stein, 1996, "Budget Institutions and Fiscal Performance in Latin America," NBER Working Paper, 5586, National Bureau of Economic Research.

Altenstetter, Christa, 1986, "German Social Security Programs: An Interpretation of Their Development, 1883–1985," in Douglas E. Ashford and E. W. Kelley, eds., *Nationalizing Social Security in Europe and America* (Greenwich, Conn.: JAI Press), pp. 73–97.

Andic, Suphan, and Jindrich Veverka, 1964, "The Growth of Government Expenditure in Germany since the Unification," *Finanzarchiv*, Vol. 23, No. 2 (January).

Aninat, Eduardo, 1999, "Addressing Equity Issues in Policymaking: Lessons from the Chilean Experience" in Vito Tanzi, Ke-Young Chu, and Sanjeev Gupta, eds., *Economic Policy and Equity* (Washington: International Monetary Fund).

Ashford, Douglas E., and E. W. Kelley, 1986, *Nationalizing Social Security in Europe and America* (Greenwich, Conn.: JAI Press).

Asiamoney, 1994, "Malaysia, Strong Fundamentals," Supplement (June).

Atkinson, Anthony B., Lee Rainwater, and Timothy M. Smeeding, 1995, *Income Distribution in OECD Countries: Evidence from Luxembourg Income Study* (Paris: OECD).

Australia Bureau of Census and Statistics, 1938, *Official Year Book* (Canberra).

Australia Office of Regulation Review, 1995, *A Guide to Regulation Impact Statements* (Canberra).

Australian Minister for Industrial Relations and Minister Assisting the Prime Minister for the Public Service, 1996, *Towards a Best Practice Australian Public Service: Discussion Paper* (Canberra: Australian Government Publishing Service).

Banca d'Italia, 1994, *Nuovo Sistema di Controlli Sulla Spesa Pubblica* (Rome).

Barro, Robert J., 1979, "On the Determination of the Public Debt," *Journal of Political Economy*, 87: 940–71.

Bastiat, Frederic, 1944–5, *Harmonies of Political Economy*, 2 vols. (Santa Ana, Calif.: Register Publishing Co.).

Bator, Francis M., 1960, *The Question of Government Spending: Public Needs and Private Wants* (New York: Harper).

Baumol, William J, 1967, "Macroeconomics of Unbalanced Growth: The Anatomy of Urban Crisis," *American Economic Review*, 57 (June): 415–26.

Bercuson, Kenneth, ed., 1995, "Singapore: A Case Study in Rapid Development," IMF Occasional Paper No. 119, International Monetary Fund, Washington.

Berman, Harold J., 1983, *Law and Revolution, The Formation of the Western Legal Tradition* (Cambridge, Mass.: Harvard University Press).

Bird, Richard, 1970, *The Growth of Government Spending in Canada* (Toronto: Canadian Tax Foundation).

Bird, Richard M., Meyer W. Bucovetsky, and David K. Foot, 1979, *The Growth of Public Employment in Canada* (Toronto: Institute for Research on Public Policy).

Bishop, Matthew, John Kay, and Colin Mayer, eds., 1994, *Privatization and Economic Performance* (Oxford: Oxford University Press).

1995, *The Regulatory Challenge* (Oxford: Oxford University Press).

Bismut, Claude, and Pierre Jacquet, 1997, "Fiscal Consolidation in Europe," *Les Cahiers de L'IFRI*, No. 18.

Bitran, Eduardo, and Raul E. Saez, 1994, "Privatization and Regulation in Chile," in Barry Bosworth, Rudiger Dornbush, and Raul Laban, eds. *The Chilean Economy: Policy Lessons and Challenges* (Washington: The Brookings Institution, 1994), pp. 379–429.

Blejer, Mario I., and Adrienne Cheasty, eds., 1993, *How to Measure the Fiscal Deficit: Analytical and Methodological Issues* (Washington: International Monetary Fund).

Blomqvist, Ake, and Emmanuel Jimenez, 1989, *The Public Role in Private Post-Secondary Education*, World Bank WPS 240 (Washington: The World Bank).

Bohn, H., and R. P. Inman, 1996, "Balanced-Budget Rules and Public Deficits: Evidence from the U.S. States," Carnegie-Rochester Conference Series on Public Policy, 45: 13–76.

Borcherding, Thomas E., Werner W. Pommerehne, and Friedrich Schneider, 1982,

"Comparing the Efficiency of Private and Public Production: The Evidence from Five Countries," *Zeitschrift für Nationalokonomie* (Supplement 2): 127–56.

Borner, Silvio, Aymo Brunetti, and Beatrice Weder, 1995, *Political Credibility and Economic Development* (New York: St. Martin's Press).

Bosworth, Barry, Rudiger Dornbusch, and Raul Laban, eds., 1994, *The Chilean Economy: Policy Lessons and Challenges* (Washington: The Brookings Institution).

Bottani, Norberto, 1996, *Education at a Glance: OECD Indicators* (Paris: OECD).

Bourdieu, Pierre, 1993, *La Misère du Monde* (Paris: Editions du Seuil).

Brandolini, Andrea, and Nicola Rossi, 1998, "Income Distribution and Growth in Industrial Countries," in Vito Tanzi and Ke-Young Chu, eds., *Income Distribution and High-Quality Growth* (Cambridge, Mass.: MIT Press).

Brennan, Geoffrey, and James M. Buchanan, 1985, *The Reason of Rules: Constitutional Political Economy* (Cambridge: Cambridge University Press).

Breton, Albert, 1984, "An Analysis of Constitutional Change, Canada, 1980–2," *Public Choice,* 44: 251–72.

Breton, Albert, Gianluigi Galeotti, Pierre Salmon, and Ronald Wintrobe, 1991, *The Competitive State*, Villa Colombella Papers on Competitive Politics (Dordrecht: Kluwer Academic Publishers).

Brosio, Giorgio, and Carla Marchese, 1986, *Il Potere di Spendere: Economia e Storia della Spesa Pubblica dell'unificazione ad oggi* (Bologna: Il Mulino).

Brown, Frank, 1995, "Privatization of Public Education: Theories and Concepts," *Education and Urban Society*, 27: 114–26.

Brunetti, Aymo, Gregory Kisunko, and Beatrice Weder, 1997a, "Institutional Obstacles to Doing Business," World Bank Policy Research Working Paper 1759, Washington.

   1997b. "Credibility of Rules and Economic Growth: Evidence from a World-wide Survey of the Private Sector," World Bank Policy Research Working Paper 1760 Washington.

Bruni, Franco, Alesandro Penati, and Angelo Porta, 1989, "Financial Regulation, Implicit Taxes, and Fiscal Adjustment in Italy," in Mario Monti, ed., *Fiscal Policy, Economic Adjustment, and Financial Markets* (Washington: International Monetary Fund), pp. 197–230.

Bruno, Michael, Martin Ravallion, and Lyn Squire, 1996, "Equity and Growth in Developing Countries: Old and New Perspectives on the Policy Issues," World Bank Policy Research Working Paper 1563, Washington.

Buchanan, James M., 1975, *The Limits of Liberty. Between Anarchy and Leviathan* (Chicago: University of Chicago Press).

   1985, "The Moral Dimension of Debt Financing," *Economic Inquiry*, 23: 1–6.

   Charles K. Rowley, and Robert D. Tollison, eds., 1987, *Deficits* (New York: Basil Blackwell).

Buchanan, James M., and Gordon Tullock, 1962, *The Calculus of Consent, Logical Foundations of Constitutional Democracy* (Ann Arbor: University of Michigan Press).

Burki, S. J., and Guillermo Perry, 1997, "The Long March: A Reform Agenda for Latin America and the Caribbean in the Next Decade," *World Bank Latin American and Caribbean Studies* (Washington: The World Bank).

Business Week, February 24, 1997, "A Continent at the Breaking Point," Byline: Gail Edmondson, New York, p. 50.

Butlin, N. G., 1984, *Select Comparative Economic Statistics 1900–1940: Australia and Britain Canada, Japan, New Zealand and U.S.A.* (Canberra: Australian National University).

Calvo, Guillermo, 1978, "On the Time Consistency of Optimal Policy in a Monetary Economy," *Econometrica*, Vol. 46 (November): 1411–28.

Campos, José Edgardo L., and Sanjay Pradhan, 1996, "Budgetary Institutions and Expenditure Outcomes: Binding Governments to Fiscal Performance," World Bank Policy Research Working Paper 1646, Washington.

Cangiano, Marco, 1996, "Accountability and Transparency in the Public Sector: The New Zealand Experience," IMF Working Paper 96/122, International Monetary Fund, Washington.

Caragata, Patrick James, 1998, *The Economic and Compliance Consequences of Taxation. A Report of the Health of the Tax System in New Zealand* (Boston: Kluwer Academic Publishers).

Cardoso, Teodora, 1985, "As Empresas Públicas e o Ajustamento Macroeconómico im Portugal," in José da Silva Lopes, ed., *Ajustamento e Crescimento na Actual Conjuntura Económica Mundial* (Washington: International Monetary Fund), pp. 150–66.

Chand, Sheetal, and Albert Jaeger, 1996, "Aging Populations and Public Pension Schemes," IMF, Occasional Paper No. 147, Internaternal Monetary Fund, Washington.

Chau, Leung Chuen, 1993, *Hong Kong: A Unique Case of Development* (Washington: The World Bank).

Chu, Ke-Young, and Sanjeev Gupta, eds., 1998, *Social Safety Nets: Issues and Recent Experiences* (Washington: International Monetary Fund).

Clark, Colin, 1964, *Taxmanship: Principles and Proposals for the Reform of Taxation*, Hobart paper 26 (London: Institute of Economic Affairs).

Coe, David, and Dennis Snower, 1996, "Policy Complementarities: The Case for Fundamental Labor Market Reform," IMF Working Paper 96/93, International Monetary Fund, Washington.

Commander, Simon, Hamid Davoodi, and Une J. Lee, 1997, "The Causes of Government and the Consequences for Growth and Well-being," World Bank Policy Research Working Paper 1785, Washington.

Connell, W. F., 1980, *A History of Education in the Twentieth Century World* (New York: Teachers College Press).

Coopers & Lybrand Global Tax Network, 1997, *International Tax Summaries 1997: A Guide for Planning and Decisions,* George J. Yost, III, Chairman, International Tax Board, ed. (New York: John Wiley & Sons, Inc.).

Corsetti, Giancarlo, and Nouriel Roubini, 1996, "European versus American Perspectives on Balanced-Budget Rules," *American Economic Review*, 86: 408–13.

Daveri, Francesco, and Guido Tabellini, 1997, "Unemployment, Growth, and Taxation in Industrial Countries," Working Paper No. 122, IGIER, Università Bocconi, Milan, November.

Davis, E. P. 1993, "The Structure, Regulation, and Performance of Pension Funds in Nine Industrial Countries," World Bank Policy Research Working Paper 1229, Washington.

De Haan, Jakob, Wim Moessen, and Bjorn Volkerink, 1997, "Budgetary Procedures: Aspects and Changes. New Evidence for some European Countries," University of Groningen, mimeo.

De Jouvenel, Bertrand, 1952, *The Ethics of Redistribution* (Cambridge: Cambridge University Press).

Delorme, Robert, and Christine André, 1983, *L'État et l'économie: un essai d'explication de l'évolution des dépenses publiques en France 1870–1980* (Paris: Seuil).

Diamond, Peter, and Salvador Valdés-Prieto, 1994, "Social Security Reforms," in Barry Bosworth, Rudiger Dornbush, and Raul Laban, eds. *The Chilean Economy: Policy Lessons and Challenges*, (Washington: The Brookings Institution, 1994), pp. 379–429.

Domberger, Simon, and Paul Jensen, 1997, "Contracting Out by the Public Sector: Theory, Evidence, Prospects," *Oxford Review of Economic Policy*, Vol. 13, No. 4: 67–78.

Dornbusch, Rudiger, and Mario Draghi, 1990, eds, *Public Debt Management: Theory and History* (New York: Cambridge University Press).

Easterlin, Richard A., ed., 1980, *Population and Economic Change in Developing Countries* (Chicago: University of Chicago Press).

Eichengreen, Barry, Ricardo Hausmann, and Juergen Von Hagen, 1996, "Reforming Budgetary Institutions in Latin America: The Case for a National Fiscal Council," paper presented at Annual Meetings of the Inter-American Development Bank, Buenos Aires.

Eijffinger, Sylvester, and Jakob De Haan, 1996, "The Political Economy of Central Bank Independence," Princeton University Special Papers in International Economics, No. 19, Princeton, N. 5.

Engel, Eduardo, Ronald Fischer, and Alexander Galetovic, 1998, "Infrastructure Franchising and Government Guarantees," paper presented at the X Regional Seminar on Fiscal Policy, CEPAL, Chile, January 26–8.

Eurostat, 1992, Digest of Statistics on Social Protection in Europe, Luxembourg.

Eusepi, Giuseppe, and Eugenio Cerioni, 1989, "Constitutional Constraints on Government: The Impact of Article 81 of the Italian Constitution," paper presented at the European Public Choice Society Meeting, Linz, Austria.

Evans, Lewis, Arthur Grimes, and Bryce Wilkinson with David Teece, 1996, "Economic Reform in New Zealand 1984–95: The Pursuit of Efficiency," *Journal of Economic Literature*, Vol. 34 (December): pp. 1856–1902.

Feld, Lars, and Gebhard Kirchgaessner, 1997, "Public Debt and Budgetary Procedures: Top Down or Bottom Up? Some Evidence from Swiss Municipalities" Switzerland: University of St. Gallen, mimeo.

Fernández Acha, Valentin, 1976, *Datos Básicos para la historia financiera de*

España (1950–1975) (Madrid: Ministerio de Hacienda, Instituto de Estudios Fiscales).

Field, Frederick Vanderbilt, ed., 1934, *Economic Handbook of the Pacific Area* (Garden City, NY: Doubleday, Doran).

Flora, Peter, Franz Kraus, and Winfried Pfennig, 1983 and 1987. *State, Economy and Society in Western Europe, 1815–1975*, Vol. I, 1983, Vol. II, 1987 (Chicago: St. James Press).

Foot, David K., 1989, "Public Expenditure, Population Aging and Economic Dependency in in Canada, 1921–2021," *Population Research and Policy Review*, 8: 97–117.

Ford, Robert, and Douglas Laxton, 1995, "World Public Debt and Real Interest Rates," IMF Working Paper 95/30, International Monetary Fund, Washington.

Forrester, Vivane, 1996, *L'horreur Economique* (Paris: Librairie Artième Fayard).

Forte, Francesco, 1998, *Le Regole della Constituzione Fiscale*, Notizie di Politeia, Anno 14, No. 49, 150.

    1989, "Costituzione Tributaria e Riforma Tributaria," in Victor Uckmar, ed., *Esperienze Straniere e Prospettive per l'Ordinamento Tributario Italiano* (Padua: CEDAM).

    and Alan T. Peacock, 1985, *Public Expenditure and Government Growth* (Oxford: Basil Blackwell).

Foster, R. A., and Stewart, S. E., 1991, *Australian Economic Statistics, 1949–50 to 1989–90*, Reserve Bank of Australia, Occasional Paper No. 8 (Sydney, N.S.W.: Reserve Bank of Australia).

Frey, Bruno, 1988, "Explaining the Growth of Government: International Perspectives in Lybeck," J. A. and M. Henrekson, eds., *Explaining the Growth of Government*, (Amsterdam: North-Holland), pp. 21–8.

Friedman, Milton, 1955, "The Role of Government in Education," in Robert Solo, ed., *Economics and the Public Interest* (New Brunswick, N.J.: Rutgers University Press).

Fry, Maxwell J., 1997, "The Fiscal Abuse of Central Banks," in *Macroeconomic Dimensions of Public Finance: Essays in Honor of Vito Tanzi* (London and New York: Routledge).

Galbraith, John Kenneth, 1958, *The Affluent Society* (Boston: Houghton Mifflin).

Giavazzi, Francesco, and Marco Pagano, 1990, "Can Severe Fiscal Contractions Be Expansionary?" in Olivier Blanchard and Stanley Fischer, eds., NBER *Macroeconomics Annual* (Cambridge: Mass.: MIT Press), pp. 75–110.

Giovannini, Alberto, and Martha De Melo, 1993, "Government Revenue from Financial Repression," *American Economic Review*, 83: 953–63.

Gómez-Ibáñez, José, and John R. Meyer, 1993, *Going Private: The International Experience with Transport Privatization* (Washington: The Brookings Institution).

Goode, Richard, 1964, *The Individual Income Tax* (Washington: The Brookings Institution).

Gradstein, Mark, and Moshe Justman, 1996, *Public Choice of an Education*

System: Implications for Growth and Income Distribution (Israel: Ben Gurion University).

Group of Ten, 1998, "The Macroeconomic and Financial Implications of Ageing Populations" (s.l.: The Group) April.

Gulhati, Ravi, and Raj Nallari, 1990, "Successful Stabilization and Recovery in Mauritius," World Bank EDI Development Policy Case Series No. 5, Washington.

Gwartney, James D., Richard Lawson, and Walter Block, 1996, *Economic Freedom of the World* (Vancouver: Fraser Institute).

Haddon-Cave, Philip, 1984, "The Making of Some Aspects of Public Policy In Hong Kong," in D. Lethbridge, ed., *The Business Environment in Hong Kong* (Hong Kong: Oxford University Press).

Hagemann, Robert, and Christoph John, 1995, "The Fiscal Stance in Sweden: A Generational Accounting Perspective," IMF Working Paper, WP/95/105, International Monetary Fund, Washington.

Halligan, John, 1997, "New Public Sector Models: Reform in Australia and New Zealand," in Jan-Erïk Lane, ed., *Public Sector Reform: Rationale, Trends, and Problems* (London: Sage Publications), pp. 17–46.

Hammond, Bray, 1957, *Banks and Politics in America, From the Revolution to the Civil War* (Princeton, N.J.: Princeton University Press).

Harberger, Arnold, 1998, "Monetary and Fiscal Policy for Equitable Economic Growth," in Vito Tanzi and Ke-Young Chu, eds., *Income Distribution and High-Quality Growth* (Cambridge, Mass.: MIT Press).

Hayek, Friedrich A. von, 1960, *The Constitution of Liberty* (Chicago: University of Chicago Press).

Heald, David, 1997, "Privately Financed Capital in Public Services," *The Manchester School of Economic and Social Studies*, Vol. 65, No. 5 (December): 568–98.

Helbling, Thomas, and Robert Wescott, 1995, "The Global Real Interest Rate," in IMF Staff Studies for the World Economic Outlook, September International Monetary Fund, Washington.

Heller, Walter W., 1966, *New Dimensions of Political Economy* (Cambridge, Mass.: Harvard University Press).

Holsey, Cheryl M., and Thomas E. Borcherding, 1997, "Why Does Government's Share of National Income Grow? An Assessment of the Recent Literature on the U.S. Experience," in Dennis C. Mueller, ed., *Perspectives on Public Choice: A Handbook* (New York: Cambridge University Press).

Holzmann, Robert, 1988, *Reforming Public Pensions* (Paris: OECD).

———, 1996, "The Economic Usefulness and Fiscal Requirements of Moving from Unfunded to Funded Pensions" (Saarbrücken, University of the Saarland).

———, 1997a, "Pension Reform, Financial Market Development and Economic Growth: Preliminary Evidence from Chile," IMF *Staff Papers,* Vol. 44, No. 2 (June): 149–78.

———, 1997b, *On the Economic Benefits and Fiscal Requirements of Moving from Unfunded to Funded Pensions,* AICGS Research Report No. 4 (Washington: American Institute of Contemporary German Studies).

Homer, Sidney, and Richard Sylla, 1991, *A History of Interest Rates* (New Brunswick, N.J.: Rutgers University Press).

Institut National de Statistique, 1952, *Annuaire statistique de la Belgique* (Brussels: INS).

Institute National de la statistique et des études économiques, *Annuaire statistique de la France* (Paris: L'Institut).

Inter-American Development Bank, 1997, *Economic and Social Progress in Latin America: Part II* (Washington).

International Monetary Fund, 1995a, *Argentina: Recent Economic Developments*, IMF Staff Country Report 95/110, International Monetary Fund, Washington.

1995b, *World Economic Outlook* (Washington: International Monetary Fund).

1996a, *Mauritius, Background Papers and Statistical Annex*, IMF Staff Country Report 96/1, International Monetary Fund, Washington.

1996b, *New Zealand: Recent Economic Developments*, IMF Staff Country Report. 96/14, International Monetary Fund, Washington.

1996c, *Belgium: Recent Economic Developments*, IMF Staff Country Report 96/25, International Monetary Fund, Washington.

1996d, *Switzerland: Recent Economic Developments*, IMF Staff Country Report 96/31, International Monetary Fund, Washington.

1996e, *Ireland: Recent Economic Developments*, IMF Staff Country Report 96/78, International Monetary Fund, Washington.

1996f, *Thailand: Statistical Appendix*, IMF Staff Country Report 96/83, International Monetary Fund, Washington.

1996g, *Finland: Selected Issues and Statistical Appendix*, IMF Staff Country Report 96/95, International Monetary Fund, Washington.

1996h, *Sweden: Selected Issues*, IMF Staff Country Report. 96/112, International Monetary Fund, Washington.

1996i, *Portugal: Recent Economic Developments*, IMF Staff Country Report 96/129, International Monetary Fund, Washington.

1996j, *United Kingdom: Recent Economic Developments*, IMF Staff Country Report 96/130, International Monetary Fund, Washington.

1996k, *New Zealand: Selected Issues and Statistical Appendix*, IMF Staff Country Report 96/144, International Monetary Fund, Washington.

1997a, *Australia: Recent Economic Developments*, IMF Staff Country Report 97/22, International Monetary Fund, Washington.

1997b, *World Economic Outlook*, International Monetary Fund, Washington.

1997c, *International Financial Statistics* (Washington: International Monetary Fund), August.

Government Finance Statistics Yearbook (Washington: International Monetary Fund) (various).

Irwin, Timothy, Michael Klein, Guillermo Perry, and Mateen Thobani, 1998, "Managing Contingent Liabilities in Infrastructure Privatization." Paper presented at the X Regional Seminar on Fiscal Policy, CEPAL, Chile, January 26–8.

Italy, Istituto Nazionale di Statistica (various years) *Annuario statistico italiano* (Rome: ISTAT).

James, Estelle, 1984, "Benefits and Costs of Privatized Public Services: Lessons from the Dutch Educational System," *Comparative Education Review* 28: 605–24.

1987, "The Public/Private Division of Responsibility for Education: An International Comparison," *Economics of Education Review* 6(1): 1–14.

Japan Statistical Association (various years), *Historical Statistics of Japan*.

Johansen, Leif, 1965, *Public Economics* (Amsterdam: North-Holland).

Kanbur, S. M. Ravi, 1991, "Poverty and Development: The Human Development report and the World Development Report," World Bank Policy Research Working Paper 1759, Washington.

Kapur, Anil, 1995, "Airport Infrastructure. The Emerging Role of the Private Sector," World Bank Technical Paper No. 313, Washington.

Kelsey, Jane, 1997, *The New Zealand Experiment: A World Model for Structural Adjustment*? (Auckland, New Zealand: Auckland University Press, Bridget Williams Books).

Keynes, John Maynard, 1926, *The End of Laissez-Faire* (London: Hogarth Press).

1936, *The General Theory of Employment, Interest, and Money* (San Diego: Harcourt Bruce Janovich).

Kindleberger, Charles Poor, 1993, *A Financial History of Western Europe* (New York: Oxford University Press).

King, Mervyn, 1997, "Tax Systems in the XXIst Century," in International Fiscal Association, ed., *Visions of the Tax Systems of the XXIst Century* (Boston: Kluwer Law International), pp. 53–64.

Kopits, George, and Jon Craig, 1998, *Transparency in Government Operations*, IMF Occasional Paper No. 158 (Washington: International Monetary Fund).

Kopits, George, and Steven Symansky, 1998, *Fiscal Policy Rules*, IMF Occasional Paper 162 (Washington: International Monetary Fund).

Kotlikoff, Laurence, 1995, "Privatization of Social Security: How It Works and Why It Matters," in *Tax Policy and the Economy*, NBER Conference Report. James Poterba, ed.

Krueger, Anne O., 1974, "The Political Economy of the Rent-Seeking Society," *The American Economic Review*, Vol. 64, No. 3 (June): 291–303.

1993, *Economic Policies at Cross Purposes: The United States and Developing Countries* (Washington: The Brookings Institution).

Kwon, Soonwon, 1993, "Social Policy in Korea: Challenges and Responses" (Seoul: Korea Development Institute), Research Monograph 93–01.

Lancaster, H. O., 1990, *"Expectations of Life: A Study in the Demography, Statistics, and History of World Mortality"* (New York: Springer-Verlag).

Lane, Jan-Erik, ed., 1997, *Public Sector Reform: Rationale, Trends, and Problems* (London: Sage Publications).

Larosière, Jacques de, 1984, *The Growth of Public Debt and the Need for Fiscal Discipline* (Washington: International Monetary Fund).

League of Nations, Economic Intelligence Service, *Statistical Yearbook of the League of Nations, 1926–1944* (Geneva: League of Nations).

Leroy-Beaulieu, Paul, 1888, *Traité de la Science des Finances* (Paris: Guillaumin).

Levitt, M. S., and M. A. S. Joyce, 1987, *The Growth and Efficiency of Public Spending* (Cambridge: Cambridge University Press).

Liesner, Thelma, 1985, *Economic Statistics, 1900–1983: United Kingdom, United States of America, France, Germany, Italy, Japan* (London: Economist Publications).

Lindbeck, Assar, 1996, "The West European Employment Problem," *Weltwirtschaftliches Archiv*, Vol. 132, No. 4, pp. 609–37.

1997, *The Swedish Experiment* (Stockholm: SNS Förlag).

Lindert, Peter H., 1994, "The Rise of Social Spending, 1880–1930," *Explorations in Economic History* 31: 1–37.

Lucas, Robert E., Jr., 1973, "Some International Evidence on Output-Inflation Tradeoffs," *The American Economic Review* (June).

1976, "Econometric Policy Evaluation: A Critique," Carnegie-Rochester Conference Series on Public Policy, Vol. 1.

Lybeck, J. A., and M. Henrekson, 1988, *Explaining the Growth of Government* (Amsterdam: North-Holland).

Macaulay, Frederick, 1938, *Some Theoretical Problems Suggested by the Movements of Interest Rates, Bond Yields and Stock Prices in the United States since 1856* (New York; National Bureau of Economic Research).

Mackenzie, G. A., and Peter Stella, 1996, "Quasi-Fiscal Operations of Public Financial Institutions," IMF Occasional Paper No. 142 (Washington: International Monetary Fund).

Maddison, Angus, 1995, *Monitoring the World Economy, 1820–1992* (Paris: OECD).

Marcel, Mario, and Andres Solimano, 1994, "The Distribution of Income and Economic Adjustment," in Barry Bosworth, Rudiger Dornbusch, and Raul Laban, eds., *The Chilean Economy: Policy Lessons and Challenges* (Washington: The Brookings Institution), pp. 379–429.

Massey, Patrick, 1995, *New Zealand, Market Liberalization in a Developed Economy* (New York: St. Martin's Press).

Masson, Paul, and Michael Mussa, 1995, "Long-Term Tendencies in Budget Deficits and Debt," IMF Working Paper 95/128, International Monetary Fund, Washington.

Mauro, Paolo, 1995, "Corruption and Growth," *Quarterly Journal of Economics*, 110: (August): 681–712.

McDermott, John, and Wescott, Robert, 1996, "An Empirical Analysis of Fiscal Adjustments," IMF Working Paper 96/59, International Monetary Fund, Washington.

Merewitz, Leonard, and Stephen H. Sosnick, 1971, *The Budget's New Clothes* (Chicago: Markham Publishing Company).

Milesi-Ferretti, Gian-Maria, 1996, "Fiscal Rules and the Budget Process," IMF Working Paper 96/60, International Monetary Fund, Washington.

Mitchell, B. R., 1998, *International Historical Statistics: Africa, Asia and Oceania, 1750–1988*, 2nd rev. ed. (New York: Stockton Press).

1998, *International Historical Statistics: Europe, 1750–1993*, 4th ed. (New York: Stockton Press).

1976, *Abstract of British Historical Statistics* (New York: Cambridge University Press).

Moser, Peter, 1994, "Constitutional Protection of Economic Rights: The Swiss and U.S. Experience in Comparison," *Constitutional Political Economy*, Vol. 5: 61–79.

Mueller, Dennis C., 1986, *The Growth of Government: A Public Choice Perspective*, DM/86/33 (Washington: International Monetary Fund).

1991, "Choosing a Constitution in East Europe: Lessons from Public Choice," *Journal of Comparative Economics*, 15: 325–48.

1989, *Public Choice II* (Cambridge: Cambridge University Press).

ed., 1997, *Perspectives on Public Choice: A Handbook* (Cambridge: Cambridge University Press).

Mullard, Maurice, 1993, *The Politics of Public Expenditure* (London: Routledge).

Musgrave, Richard A., 1959, *The Theory of Public Finance: A Study in Public Economy* (New York: McGraw-Hill).

1965, *Essays in Fiscal Federalism* (Washington: The Brookings Institution).

Neck, Reinhard, and Friedrich Schneider, 1988, "The Growth of the Public Sector in Austria: An Exploratory Analysis," in J. A. Lybeck and M. Henrekson, eds, *Explaining the Growth of Government* (Amsterdam: North Holland).

Netherlands, Centraal Bureau voor de Statistiek, 1956, *Statistical Yearbook of the Netherlands* (The Hague: Staatsuitgveri).

New Zealand, Department of Statistics, 1998, *The New Zealand Official Yearbook* (Wellington).

New Zealand, State Services Commission, 1998, *Assessment of the State of the New Zealand Public Service*, Occasional Paper No. 1 (October).

Niskanen, William A., 1992, "The Case for a New Fiscal Constitution," *Journal of Economic Perspectives*, 6: 13–24.

Noord, Paul Van den, and Richard Herd, 1993, *Pension Liabilities in the Seven Major Economics*, OECD Economics Department Working Papers No. 142 (Paris: OECD).

North, Douglass, 1994, "Economic Performance through Time," *American Economic Review*, 84: 359–68.

Norway, Statistisk Sentralbyrå, 1969 and 1978, *Historical Statistics, 1968* (Oslo: Statistisk Sentralbyrå).

Nozick, Robert, 1974, *Anarchy, State and Utopia* (Basic Books).

Okawa, Kazushi, Miyohei Shinohara, Mataji Umemura, eds., 1965–79, *Estimates of Long-Term Economic Statistics of Japan since 1868* (Tokyo: Toyo Keizai Shinpo Sha).

Okun, Arthur M., 1970, *The Political Economy of Prosperity* (Washington: Brookings Institution).

Olson, Mancur, 1965, *The Logic of Collective Action* (Cambridge, Mass.: Harvard University Press).

1982, *The Rise and Decline of Nations: Economic Growth, Stagflation and Social Rigidities* (New Haven, Conn.: Yale University Press).

Organisation for Economic Cooperation and Development, 1985, *Social Expenditure, 1960–1990: Problems of Growth and Control* (Paris: OECD).

1987, Toll Financing and Private Sector Involvement in Road Infrastructure Development (Paris: OECD).

1988, *Reforming Public Pensions* (Paris: OECD).

Directorate for Social Affairs, Manpower and Education, 1990, *Labour Market Policies for the 1990s* (Paris: OECD).

1992a, *Private Pensions and Public Policy* (Paris: OECD).

1992b, "The Reform of Health Care Systems. A Comparative Analysis of Seven OECD Countries," *Health Policy Studies*, No. 2 (Paris: OECD).

1994a, "The Reform of Health Care Systems. A Review of Seventeen OECD Countries," *Health Policy Studies*, No. 5 (Paris: OECD).

1994b, *New Orientations for Social Policy* (Paris: OECD).

1995a, *Social Expenditure Database* (SOC) (Paris: OECD).

1995b, *OECD Environmental Data: Compendium* (Paris: OECD).

Directorate for Social Affairs, Manpower, and Education, 1996a, *Trends in International Migration: Continuous Reporting System on Migration: Annual Report 1994* (Paris: OECD).

1996b, "Social Expenditure Statistics of OECD Member Countries, Labour Market and Social Policy," Occasional Paper No. 17 (Paris: OECD).

1996c, *National Accounts, Main Aggregates* (Paris: OECD).

1996d, *Social Expenditure Statistics of OECD Members Countries* (Provisional Version), Labour Market and Social Policy Occasional Papers, No. 17 (Paris: OECD).

1996e, *Revenue Statistics of OECD Member Countries, 1965/95* (Paris: OECD).

1997, *Making Work Pay: Taxation, Benefits, Employment, and Unemployment* (OECD: Paris).

(various years), *Economic Surveys* (Paris: OECD).

(various years), *Economic Outlook* (Paris: OECD).

(various years), *Historical Statistics* (Paris: OECD).

(various years), *Main Economic Indicators* (Paris: OECD).

(various years), *Main Science and Technology Indicators* (Paris: OECD).

(various years), *National Accounts* (Paris: OECD).

(various years), *Private Pensions in OECD Countries (Canada, Ireland, New Zealand, the United States)* (Paris: OECD).

Osborne, David, and Ted Gaebler, 1992, *Reinventing Government: How the Entrepreneurial Spirit Is Transforming the Public Sector* (Reading, Mass.: Addison-Wesley Publishing Company).

Österreichisches Statistiches Zentralamt, 1935 (Republik Österreich).

Owens, Jeffrey, 1997, "Emerging Issues in Tax Reform: The Perspective of an International Administrator," Paper presented at the 53rd Congress on Public Investment and Public Finance in Kyoto, Japan.

Oxley, Howard, and Maitland MacFarlan, 1995, "Health Care Reform: Controlling Spending and Increasing Efficiency," OECD *Economic Studies* No. 24, 1: 7–56.

Palacios, Robert J., 1996, *Averting the Old Age Crisis*: Technical Annex (Washington: World Bank).

Palda, Filip, 1997, "Fiscal Churning and Political Efficiency," *Kyklos* (Switzerland), 50: 189–206.

Parker, David, 1994, "International Aspects of Privatisation: A Critical Assessment of Business Restructuring in the UK, Former Czechoslovakia and Malaysia," *British Review of Economic Issues*, 16: 1–32.

Peacock, Alan, 1986, "The Political Economy of the Public Expenditure," in John A. Bristow and Declan McDonagh, eds., *Public Expenditure: The Key Issues* (Dublin: Institute of Public Administration), pp. 42–63.

Peacock, Alan, and Jack Wiseman, 1961, *The Growth of Public Expenditure in the United Kingdom* (Princeton, N.J.: Princeton University Press).

Perotti, Roberto, 1998a, "The Political Economy of Fiscal Consolidations," in the *Scandinavian Journal of Economics* (Sweden), 100, No. 1: 367–404.

   1998b, "Fiscal Policy When Things Are Going Badly," mimeo, January 12, Columbia University and Centre For Economic Policy Research.

Perotti, Roberto, Rolf Straunch, and Juergen von Hagen, 1998, *Sustainability of Public Finances*, CEPR (London).

Peters, G. H., 1973, *Cost-benefit Analysis* (Westminister: Institute of Economic Affairs).

Poullier, Jean-Pierre, 1993, *OECD Health Systems* (Paris: OECD).

Pommerehne, Werner W., and Friedrich Schneider, 1982, "Unbalanced Growth between Public and Private Sectors: An Empirical Examination," in Robert H. Haveman, ed., *Public Finance and Public Employment* (Detroit, Mich.: Wayne State University Press) pp. 309–26.

Premchand, A., 1983, *Government Budgeting and Expenditure Controls. Theory and Practice* (Washington: International Monetary Fund).

   1996, Issues and New Directions in Public Expenditure Management, IMF Working Paper 96/123, International Monetary Fund, Washington.

Prescott, Edward C., 1986, "Theory Ahead of Business-Cycle Measurement," Carnegie-Rochester Conference Series on Public Policy, Vol. 25.

Psacharopoulos, George, 1992, "The Privatization of Education in Europe," *Comparative Education Review* 36: 115–26.

PUMA (OECD), 1997a, *Modern Budgeting* (Paris: OECD).

   1997b, *Budgeting for the Future* (Paris: OECD).

   1997c, *Contracting Out Government Services: Best Practice Guidelines and Case Studies*, Occasional Paper No. 20 (Paris: OECD).

Putnam, Robert D., 1993, *Making Democracy Work: Civic Traditions in Modern Italy* (Princeton, N.J.: Princeton University Press).

Rafuse, Robert, 1965, "Cyclical Behaviour of State-Local Finances," in Richard A. Musgrave, ed., *Essays in Fiscal Federalism* (Washington: The Brookings Institution).

Remnick, David, 1994, *Lenin's Tomb: The Last Days of the Soviet Empire* (New York: Vintage Books).

Rimlinger, Gaston V., 1971, *Welfare Policy and Industrialization in Europe, America and Russia* (New York: Wiley).

Robbins, Lionel, 1962, "What Role for Government Expenditure?" in Edmund Phelps, ed. (New York: W. W. Norton & Company, Inc.).

Roberti, Paolo, 1989, "Some Critical Reflections on the Principles and Instruments of the Welfare State," *Labour: Review of Labour Economics and Industrial Relations*, Vol. 3: 95–125.

Robinson, David, and others, 1991, *Thailand: Adjusting to Success: Current Policy Issues*, IMF Occasional Paper No. 85 (Washington: International Monetary Fund).

Rodrik, Dani, 1996, "Understanding Economic Policy Reform," *Journal of Economic Literature*, 34: 9–41.

Roseveare, Deborah, Willi Leibfritz, Douglas Fore, and Eckhard Wurzel, 1996, "Ageing Populations, Pension Systems, and Government Budgets: Simulations for 20 OECD Countries," OECD Economics Department, Working Paper No. 168 (Paris: OECD).

Rothbard, Murray N., 1962, *The Panic of 1819. Reaction and Policies* (New York: Columbia University Press).

Sadka, Efraim, and Vito Tanzi, 1998, "Increasing Dependency Ratios, Pensions, and Tax Smoothing," Working Paper 98/129, International Monetary Fund, Washington.

Scherer, Peter, 1996, "The Myth of the Demographic Imperative," in C. Eugene Steuerle and Masahiro Kawai, eds., *The New World Fiscal Order: Implications for Industrialized Nations* (Washington: The Urban Institute Press), pp. 61–83.

Schick, Allen, 1998, "Why Most Developing Countries Should Not Try New Zealand's Reforms," *World Bank Research Observer*, February: 123–31.

Schneider, Friedrich, 1997, "Empirical Results for the Size of the Shadow Economy of Western European Countries over Time," University of Linz, mimeo.

Schuknecht, Ludger, 1992, *Trade Protection in the European Community* (Chur: Harwood Academic Publishers).

Schwartz, Gerd, and Paulo Silva Lopes, 1993, "Privatization: Expectations, Trade-offs, and Results," *Finance and Development*, 30 (June): 14–17.

Scott, Graham, 1996, *Government Reform in New Zealand*, IMF Occasional Paper No. 140 (Washington: International Monetary Fund).

Siebert, Horst, 1998, *Redesigning Social Security* (Tübingen: Mohr Siebeck).

Singh, Anoop, Josh Felman, Ray Brooks, Tim Callen, and Christian Thimann, 1998, *Australia: Benefiting from Economic Reform* (Washington: International Monetary Fund).

Slesnick, Daniel T., 1998, "Empirical Approaches to the Measurement of Welfare," *Journal of Economic Literature*, Vol. 36 (December): 2108–65.

Smith, Adam, 1937, *An Inquiry into the Nature and Causes of the Wealth of Nations* (New York: The Modern Library).

Smithies, Arthur, 1964, "A Conceptual Framework for the Program Budget" (Santa Monica, Calif.: The Rand Corporation).

Social Protection Expenditure and Receipts, 1994 (Luxembourg: Office des publications officielles des Communautés européenes).

Solimano, Andrés, Osvaldo Sunkel, and Mario Blejer, eds., 1994, Rebuilding Capitalism: Alternative Roads after Socialism and Dirigisme (Ann Arbor: University of Michigan Press).

Statistisches Jahrbuch für die Republic Österreich, 1935 (Vienna: Das Zentralamt).

Steuerle, C. Eugene, and Masahiro Kawai, eds., 1996, *The New World Fiscal Order: Implications for Industrialized Nations* (Washington: The Urban Institute Press).

Stockholm International Peace Research Institute, 1996, *Armaments, Disarmament and International Security: SIPRI Yearbook, 1996* (New York: Oxford University Press).

Tanzi, Vito, 1970, *Taxation: A Radical Approach. A Reassessment of the High Level of British Taxation and the Scope for Its Reduction* (London: The Institute of Economic Affairs).

—— 1986, "Public Expenditure and Public Debt," in John Bristow and Declan McDonagh, eds. *Public Expenditure: The Key Issues* (Dublin: Institute of Public Administration), pp. 6–37.

—— 1988, 'Trends in Tax Policy as Revealed by Recent Developments and Research," *Bulletin for International Fiscal Documentation* 42 (March): 97–103.

—— 1995, *Taxation in an Integrating World* (Washington: The Brookings Institution).

—— 1996, "Fiscal Policy and Income Distribution," paper presented at the Conference on Economic Growth and Equity: International Experience and Polices, July 12–13, Santiago.

—— 1996b, "Fiscal Federalism and Decentralization: A Review of Some Efficiency and Macroeconomic Aspects," in *Annual World Bank Conference on Development Economics 1995* (Washington: World Bank).

—— 1997, "The Changing Role of the State in the Economy: A Historical Perspective," IMF Working Paper 97/114, International Monetary Fund, Washington.

—— 1998a, "Globalization, Tax Competition, and the Future of Tax Systems," in Gerold Krause-Junk, ed., *Steuersysteme der Zukunft* (Berlin: Duncker & Humbolt).

—— 1998b, "Corruption around the World," IMF *Staff Papers*, Vol. 45, No. 4, (December): 559–94.

—— 1998c, "Government Role and the Efficiency of Policy Instruments," in Peter Birch Sorensen, ed. *Public Finance in a Changing World* (Macmillan Press, Ltd.), pp. 51–79.

—— 1998d, "Fundamental Determinants of Inequality and the Role of Government," IMF Working Paper 98/178, International Monetary Fund, Washington.

—— 1999, "Is There a Need for a World Tax Organization? in Assaf Razin and Efraim Sadka, eds., *The Economics of Globalization: Policy Perspectives from Public Economics* (Cambridge: Cambridge University Press).

Tanzi, Vito, and Domenico Fanizza, 1995, "Fiscal Deficit and Public Debt in

Industrial Countries, 1970–1994, IMF, Working Paper 95/49, International Monetary Fund, Washington.

Tanzi, Vito, and Ludger Schuknecht, 1997a, "Reconsidering the Fiscal Role of Government: The International Perspective," *American Economic Review*, 87: 164–8.

1997b, "Reforming Government: An Overview over the Recent Experience," *European Journal of Political Economy*, 13: 395–417.

1998a, "The Growth of Government and the Reform of the State in Industrial Countries," in Andres Solimano, ed., *Social Inequality: Values, Growth, and the State* (Ann Arbor: University of Michigan Press), pp. 171–207.

1998b, "Can Small Governments Secure Social and Economic Well-Being?" in Herbert Grubel, ed., *How to Spend the Fiscal Dividend: What Is the Optimal Size of Government?* (Vancouver: Fraser Institute).

Tanzi, Vito, and Howell Zee, 1997, "Fiscal Policy and Long-Run Growth" IMF *Staff Papers*, Vol. 44, No. 4 (June): 179–209.

1998, "Taxation and the Household Saving Rate: Evidence from OECD Countries," IMF Working Paper, WP/98/36, International Monetary Fund, Washington.

Ter-Minassian, Teresa, ed. 1997, *Fiscal Federalism in Theory and Practice* (Washington: International Monetary Fund).

The Independent, October 1, 1996, "Time to Change the Rules of the Fiscal Game," Byline: Hamish McRae (London), p. 20.

Tinbergen, Jan, 1952, *On the Theory of Economic Policy* (Amsterdam: North-Holland).

Tobin, James, 1966, *National Economic Policy*: Essays (New Haven, Conn.: Yale University Press).

Transparency International, 1996, Transparency International Annual Report 1996: "Sharpening the Responses against Global Corruption" (Berlin: Transparency International).

Tullock, Gordon, 1967, "The Welfare Costs of Tariffs, Monopolies, and Theft," *Western Economic Journal* (June): 224–32.

1989, *The Economics of Special Privilege and Rent-Seeking* (Boston: Kluwer Academic Publishers).

United Nations Development Programme, 1995, *Human Development Report*, 1995 (New York: Oxford University Press).

1996, *Human Development Report*, 1996 (New York: Oxford University Press).

1997, *Human Development Report*, 1997 (New York: Oxford University Press).

United Nations, 1997, *World Economic and Social Survey: Current Trends and Policies in in the World Economy* (New York: United Nations).

United Nations (various years), *National Accounts Statistics: Main Aggregates and Detailed Tables*, Vol. 1, parts 1 and 2 (New York: United Nations).

UNESCO, 1993, *World Education Report* (Paris: UNESCO).

United States, Arms Control and Disarmament Agency, 1996, *World Military Expenditures and Arms Transfers* (Washington: GPO).

United States, Bureau of the Census, 1975, *Historical Statistics of the United States, Colonial Times to 1970*, Bicentennial edition (Washington: GPO).

United States Social Security Administration, 1993, *Social Security Programs throughout the World.*

Van den Noord, P., and R. Herd, 1993, *Pension Liabilities in the Seven Major Economies*, (Paris: OECD).

Velasco, Andres, 1994, "The State and Economic Policy: Chile 1952–92," in Barry Bosworth, Rudiger Dornbush, and Raul Laban, eds., *The Chilean Economy: Policy Lessons and Challenges* (Washington: The Brookings Institution), pp. 379–429.

Von Hagen, Juergen, 1992, "Budgeting Procedures and Fiscal Performance in the European Communities," Brussels: EC Economic Papers No. 96.

Von Hagen, Juergen, and Ian Harden, 1994, "National Budget Processes and Fiscal Performance," in European Economy Reports and Studies, No. 3, *Towards Greater Fiscal Discipline* (Brussels).

1996, Budget Processes and Commitments to Fiscal Discipline, IMF Working Paper 96/78, International Monetary Fund, Washington.

Wagner Adolf H., 1892, *Grundlegung der Politischen Oekonomie*, Pt. I: Grundlagen der Volkswirtschaft, 3rd ed. (Leipzig: Winter).

Wagner, Richard E., and Tollison Robert D., 1987, "Balanced Budgets, Fiscal Responsibility and the Constitution," in Richard Fink and Jack High, eds., *A Nation in Debt: Economists Debate the Federal Budget Deficit* (Frederick, Md.: University Publications of America).

Walford, Geoffrey, ed., 1989, *Private Schools in Ten Countries: Policy and Practice* (London: Routledge).

Weck-Hannemann, Hannelore, Werner W. Pommerehne, and Bruno S. Frey, 1984, *Schattenwirtschaft* (Munich: Vahlen).

West, Edwin G. 1970, *Education and the State: A Study in Political Economy*, 2nd ed. (London: The Institute of Economic Affairs).

1992, "The Benthamites as Educational Engineers: The Reputation and The Record," *History of Political Economy*, 24: 595–621.

1997, "Education Vouchers in Principle and Practice: A Survey," World Bank, *Research Observer*, Vol. 12: 83–104.

Wildavsky, Aaron 1985, "A Cultural Theory of Expenditure Growth and (Un)Balanced Budgets," *Journal of Public Economics* 28: 349–57.

Williams, Gareth L., and Dorothea Furth, 1990, *Financing Higher Education: Current Patterns* (Paris: OECD).

Winer Stanley L., and Walter Hettich, 1991a, "Debt and Tariffs: An Empirical Investigation of the Evolution of Revenue Systems," *Journal of Public Economics*, 45: 215–42.

1991b, "Political Checks and Balances and the Structure of Taxation in the United States and Canada," in Breton, Albert, Gianluigi Galeotti, Pierre Salmon, and Ronald Wintrobe, eds., *The Competitive State*, Villa Colombella Papers on Competitive Politics (Dordrecht: Kluwer Academic Publishers).

World Bank, 1993, *World Development Report: Investing in Health* (New York: Oxford University Press).

1994a, *Averting the Old Age Crisis: Policies to Protect the Old and Promote Growth* (New York: Oxford University Press).

1994b, *World Development Report* (New York: Oxford University Press).

1995, *Bureaucrats in Business: The Economics and Politics of Government Ownership* (New York: Published for the World Bank by Oxford University Press).

1996, *Social Indicators of Development* (Baltimore: Johns Hopkins University Press).

1997, *World Development Report* (New York: Oxford University Press).

Wunder, Haroldene F., and Stephen R. Crow, 1997, "International Tax Reform since 1986: An Update," in *Tax Notes International* (April 7).

Zandvakili, Sourushe, 1994, "Income Distribution and Redistribution through Taxation: An International Comparison," *Empirical Economics*, Vol. 19, No. 3: 473–91.

Zee, Howell, 1996, "Taxation and Unemployment," IMF Working Paper 96/45, International Monetary Fund, Washington.

Author Index

273

Subject Index

accountability: with buyer-provider link to performance contracts, 163; in Economic and Monetary Union (EMU), 159; of executive to the legislature, 154; of ministry of finance, 165; with quasi-fiscal regulations, 204; strengthening, 153

administration, public: antitrust agency, 165–6; core fiscal agencies, 165; core implementation agencies, 165–7; corruption, 165–7; management of public spending, 161–4; in newly industrialized countries (NICs), 129–30; restructuring in New Zealand, 210–13

African countries: centralized budget process in, 157; levels of public sector employment, 240

Argentina: fiscal reform, 226–7; pension reform, 195; private universities in, 185; privatization in, 180n10

Asian countries: centralized budget process, 157

Australia: education (1870–1994), 92–3; employment in public sector (1870–1994), 28; fiscal balance (1960–1996), 62; fiscal churning,

140–1; fiscal reform, 216–18; fiscal transparency, 139; government real spending (1870–1995), 27; government size and public spending (1960, 1990), 100; health indicators (1870–1995), 90–1; income distribution (1930s, 1960, 1980s), 94–8; interest payments (1870–1995), 45–6; interest payments (1960–1990), 85–6; per capita GDP (1870–1990), 79; post-World War II public spending, 16; public debt (1870–1996), 64–5; public spending (1870s), 5, 21; public spending (1920s), 8; public spending (1930s), 9–10; public spending (1991, 1996), 216–18; public spending trend (1980–1996), 21; rejection of education vouchers, 187; resource accounting, 205; revenues (1870–1996), 51–5; social insurance coverage (1910–1975), 36, 39; spending for education (1870–1993), 33–4; tax rates, 59–60

Austria: cost of health care, 199–200; employment in public sector, 25; government size and public spending (1960, 1990), 100; health indicators (1870–1995), 89–90;

278

Mexico: controls on financial markets, 203–4; health indicators, 91; pension reform, 195; per capita GDP, 79; premiums on Eurobond issues, 88; privatization in, 180n10
ministry of finance: effect of strong, 165
monetary policy: effect of tight (1980s), 86. *See also* fiscal policy

Netherlands: attendance at private primary and secondary schools, 185; budget targets, 156; expenditure ceilings on fiscal plans, 161; fiscal balance (1960–1996), 62, 64; fiscal reform, 220–1; government real spending (1870–1995), 29; government size and public spending (1960, 1990), 99; health indicators (1870–1995), 89–91; income distribution (1930s, 1960, 1980s), 94–8; other transfer programs, 43–4, 202; pension liabilities, 68; pension reform, 195; public spending (1870), 5; public spending (1920s), 8; public spending (1930s), 9; public spending trend (1980–1996), 20; public spending after World War II, 16; public spending reform, 221; recent fiscal position, 64; revenue composition (1870–1994), 56–8; revenues (1870–1996), 52–4; subsidies and transfers (1870–1995), 30–2; unemployment insurance spending (1937–1996), 42–3; unemployment rate (1870–1996), 80–1
newly industrialized countries (NICs): distributional and social stability indicators (1960, 1990), 112–15; economic and labor market indicators, 124–7; economic growth (1960, 1990), 102–6; economic performance (1960, 1990), 102–8;

educational standards, 128; environmental indicators (1960, 1990), 110–12; fiscal reform, 225–9; focus of public spending, 133–4; governance-related indicators, 115–19, 129–30; government performance indicators (1990s), 121–30; growth rates (1990s), 126; income distribution, 128; infant mortality rates, 89, 91; interest rates (1960s–1990s), 107; labor market indicators (1960, 1990), 102–8; privatization in, 180n10; public debt (1960, 1990), 102–8; public spending (1960, 1990), 100–2; public spending patterns, 121–4; social and distributional indicators, 127–9; social indicators (1960, 1990), 108–10; unemployment rates (1960, 1990), 107–8. *See also* Chile; Hong Kong; Korea; Singapore
New Zealand: changes in economic policy, 210; education (1870–1994), 93; fiscal balance (1960–1996), 62, 64; fiscal reforms, 207–8, 210–13; fiscal transparency, 139; government real spending (1870–1995), 29; government size and public spending (1960, 1990), 100; health indicators (1870–1995), 90–1; implementation of fiscal reform, 150; interest on public debt (1960–1990), 85; per capita GDP (1870–1990), 79; public debt (1870–1996), 64–6; recent fiscal position, 64; resource accounting, 205; revenues (1870–1996), 51–4; spending for education (1870–1993), 33–4; subsidies and transfers, 134–5; subsidies and transfers (1870–1995), 32; tax rates, 59–60; trend in public spending (1980–1996), 20–1; using market forces, 209
Norway: educational spending (1870–1993), 33–4; employment in